THE GENIUS
OF LUTHER'S
THEOLOGY

THE GENIUS
OF LUTHER'S
THEOLOGY

A WITTENBERG WAY OF THINKING
FOR THE CONTEMPORARY CHURCH

Robert Kolb
and Charles P. Arand

B
Baker Academic
Grand Rapids, Michigan

Published by Baker Academic
a division of Baker Publishing Group
P.O. Box 6287, Grand Rapids, MI 49516-6287
www.bakeracademic.com

Printed and bound by CPI Group (UK) Ltd, Croydon, CR0 4YY

Library of Congress Cataloging-in-Publication Data
Kolb, Robert, 1941–
    The genius of Luther's theology : a Wittenberg way of thinking for the contemporary church / Robert Kolb and Charles P. Arand.
       p.   cm.
    Includes bibliographical references and index.
    ISBN 978-0-8010-3180-9 (pbk.)
    1. Luther, Martin, 1483–1546. I. Arand, Charles P. II. Title.
BR333.3.K65 2007
230′.41—dc22   2007027387

CONTENTS

Abbreviations   7
Introduction: The Genius of Luther's Thought   9

Part 1 "Our Theology": Luther's Definition of the Human Creature through "Two Kinds of Righteousness"   21

1. Luther's Anthropological Matrix   23
2. The Core of Human Identity   33
3. The Shape of Human Performance   53
4. The Subversion of Our Human Identity   77
5. The Dynamic of Faith   101

Part 2 When the Word Is Spoken, All Things Are Possible: Luther and the Word of God   129

6. The Functions of the Word   131
7. The Enfleshed and Written Forms of God's Word   161
8. The "Means of Grace" as Forms of God's Word   175
9. God's Word Takes Form as His People Convey It to One Another   205

Conclusion: Thinking with Luther in the Twenty-first Century   221
Bibliography   225
Index   235

ABBREVIATIONS

Book of Concord	*The Book of Concord.* Edited by Robert Kolb and Timothy J. Wengert. Minneapolis: Fortress, 2000.
BSLK	*Die Bekenntnisschriften der evangelisch-lutherischen Kirche.* Göttingen: Vandenhoeck & Ruprecht, 1930, 1991.
CR	Philip Melanchthon. *Corpus Reformatorum: Opera quae supersunt omnia.* Edited by C. G. Bretschneider and H. E. Bindseil. Vols. 1–28. Halle and Braunschweig: Schwetschke, 1834–60.
KJV	King James Version of the Holy Bible.
LW	Martin Luther, *Luther's Works.* Saint Louis and Philadelphia: Concordia and Fortress, 1958–1986.
NIV	New International Version.
RSV	Revised Standard Version
WA	Martin Luther. *D. Martin Luthers Werke.* Weimarer Ausgabe. 127 vols. Weimar: Böhlau, 1883–1993.
WA DB	Die Deutsche Bibel. 1522–46. In *WA.* 12 vols. in 15. Weimar: Böhlau, 1906–61.
WA TR	Martin Luther. In *WA. D. Martin Luthers Werke: Tischreden.* 6 vols. Weimar: Böhlau, 1912–21.

Introduction

The Genius of Luther's Thought

Two Presuppositions of Wittenberg Theology

People are known by the company they keep. What are we then to make of the company Martin Luther has kept over the years? A list of his conversation partners in recent decades presents a strange mosaic. Professor Claus Schwambach of Sao Bento du Sul in Brazil has recently brought the sixteenth-century exegete into dialogue with the twentieth-century liberation theologian Leonardo Boff in his book on "the event of justification and the process of liberation, the eschatologies of Martin Luther and Leonardo Boff in critical conversation."[1] In his work on "theosis in the thought of Palamas and Luther," the German church historian Reinhard Flogaus joined the Wittenberg reformer in interchange with the fourteenth-century Thessalonican monk Gregory of Palamas.[2] These are only among the latest in a long line of such books, including *Luther*

1. Leonardo Boff, *Rechtfertigungsgeschehen und Befreiungsprozess: Die Eschatologien von Martin Luther und Leonardo Boff im kritischen Gespräch* (Göttingen: Vandenhoeck & Ruprecht, 2004).
2. Reinhard Flogaus, *Theosis bei Palamas und Luther: Ein Beitrag zum ökumenischen Gespräch* (Göttingen: Vandenhoeck & Ruprecht, 1997).

und Hegel,[3] *Ritschl and Luther,*[4] and *Aquinas and Luther.*[5] Constructive efforts continue to take seriously the thought of this man, who departed this earth four hundred and sixty years ago, not only as a historical figure but also as a conversation partner in the context of the late twentieth and early twenty-first century. This fact suggests that the study of Luther's life and thought may be quite worthwhile for those seeking to bring the biblical message to the people of the twenty-first century.

Many elements provide the raw material for such conversations, both from Luther's thought and from the thought of his conversation partners, such as Palamas, long since dead, and the authors of other books, writing from amid their contemporary concerns. In this volume we focus on two elements of Luther's way of understanding the biblical message: his fundamental presuppositions regarding what it means to be human (part 1) and his understanding of the way God works in his world (part 2). We believe these to be the genius—the pervading and animating orientation, the particular character—that shapes the course of his teaching of every part of the Christian message. These two elements provide the matrix within which the sixteenth-century reformer from Wittenberg studied and proclaimed his faith and conversed about it with his contemporaries.

Martin Luther, Conversation Partner for Twenty-first-Century Christians

In our time, many Christians are involved in conversations with other Christians and with people outside the Christian faith. Some of those conversations project confidence; some are more questioning and reflect a sense of crisis. At the beginning of the twenty-first century, Christian churches around the world are in crisis. New challenges to the church's right to proclaim its message and even to exist in certain societies, aggressive opposition to its way of life, questions from inside as well as outside—all are bringing believers to reflect anew on the best ways to bring the gospel of Jesus Christ to their ever-changing surroundings.

Lutheran churches share in this confrontation with crises. Certainly, Lutherans have always thought themselves to be in the midst of crisis. *Krisis* is the Greek word for judgment, and Martin Luther experienced the world around him as a world under judgment, at the edge of liberation

3. Ulrich Asendorf, *Luther und Hegel: Untersuchungen zur Grundlegung einer neuen systematischen Theologie* (Wiesbaden: Steiner, 1982).

4. David Lotz, *Ritschl and Luther: A Fresh Perspective on Albrecht Ritschl's Theology in the Light of His Luther Study* (Nashville: Abingdon, 1974).

5. Stephanus Pfurtner, *Aquinas and Luther* (New York: Sheed & Ward, 1964).

from all its ills. Luther believed that the God who had revealed himself in the judgment of the cross was present in quite real ways amid all that was going wrong with church and society in the early sixteenth century. He counted on the God of the cross to deliver him, with all those faithful people whom God had chosen to be his children, from the manifold evils of their time. His certain hope and absolute confidence that his Lord is Lord of the world drove him to proclaim that hope for God's people, as Paul had (Col. 1:15–29).

So Luther lived as a free man even though for the last quarter century of his life he stood under the condemnation of emperor and pope, under the threat of execution at the stake. His thoughts on how the gospel of Jesus Christ liberates people caught in the entanglement of evils of all sorts offer twenty-first-century believers, as well as their neighbors who do not know Jesus Christ, fresh ways of examining the biblical message. His reflections on Scripture and the world around him can contribute significantly to the conversation on the propagation and practice of God's Word among Christians of all traditions in this age.

Luther believed that the church of his youth had played power games that obscured the simple truth of Christ's victory over evil through death and resurrection. In so doing, the reformer and his associates charged church leaders with neglecting the care of the people of God. The Reformation Luther led with his colleagues at the University of Wittenberg arose out of the crisis of pastoral care that plagued the late medieval church. That crisis had its roots in a crisis of proclamation: there was too little preaching in the fifteenth century, largely because pastors were ill trained or not trained at all. Most knew little theology and had little idea of how the gospel might make a difference in people's lives. Theologians lived trapped in their own intellectual constructs—although Luther's instructors from the theological school labeled "Ockhamist" or "nominalist" gave him much of the raw material that helped him mine the Scriptures. From that study of the Word, he was able to teach and proclaim the richness of the good news of Jesus Christ.

Luther did not learn alone, and he did not think and teach alone. Together with his Wittenberg colleagues and others from his circle of conversation partners, he developed his approach to the Word of God. With his way of thinking theologically and within a framework of presuppositions, Luther approached Scripture and the world, to which his doctoral oath obligated him to bring the message of the Bible. Because these presuppositions are embedded in the conceptual matrix within which the various elements of his teaching were presented and related to each other, they sometimes escape our notice when we look at what the faculty at Wittenberg taught. Nevertheless, these presuppositions guided the ways in which Luther, his closest colleague and most significant contributor to his reform program, Philip Melanchthon, and their circle treated the various topics of biblical teaching.

Presuppositions as the Framework of the Wittenberg Way of Practicing Theology

This volume looks at two vital elements that constituted the matrix within which Luther developed other topics from biblical revelation and the genius that channeled their unfolding: the anthropological presupposition that God shaped human life according to two dimensions (two kinds of righteousness), and the theological presupposition that God works through his Word in its manifold forms. The first presupposition posits that what makes human beings genuine human creatures of God in his sight is his grace and favor alone, to which we respond with total trust in him; what makes us genuinely human in relationship to other creatures is our performance of the works of love, which God designed to be our way of living out our trust in him. The second presupposition posits that his Word does not merely provide us with information about his heavenly disposition. Instead, the God who spoke the worlds into being (Gen. 1) speaks through his Word in oral, written, and sacramental forms as it actually effects and delivers new life on the basis of the Word made flesh, the crucified and risen Jesus Christ.

These two presuppositions formed vital elements of Luther and Melanchthon's practice of theology and the delivery of the biblical message to their contemporaries in the sixteenth century. In this volume, we intend to present these presuppositions in such a way that they become useful for pastors and laypersons in the twenty-first century as they bring the promise of life in Christ to their neighbors in our time. The matrix offered in these two presuppositions enables us to evaluate our own formulations. Such a matrix aids us as we construct our own formulations of God's truth and interface in ways appropriate to our time and place with the unchanging edifice of God's biblical message and formulate our applications of the Word's power to the situations confronting us. These principles help us sort out Scripture passages that our ways of posing questions may put in conflict (Paul's and James's statements on faith and works, for example) or to frame a fresh approach to questions from our society that do not seem to fit a biblical worldview at all. These presuppositions guide our thinking as we tread the path of the sometimes strange and occasionally forbidding future that God presents us.

The practice of theology Wittenberg style involves a regular pattern of searching the Scriptures, looking at the world around us, and examining ourselves and the manner in which we engage the thought world into which God has called us, here and now applying the good news of God's promise of life in Christ. With Luther we must honestly confront the inevitable tendency of Christians to mix the sound of God's Word with other sounds from the world around them. Therefore, he believed that the entire life of believers, individually and as a group gathered together, the church, is a life of being called back from the way misrepresentations of reality divert us from the truth of God. The whole life of the Christian, he wrote as he began his call for reform in the church, is a life of repentance.[6] By repentance Luther meant a life lived out in the rhythm that God set in motion through his baptismal Word of life. Using Paul's words in Romans 6, Luther described the ongoing significance of the Holy Spirit's baptismal action in his Small Catechism. He summarized the Christian life as a life in which "the Old Adam in us is drowned through daily remorse and repentance and dies with all sins and evil lusts, and a new human creature daily arises, who lives eternally in God's sight in righteousness and purity."[7]

Luther's reminder that God calls Christians in the midst of a sinful world to turn from their mistakes, failures, and disobedience each day of their lives reminds theologians of their need to return to Scripture continually to check out whether they are faithfully reproducing God's message. This is true not only because students of God's Word can make false formulations but also because Satan's deceptions take so many forms and God's gift of humanity has so many facets. In different situations and in confrontation with various forms of evil, God's message for a fallen world takes on new and different expressions. The unchangeable truths of Scripture must be proclaimed to specific human beings in their specific environments as the gospel addresses their realities and brings its power to change those realities through forgiveness and the promise of new life in Christ. God's Word not only describes reality but also creates it. In the beginning God said, "Let there be . . . ," and reality came into existence. God says, "I forgive," and the reality of a new creature comes into existence or is sustained in life as a child of God. Luther risked his life, and many of his disciples laid down their lives, in order to bring this message—this act of God—to reality in the lives of others.

The Form and Framework for Teaching the Biblical Message

This volume does not follow a traditional model of presenting Lutheran doctrine, namely, one topic at a time. That mode of summarizing

6. The first of the Ninety-five Theses, *LW* 31:25; *WA* 1:233.10–11.
7. Small Catechism, Baptism, question 4, *Book of Concord*, 360; *BSLK*, 516.

Lutheran teaching has served the church since the days Philip Melanchthon first followed the models of Peter Lombard and John of Damascus in devising his *Theological Topics* (*Loci communes theologici*) nearly five hundred years ago. Instead, readers will find in these pages two extensive essays (parts 1 and 2) that portray the genius that guided the crafting of Wittenberg teaching, sketching a "Wittenberg way" of thinking biblically and theologically. Both essays intend to anchor their framework for such thinking historically, and both intend to offer readers foundational insights for the practice of theology, a matrix for the faithful formulation of the message of Scripture in the twenty-first century. As mentioned above, these two essays deal with two presuppositions the Wittenberg reformers formulated to guide their expression of biblical teaching.

We presume that the formal, public teaching of the people of God may best be described as Luther and Melanchthon themselves described it, through the metaphor of the body.[8] The whole of biblical teaching that commends itself for presentation to the people of God and those outside the faith is constituted, as Melanchthon envisioned it, as a series of "articles" or "members" of a body that functions as an organic whole.[9] But the church's body of public teaching is not composed merely of these topics with which every Christian is familiar: God, the human creature, sin, salvation, church, the end times, and many others. The way in which believers teach these topics is governed by principles or guidelines that we may compare to a nervous system or a circulatory system. These presuppositions or governing principles provide the energy and the direction for our formulation and application of the truths of Scripture as expressed in the many articles of faith or doctrinal topics that help us organize our processing and delivery of the biblical witness to God and his interaction with his human creatures. This is the manner in which Luther's anthropological presupposition of two kinds of human righteousness and his theological presupposition of the Word of God serving as God's instrument of presence and power in the world function in the Wittenberg theology.

To use another metaphor, these essays provide discussions of two road maps that Luther designed to help travelers move through the landscape of biblical revelation, or two systems of lighting and signage that the traveler needs to traverse the territory of Scripture's content and engage the adventure of exploring how God is bringing his message to the people of our time and our places. Like all other Christians, Luther,

---

8. Irene Dingel, "Philip Melanchthon and the Establishment of Confessional Norms," *Lutheran Quarterly* 20 (2006): 146–69, esp. 152–59.

9. *Book of Concord*, 7 (par. 7).

along with Melanchthon and their colleagues, mapped out their way of understanding what God has said in Scripture to his people, and they also shaped their own way of formulating and conveying that message. They conducted their instruction of theological students largely through lectures on books of the Bible, but their lectures went beyond examination of exegetical details of the text. For their students they constructed a scaffold on which these future preachers learned to climb around on the edifice of God's Word, so that they might better present it, in all its power, fresh and appealing in its fundamental delivery of God's saving will for humankind. The content of the Wittenberg reformers' understanding of the biblical message also dictated its own method for applying it to the lives of individuals. We dedicate this little volume to helping readers grasp how Luther and his colleagues practiced the study and the proclamation of God's Word.

Luther and his colleagues committed themselves to honest intellectual exploration of the world God has given into human care. They likewise committed themselves to search the Scriptures and deliver eternal life to their hearers through their mining of that Word of God. But the study of Scripture, the discipline of theology, was regarded as a thoroughly practical discipline, moving from the university to the world, where God wants his people to be at work. So even though it may be said that the Wittenberg Reformation was conceived in the university, where across its disciplines faith and intellectual curiosity and adventure combined, it must also be said that the Lutheran church was born in Augsburg, in the sixteenth-century equivalent of the halls of Congress, where the reformers delivered the public confession of their faith in the Augsburg Confession of 1530. Therefore, Luther's followers regarded themselves as called to active citizenry in their political circumstances. They also wanted to follow Martin and his wife, Käthe, in their enjoyment of marital and family life. Yet Luther's adherents believed that the life of the church and all its members emerges from God's engagement with his human creatures in the biblical text. Luther and his students committed themselves to engaging the testimony of believers from previous eras regarding what God has revealed of himself there.

At Wittenberg, Luther, Melanchthon, their colleagues, and their students listened to what God was saying through the pages of Scripture, using the best methods and material contemporary biblical scholars were supplying, with an eye always fixed on the needs of people to be called to repentance and to be given new life through the gospel of Jesus Christ. Because they believed that God's Word is an active and living agent of his re-creative activity, they emphasized the importance of publicly proclaiming that Word and privately sharing it with others in the family circle and the wider circle of acquaintances. For these Wittenberg students of the Word, confessing their faith became their way of life.

Because Luther had a price on his head and the emperor's threat of execution hanging over his life in 1530, Melanchthon got the nod as the chief negotiator when the emperor of the Holy Roman Empire, Charles V, summoned Elector John of Saxony to explain why he was not obediently returning to subjection to the bishop of Rome but instead pursuing reform of the churches in his lands according to Luther's model. Other princes and cities of the German Empire joined John in defining their cause and their church in a document Melanchthon composed for them from materials he, Luther, and their Wittenberg colleagues had been writing. To this day that document, the Augsburg Confession, remains the basic definition of what it means to be a "Lutheran."

In this document Melanchthon brought together a summary of the fundamental core of Luther's understanding of the biblical message, in a compact, concise form, resulting in twenty-one articles of faith. He added to it explanations of why followers of Luther had introduced reforms or were calling for improvements in the life and practice of the church, for Wittenberg teaching was never only theoretical. It always had pastoral and practical implications. Melanchthon considered calling his definition of the Wittenberg plan for the repentance of the church a "defense"—in Greek *apologia*—but instead he decided that this new creed should be called a "confession" of faith.

As Luther's colleague, Melanchthon understood that the Word of God is a dynamic instrument of God's power. The specific content of Wittenberg teaching demanded a specific method for bringing God's Word to people. Melanchthon's conviction that the Word of God in our mouths does things and his perception that the Holy Spirit must daily turn believers from their sinfulness back to God dictated a particular framework for preaching and teaching. God's Word, as we pronounce and proclaim it, brings the judgment of God's wrath on sin, but above all it fulfills his ultimate will for humankind. It makes sinners alive by restoring them to their status as God's children in the sight of our heavenly Father. With this understanding of both God's Word and our repetition of his message for humankind, Melanchthon made a confession. He understood that Word not merely in terms of the content of the document he was writing but also in terms of the action that necessarily conveys that content when one believes it. Melanchthon already knew what Paul tells us in Romans 10:10–17, that when we *believe*, we cannot help but *teach* and *confess* what God has done for us.

At first, Melanchthon's friends and Luther's disciples used the term "Augsburg Confession" for the entire action of explaining the Christian faith undertaken in Augsburg that spring and summer by the supporters of the Wittenberg reformation. These believers understood confessing the faith to be their way of life. Everything said and done to make clear what Jesus Christ had done for humankind in negotiation with the papal party in Augsburg constituted a confession. In the years following 1530, Lutherans came to define who they were, what it meant to be "Lutheran," first of all in terms of this document. They also used the term "Augsburg Confession" specifically to designate the content of its teaching, for they viewed biblical "teaching" as the Word of God lifted from the biblical page, full of God's power to kill the sinners who were ruining his favorite creation, humanity, and full of his power to raise these sinners up as new people through Christ's death and resurrection.

This Augsburg Confession expressed a great deal about Luther's practice of theology, both as a university course of instruction and as the nervous system that empowers the entire life of God's people. The Confession commits Luther's adherents to specific formulations of the biblical message; its spirit also guides their perception of how the people of God, his church, act as they carry God's Word from the Bible's pages into the lives of other people.

First of all, the Augsburg Confession charges its adherents to be pro-claimers of the evangel of our Lord Jesus Christ. It is not true that Luther was "Christomonic," or "Christomanic," as some charge, for he had a rich doctrine of the Trinity. His strong doctrine of creation caused him to exult in the Father's providence. Far beyond what we sometimes recognize, he emphasized how important the Holy Spirit's work is in sanctifying the church through the active use of the Word (understood as "means of grace," the instrument of God's re-creating sinners into his children) and by guiding Christians into new obedience. But finally at the center of his catechism are those five words in his explanation of the second article, "Jesus Christ is our Lord." Luther believed that one cannot be a faithful hearer of God's Word without centering life on the confession that "Jesus Christ, true God, begotten of the Father from all eternity, and also truly human, born of the virgin Mary, is my Lord, who has redeemed me, a lost and condemned creature . . . so that I might be God's own child and serve him forever."[10]

Second, the spirit of Luther's way of practicing the faith, as reflected in the Augsburg Confession, commits us to recognizing the eschatologi-cal urgency of our proclamation. Luther did expect the world to end in the sixteenth century, but he also had a continual sense of standing im-mediately in the presence of God. He knew that the last moment could dawn in any of our lives on any day. But beyond this, he knew that

10. Small Catechism, Apostles' Creed, explanation to the second article, *Book of Concord*, 355; *BSLK*, 511.

the work Jesus Christ had begun was already coming to fulfillment in our experience of the killing and resurrecting power of God's Word. He wanted as many people as possible to enjoy what life in Christ brings as soon as possible, and so he regarded it as the most urgent of tasks to proclaim the gospel. By the same token, the eschatological focus did not lead Luther to abandon earthly responsibilities or callings. According to an oft-repeated apocryphal account,[11] Luther said that if he had known that Christ would return for the last day tomorrow, he would plant an apple tree today; the story illustrates his attitude toward the goodness of each day and the callings God gives us to serve in his world.

Third, the logic of Melanchthon's call to confession compels believers in the twenty-first century toward evangelistic witness. It is true that there were relatively few people outside the Christian faith in Melanchthon's society and that few of his contemporary believers ever met an unbaptized person. Nonetheless, Lutherans were most concerned about bringing the gospel of their Lord to fellow Christians who did not truly trust in him, because we believe that it is a matter of eternal life or death for us to bring people to know Jesus Christ as their Lord and Savior. Having experienced the dynamic of God's Word in our own life, we cannot help but tell those things that we have heard and seen from the biblical witness and our experience of the Holy Spirit working in the church. Preaching in Wittenberg on 1 Peter 2:9 in 1523, Luther told the congregation that God "permits us to live here on earth in order that we may bring others to faith, just as he has brought us." He instructed his fellow citizens of Wittenberg: "You must, says Peter, exercise the chief function of a priest, that is, to proclaim the wonderful deed God has performed for you to bring you out of darkness into the light. Your preaching should be done in such a way that one brother proclaims the mighty deed of God to the other, how you have been delivered through him from sin, hell, death, and all misfortune, and have been called to eternal life. . . . Let it be your chief work to proclaim this publicly and to call everyone into the light into which you have been called."[12]

Fourth, Melanchthon spoke for Luther and his other colleagues when he endeavored to explain the Wittenberg concern for reform in the church's teaching and life. The spirit of the Augsburg Confession embodies Luther and Melanchthon's commitment to ecumenical witness within the household of faith. Melanchthon went, his contemporaries said, like Daniel going into the lions' den, carrying the witness of the gospel to the leaders of the Roman Catholic party in Augsburg. He

11. See Martin Schloemann, *Luthers Apfelbäumchen? Ein Kapitel deutcher Mentalitäts-geschichte seit dem Zweiten Weltkrieg* (Göttingen: Vandenhoeck & Ruprecht, 1994).
12. *LW* 30:11; *WA* 12:267.3–7.

made strenuous efforts to convince them of the truth of what Luther, he, and their colleagues had been teaching in Wittenberg. Such a bold and fearless testimony was aimed at restoring the unity of the church in its confession of the saving gospel. What Timothy Wengert has written about Melanchthon's continuing engagement with other Christians in his Apology of the Augsburg Confession is also true of Lutheran witness as it is voiced as an echo of the Augsburg Confession, which understood itself as an echo of Scripture: "Melanchthon wanted to do nothing other than remain true to his confession of faith. This brand of honest confession and encounters with other Christians may not stand him in good stead with some ecumenically minded Christians today. However, it accurately portrays the unwavering behavior of the author of the chief confession of the Lutheran church, for whom compromise never meant capitulation and conversation about faith always entailed confession of the same."[13] He and Luther alike understood that God had called them and all other members of his church to clear and faithful witness to the biblical revelation of God's saving goodness and power in Christ Jesus.

We have written this book for our students and for people around the world who wish to explore the basic elements of Luther's teaching, though not in detail, topic by topic. Instead, we explore the genius of his way of thinking, the matrix within which he explored the text of Scripture and applied its truths to the everyday lives of people. The goal is to aid readers in constructing their own matrix for reading and proclaiming Scripture out of the material left by these Wittenberg thinkers. We are setting out to do that, conscious of the twenty-first-century world in which we are listening to these students of the Word of God who lived a half millennium ago.

Our essays betray the differing approaches of the systematic theologian and the historian. Since the authors believe that the Wittenberg theology can serve our contemporary church well when properly translated across the centuries and cultural barriers, the historical assessment is not, strictly speaking, an academic analysis but rather a use of Luther's thought to offer a pattern for contemporary use of God's Word. The systematic treatments are squarely anchored in historical research and demonstrate how the historic tradition of the Lutheran confession comes alive in this new millennium. We hope that readers will therefore learn

13. Timothy J. Wengert, "Philip Melanchthon's Last Word to Cardinal Lorenzo Campeggio, Papal Legate at the 1530 Diet of Augsburg," in *Dona Melanchthoniana: Festgabe für Heinz Scheible zum 70. Geburtstag*, ed. Johanna Loehr (Stuttgart-Bad Cannstatt: Frommann-Holzboog, 2001), 483.

something about the practice of Lutheran theology from the differing styles of conveying these summaries and applications for proclaiming the Lutheran tradition. In these discourses, readers will find suggestions out of the Wittenberg tradition for the way the message of new life in Christ is to be proclaimed, taught, and lived.

This volume, therefore, is not a textbook on Christian doctrine but a conversation about the genius of Luther and Melanchthon's way of thinking. It is an exploration of decisive elements in the matrix or conceptual framework, the nervous system, of Wittenberg theology. It aims to prepare Lutherans and non-Lutherans alike for viewing God's world through biblical lenses, lenses ground by the Wittenberg reformation. For amid the crises that the people of God face in various parts of the world at the beginning of the twenty-first century, we believe that Luther's approach to the questions of the meaning of our humanity and God's way of communicating with us can guide the formulation of our thought in decisive ways. We believe that these essays will demonstrate that Martin Luther is indeed a man for this season in the history of Christ's church.

PART ONE

"OUR THEOLOGY"

Luther's Definition of the Human Creature through "Two Kinds of Righteousness"

We set forth two worlds, as it were, one of them heavenly and the other earthly. Into these we place these two kinds of righteousness, which are distinct and separated from each other. The righteousness of the law is earthly and deals with earthly things; by it we perform good works. . . . But this righteousness [of the gospel] is heavenly and passive. We do not have it of ourselves; we receive it from heaven. We do not perform it; we accept it by faith, through which we ascend beyond all laws and works.

Luther, "Lectures on Galatians, 1531–1535"

This is our theology, by which we teach a precise distinction between these two kinds of righteousness, the active and the passive, so that morality and faith, works and grace, secular society and religion may not be confused. Both are necessary, but both must be kept within their limits.

Luther, "Lectures on Galatians, 1531–1535"

For nearly five hundred years Lutheran identity has been indelibly linked to the teaching that sinners are justified by God's favor because of Christ, a justification that is received through faith alone. This is the teaching by which the church stands and falls, Lutherans confess. Not surprisingly then, the question of how a sinner is justified occupied center stage in Lutheran thought and life. Over the years, Lutheran systematic theologians have tried to show how all theology centers on and revolves around this single question.[1] They have explored how the answer to that question is expressed in a wide variety of biblical images, including reconciliation, new creation, and forgiveness of sins.[2]

While Lutheran biblical theologians have often focused on Paul's letter to the Romans or Galatians, they have also shown how the Scriptures as a whole are anchored in the teaching of justification. Lutheran pastoral theologians have shown how justification, brought about by maintaining the proper distinction between law and gospel, expresses itself in pastoral care.[3] Here in part 1 we explore the Lutheran anthropological presupposition that God shaped human life according to two dimensions, with two kinds of righteousness.

What is not readily recognized or sufficiently appreciated is how the entire discussion on justification is not limited to the question regarding one's salvation, or to the issue of whether or not a person is on God's good side. In large part, the doctrine of justification, like the closely related doctrine of original sin, is a question of anthropology: How do we define a human being? Although the early church focused on the mystery of the Trinitarian relations along with the unity of the natures in Christ, the Reformation focused on issues related to human existence. These included such topics as the image of God, original sin, whether the human will is free or bound, justification, sanctification, and the final beatification of the human being. From different perspectives, these issues address questions of the origin and purpose of human life. Their answers shape how we see ourselves, define our identity, and provide a framework within which we make sense of our lives.

1. This is especially true in works on the distinction of law and gospel, such as C. F. W. Walther, *Law and Gospel*, trans. Herbert J. A. Bouman (St. Louis: Concordia, 1981); or Werner Elert, *Law and Gospel*, trans. Edward H. Schroeder (Philadelphia: Fortress, 1967); among many others.

2. J. A. O. Preus, *Just Words: Understanding the Fullness of the Gospel* (St. Louis: Concordia, 2000).

3. William Hulme's pioneering study of pastoral counseling, *Counseling and Theology* (Philadelphia: Muhlenberg, 1956), is one example. In a quite different genre, the short stories of pastoral care by Swedish bishop Bo Giertz (*The Hammer of God*, 2nd ed. [Minneapolis: Fortress, 2005]) illustrate how the doctrine of justification works in practice.

1

LUTHER'S ANTHROPOLOGICAL MATRIX

Every age brings with it a predominant set of beliefs about what it means to be human and how to live out that humanity. Each configuration of the human being also brings with it an analysis of the ailments that beset human life along with a proposal of the sort of cures that are needed. Most people imbibe these understandings of what it means to be a human being without giving them much thought. We seldom if ever stop to think about the foundation on which our goals for life and our decisions rest. But our attitudes and actions arise out of the axioms and principles that constitute our conception of what a human being should be and do. We learn our presuppositions about who we are at our core from our parents and the surrounding world, which has been shaped by the prevailing currents in church, university, and society. The ancient Greeks used the discipline of philosophy to think about what it means to be a human being and how human beings should live in the world. In the twentieth century, modern societies have increasingly drawn on the more recently developed disciplines of the social sciences, such as psychology, neuropsychology, sociology, cultural anthropology, political science, behavioral economics, and sociobiology, to identify the elements

that must be included in any definition of what it means to be human.
As such, contemporary thinkers have come to see the human being primarily as, among other designations, a machine, an animal, a sexual
being, an economic being, a pawn of the universe, a free being, a social
being, or a genetic product.

In spite of the multiplication of academic disciplines in the twentieth century that focus on the biological, social, psychological, and
evolutionary understanding of the human creature, these modern approaches provide a very limited perspective from which the human
person can understand the human condition. The sixteenth-century
Reformers recognized that it was not enough for human beings to study
themselves. That provided too limited a horizon. They could not stand
outside themselves to gain the necessary perspective from which they
could comprehend the totality of their being and existence. Because we
are creatures, what it means to be fully human simply lies beyond the
grasp of the human mind. Creatures cannot, by the very definition of
what it means to be a creature, comprehend and understand everything
about their Creator, and because their relationship with their Creator
stands at the heart of their existence, they cannot grasp everything about
themselves. Lacking the ability to step outside of themselves, human
beings take on a sense of self-exalted importance or find themselves
struggling with a sense of insignificance and helplessness within the
universe.

For example, many modern observers define the human creature as
a free and autonomous being who can understand and grasp the comprehensive unity of reality. They view all humans as self-constituting,
self-creating, and self-actualizing beings capable of controlling their
environment through the use of reason, thereby securing the future
from destruction for the benefit of humankind and nature. This version
of modernity gave rise to the hope of inevitable progress and the dream
of creating a utopian world as seen in TV shows like *Star Trek*. Nevertheless, modernity has failed as a system of comprehensive, redemptive
meaning. Postmodernity came to recognize that humans are not free,
autonomous beings, looking out on the universe from a privileged and
objective position; instead they are the product of local economic, social, and historical forces often outside the control of human reason.
In the process, postmodernity displaced human beings from the center
of the universe and its understanding by refusing to see the self as an
independent consciousness that is not merely the product of contextual
conditions that formed it. For many postmodern individuals, the loss of
control over meaning and history and the subsequent marginalization
this produced often led to a sense of despondency and meaningless-
ness. Thus, the postmodern person sees human beings sliding toward

more apocalyptic visions like those portrayed in *Mad Max*.[1] Because both views (modern and postmodern) lack a theological perspective, counting God as not present or active in daily life, they thereby leave the human being to oscillate between defiance and despondency, pride and despair.

For this reason we need to view anthropology theologically if we are to comprehend the full mystery of what it means to be a human being and to grasp the foundation and purpose of our existence. Sixteenth-century reformers like Martin Luther and his colleague Philip Melanchthon developed their theological perspective of the human being within a framework that Luther called the "two kinds of [human] righteousness," two distinct ways in which every human creature pursues existence, two dimensions to what it means to be human. This view provided the theological assumptions for everything they had to say about the relationship between God and the human being. This distinction between the two kinds of righteousness is one of the elements that we can describe as the "nervous system" running through the body of Christian teaching as these reformers thought of public teaching of Scripture.[2] So important was this framework that Luther refers to the two kinds of righteousness as "our theology" in his famous *Galatians Commentary* (1535).[3] In some ways, this work represents the culmination of his thinking on the two kinds of righteousness. He had first hinted at it in the Heidelberg Disputation, and then developed it in his sermons entitled "Three Kinds of Righteousness" (1518),[4] "Two Kinds of Righteousness" (1519),[5] "On Monastic Vows" (1522),[6] and his sermons on Genesis (1523/1527).[7] Similarly, Melanchthon identified the two kinds of righteousness as the heart of the issue, which then shaped his entire theological argument in his masterwork, the Apology of the Augsburg Confession, although he had

1. See Gary A. Phillips, ed., *Poststructural Criticism and the Bible: Text/History/Discourse* (Atlanta: Scholars Press, 1990), 22–24.

2. See Introduction above.

3. See Robert Kolb, "Luther on the Two Kinds of Righteousness: Reflections on His Two-Dimensional Definition of Humanity at the Heart of His Theology," *Lutheran Quarterly* 13 (1999): 449–66, esp. 453; Kolb, "God Calling, 'Take Care of My People': Luther's Concept of Vocation in the Augsburg Confession and Its Apology," *Concordia Journal* 8 (1982): 4–11; and David A. Lumpp, "Luther's 'Two Kinds of Righteousness': A Brief Historical Introduction," *Concordia Journal* 23 (1993): 27–38.

4. *WA* 2:41–47.

5. *WA* 2:9–146; *LW* 31:297–99.

6. *WA* 8:573–669. See Robert Kolb, "Mensch-Sein in zwei Dimensionen: Die zweierlei Gerechtigkeit und Luthers *De votes monasticis Iudicium*," in *Luther und das monastische Erbe*, ed. Christoph Bultmann, Volker Leppin, and Andreas Lindner (Tübingen: Mohr Siebeck, 2007).

7. *WA* 24:1–710.

also been working with the presuppositions it provided from as early as 1524.[8]

Working within the matrix of the two kinds of righteousness, the reformers clarified the nature of the relationship between the Creator, who bestows "passive righteousness" on his creatures (first in creation and then in redemption) through the creative and re-creative Word, and the human creature, who responds in faith and trust. The distinction between the two kinds of righteousness allowed the reformers without qualification to extol the gospel by removing human activity as a basis for justification before God. At the same time, it clarified the relationship of the human creature to the world in which God had placed him or her to live a life of "active righteousness" for the well-being of the human community and the preservation of the environment. The two kinds of righteousness, however, are inseparable from one another. The passive righteousness of faith provides the core identity of a person; the active righteousness of love flows from that core identity out into the world.

This framework remains an indispensable tool for dealing with the perennial temptation to consider human existence one-dimensionally. Such a single dimension occurs either when human works become the basis of justification before God or when "faith alone" appears to render human activity irrelevant and unimportant in the Christian life. Over against both tendencies, the two kinds of righteousness enable Lutherans fully and unreservedly to affirm two simultaneous and yet distinct genuine dimensions of human existence without one compromising the other.

The Contours of the Two Kinds of Righteousness

Although the term "righteousness" is no longer a part of our everyday vocabulary, it is a basic and in some ways an indispensable concept if we hope to grasp the message of the Bible. Its disuse is unfortunate since the meaning of "righteousness" is not terribly difficult or complex. Simply put, to be righteous is to be the human person God envisioned when he created us. It has to do with meeting God's "design specifications" for being a human creature and fulfilling the purpose for which God created us.[9] Integral to his design, God created us as relational beings (in Lu-

8. See Charles P. Arand, "Two Kinds of Righteousness as a Framework for Law and Gospel in the Apology," *Lutheran Quarterly* 15 (2001): 417–39. See also Timothy J. Wengert, *Human Freedom, Christian Righteousness: Philip Melanchthon's Exegetical Dispute with Erasmus of Rotterdam* (New York: Oxford University Press, 1998).

9. God's purpose is attained by conforming to a standard, or pattern, of being and behaving that has been approved by a superior, someone whose judgment is vital to us and has an important impact on our life (Apology of the Augsburg Confession IV, *Book*

ther's academic Latin, *in relatione*) who live in his presence (*coram Deo*) and at the same time in community with one another (*coram mundo*). Who I am is determined in large part by how I live with God and my fellow human creatures. As creatures we thus have an innate need to know whether or not our lives are fulfilling God's purpose.[10] We need to be justified or vindicated; we need to know that we are "measuring up." This human need expresses itself in the various life questions we ask ourselves: Why am I here? What is the purpose of my life? How and where do I fit in? Such questions give voice to the fundamental human need to connect with God and his plan for our lives. By virtue of our created nature, we need to hear God's "yes" (his original word of blessing: "very good" [Gen. 1:31]). After the fall into sin this basic element of our created humanity becomes distorted in terms of how and where we find the answers. In some instances people seek God's affirmation, but only on their own terms; in other instances people substitute the affirmation of other human beings for that of God himself.

In addition to creating us for relationship with himself, God has created us for service as his representatives within the world. As social beings we need the mutual support and recognition of the human community in which we find ourselves, to know how we are fitting in and that our contributions matter. And so, throughout life, "I am constantly trying to ascertain others' judgment about me and my own judgment of myself."[11] As Oswald Bayer has observed, the language of justification (and the verdict of guilty or not guilty) comes out of the courtroom, and we find ourselves in hundreds of smaller "courtrooms" in everyday life. With respect to other human creatures, we constantly encounter questions and challenges, such as "What were you thinking?" or "Why did you do that?" These questions require that we justify ourselves or vindicate our actions to others. Statements like these can deeply affect us: "You're hired" or "You're fired," "I love you" or "I hate you," "Welcome" or "Get out of here." The affect runs deep because as social beings we need to be accepted, acknowledged, affirmed, and noticed. Rejection, abandonment, and negative judgments cut us to the quick. These fundamentally verbal events affect how we see ourselves and understand our place within society. They determine our worth and value to others.

We can plot these two spheres of human existence on two axes: a vertical axis for life with God and a horizontal axis for life with our fellow human creatures and the goods of creation. Righteousness, or to be

---

of Concord, 164, a section from the second edition of the Apology [October 1531], which does not appear in *BSLK*).

10. Oswald Bayer, *Living by Faith: Justification and Sanctification*, Lutheran Quarterly Books (Grand Rapids: Eerdmans, 2003), 2.

11. Ibid., 3.

in a "right relationship," is determined by the nature of the respective relationships in which we find ourselves. Another way to put it is to say that God designed these relationships to function in fundamentally different ways. And so in these two relationships we encounter a twofold definition of what it means to be the person God made us to be—hence two kinds of righteousness.[12]

On one hand, human righteousness before God flows from God's activity. Like human parents, God originally gave life to his creation apart from any contribution or participation from his creatures.[13] As his handiwork, we by definition are dependent and contingent beings who have life only from the reception of God's gifts. We depend on the air we breathe, the food we eat, and the water we drink. Take these away and we die. We are receivers in the presence of God. When his human creatures lay dead in sin, God restored life to them through the death and resurrection of his Son. He bestows on us as a gift the righteousness that his Son acquired. This also took place without any contribution or cooperative participation on our part. The Holy Spirit creates faith through the gospel so that human beings can once again entrust all of life to God's care. In both instances, human beings "suffered" the work of God. In creation, God formed Adam from dust and breathed into him the breath of life. In redemption, the human creature lay on the operating table while undergoing surgery and resuscitation. Thus before God (*coram Deo*) we are entirely passive; and so our righteousness is passive, not active.[14]

On the other hand and at the same time, righteousness in the world with our fellow creatures (*coram mundo*) depends on our carrying out our God-entrusted tasks within our walks of life for the good of creation. God created human beings as male and female to complement and complete each other. Together they formed human community, and together they were given responsibility for tending God's creation. To guide them in their task, God hardwired his law into creation and engraved it on the human heart. At the same time, God gave human beings dominion in such a way that they have the freedom to figure out how best to tailor that law to the specific challenges and questions of daily life. Here human reason and imagination play critical roles in mediating the law into our daily lives in such a way as to carry out God's ongoing work of preserving and promoting creaturely well-being. Human beings carry

12. For this reason, when the Lutheran Confessions speak about righteousness, they specify which relationship they are considering by speaking about righteousness "before God" (*coram Deo*) or righteousness "before the world" (*coram mundo/hominibus*).

13. Robert Kolb, "God and His Human Creatures in Luther's Sermons on Genesis: The Reformer's Early Use of His Distinction of Two Kinds of Righteousness," *Concordia Journal* 33 (2007): 166–84.

14. "Heidelberg Disputation, 1518," thesis 25, *LW* 31:41; *WA* 1:354.29–30.

out their God-given tasks for the well-being of both the human and the nonhuman creation. As they do so, they stand accountable both to God and to their fellow creatures for the way they carry out tasks. And so in the eyes of the world (*coram mundo*), our righteousness is ever active, never passive.

Although Luther labeled the way we are to relate to God as passive righteousness, this dimension of our personhood also assumed a variety of other names such as "Christian righteousness," "the righteousness of the gospel," "the righteousness of faith," "divine righteousness," or "spiritual righteousness." In their own way, each of these phrases highlights a particular aspect of a relationship to God whereby a person's core identity is defined by a trust that lives totally from reception of God's gifts. The Wittenberg reformers constantly stressed that only the passive righteousness of faith gives all glory to Christ as our Savior and, conversely, provides the sinner with the comforting assurance of standing under the approving eye of God.

The reformers also used a rich and varied vocabulary to highlight the various activities and aspects of human life that constitute righteousness in the web of mutually constitutive human relationships. These include "human righteousness," "civil righteousness," "political righteousness," "ceremonial righteousness," "righteousness of the law," "righteousness of reason," "carnal righteousness," and similar expressions. There are almost as many specific ways to demonstrate and implement the human righteousness designed by God as there are human communities, responsibilities, and tasks (though God's elemental structure for human life hovers behind them). In each situation all these ways contribute to the well-being of life within the world.

The Relationship of the Two Kinds of Righteousness

Luther insisted that to affirm both dimensions of human existence, they must be kept distinct. But in distinguishing them, Luther also stressed that the two types of righteousness are not alternative forms of human existence. To be completely and genuinely human, people need both kinds of righteousness. Luther did not see them as alternatives to one another as if we could be fully human by possessing only one kind of righteousness, either the passive or the active. Christians need both kinds of righteousness. "We must be righteous before God and man."[15] Nor did Luther compartmentalize the human being in such a way that one could be human by partly possessing passive righteousness and partly

15. "Disputation Concerning Justification, 1536," *LW* 34:162; *WA* 39.1:93.7–10.

possessing active righteousness. To be a human being as God created us to be, a perfect human specimen, involves being totally passive, as a newborn child of God, and totally active, as a responsible neighbor to other people and to the whole of God's world. But only keeping each in its proper sphere, to use the words of Gerhard Ebeling, "truly lets creation be creation and redemption be redemption."[16]

The crux of the Lutheran reformation rested on maintaining the distinction between divine righteousness (which is salvific before God) and human righteousness (which is good for the world). In the Lutheran view, the medieval church failed to distinguish between these two kinds of righteousness. It had confused the two by giving human righteousness an ultimate significance before God that it does not and cannot possess.[17] It disparaged faith as insufficient for salvation and for our relationship with God. But we need to distinguish them: the active righteousness dare never become the basis for our righteousness *coram Deo*. Any attempt to bring works into the presence of God will lead to a rejection of the Creator-creature relationship, whereby we receive our identity and life as God's children as a sheer gift. And so these reformers argued that when standing before God in heaven, human beings must leave all works behind on earth and seek nothing but the righteousness of Christ, which is received by faith. Active righteousness must remain on earth, within the relationships of our fellow human creatures. By confusing the two kinds of righteousness, or by collapsing one into the other, the medieval church ultimately undermined salvation and failed the neighbor.

From the vantage point of the Reformation's opponents' understanding of "faith alone"—opponents such as Johann Eck and Johann Cochlaeus—the danger posed by the Lutheran reformation lay in a rejection of good works, which they believe could undermine the social order and lead to anarchy. Some even placed responsibility for the German Peasants' Revolt of 1525 squarely at the doorstep of Luther's reformation because of its emphasis on the freedom of the Christian person. In response, Luther argued that the righteousness of faith does not draw us out of the world or render life in the world as an inferior order of existence. Nor does it disparage the works of daily life as inadequate expressions of Christian living in favor of pursuing "spiritual" or so-called distinctively Christian forms of living. To the contrary, Luther stressed that the passive righteousness of faith does not remain in heaven; it descends to earth and contributes to the pursuit of active righteousness in the world. Faith

16. Gerhard Ebeling, "Das Problem des Natürlichen bei Luther," in *Lutherstudien*, vol. 1 (Tübingen: Mohr Siebeck, 1971), 278–79.

17. Mary Jane Haemig, "The Confessional Basis of Lutheran Thinking on Church-State Issues," in *Church and State: Lutheran Perspectives*, ed. John R. Stumme and Robert W. Tuttle (Philadelphia: Fortress, 2003), 16.

revitalizes and renews our life in this world so that others may for the first time see how God intended human beings to live for one another and in relation to the environment. Our relationship to God shapes our relationship to creation. And so on earth we actively pursue a life of works and virtues in accordance with God's will for creation and his reclamation of creation in Christ.

Maintaining the distinction between the two kinds of righteousness allows us to affirm both dimensions of our humanity. The passive righteousness of faith brings about our salvation by restoring our relationship with God. The active righteousness of works serves the well-being of creation by looking after our neighbor. Nevertheless, a tension does exist between affirming the gospel of the forgiveness of sins and at the same time emphasizing the Creator's expectations for his restored creatures. On this side of eternity humans will always be tempted to think only in terms of one kind of righteousness, but by doing so humans lose sight of what it means to be truly human. Maintaining a proper distinction between the two kinds of righteousness also preserves the proper relationship between them. On one hand, the passive righteousness of faith rightly understood leads to embracing earthly life as the sphere for our labors. It leads us to embrace the world as the good creation of God. On the other hand, the active righteousness of works, considered within the context of a person's earthly calling, leads to the recognition that they serve creation and not salvation; it prevents us from "using the law to justify ourselves before God or lift us above our neighbors."[18]

18. Marc Kolden, "Earthly Vocation as a Corollary of Justification by Faith," in *By Faith Alone: Essays on Justification in Honor of Gerhard O. Forde*, ed. Joseph A. Burgess and Marc Kolden (Grand Rapids: Eerdmans, 2004), 273.

2

THE CORE
OF HUMAN IDENTITY

> The righteousness of faith, which God imputes to us through Christ
> without works, . . . is a merely passive righteousness. . . . For here
> we work nothing, render nothing to God; we only receive and permit
> someone else to work in us, namely, God. Therefore it is appropriate
> to call the righteousness of faith or Christian righteousness "passive."
> This is a righteousness hidden in a mystery, which the world does not
> understand. In fact, Christians themselves do not adequately understand
> it or grasp it in the midst of their temptations. Therefore it must always
> be taught and continually exercised."
>
> Luther, "Lectures on Galatians, 1531–1535"

Luther's struggle with God took place against the backdrop of the medieval conviction that a person's entire life, present and future, depends on
what God the Creator at the last judgment will say about the way human
creatures have fulfilled their creative purposes. Every aspect of one's life
is under the judging or approving eye of God. Luther was reminded of
this fact every time he entered the city church in Wittenberg. On a stone
relief above the entrance to the cemetery that surrounded the church,
Luther saw, "carved into the mandorla (an aureole shaped like an almond),
Christ seated on the rainbow as judge of the world, so angry the veins

stand out, menacing and swollen, on his forehead." A lily hung from the right side of his mouth, while a sword emerged from the left side. Together they symbolized that Christ sat as judge over the worldly as well as the spiritual realm. In other words, "Nothing escapes his judgment."[1] Standing before this Christ, a person comes face-to-face with the judging God. Believers knew that the last day was coming; this awareness and the "apocalyptic" anticipation of its final revelation of God characterized the outlook of the entire sixteenth-century European world. In the last paragraph of the Formula of Concord, the second generation of Luther's followers state that they are prepared to give an account for their teaching on the last day before the judgment seat of Christ. Human beings already had a foretaste of that judgment. As preliminary judgments on the world, God had meted out the loss of original righteousness and the loss of life, along with all the troubles of life that hasten death. They provided constant reminders of the guilty verdict and sentence of eternal death that God would be entirely justified in pronouncing on the last day, when he finally purges his creation of all sin and evil. Once that day comes, the verdict God announces will be irrevocable, final, and binding.

In medieval piety, preparing for that final word of judgment shaped a person's entire earthly existence. Before that day, there might be a faint hope of escaping a guilty verdict if a person lived rightly. How one prepared for and survived that future encounter with God lay at the heart of the crisis of pastoral care and personal faith that brought about the Reformation. Within the creedal tradition of the ancient church, Luther had been taught that Christ became incarnate and was crucified for our salvation. He had learned that those events lived on in the preaching and sacraments of the church. They were said to bestow a transforming grace, which was given in order to assist God's fallen human creatures in cultivating the habits of love that were critical for the salvation and final beatification of the human being. From the time of Augustine of Hippo, the pious had assumed that salvation was based on the principle that "like attracts like." For a person to be saved, that person had to become like God. Since God is love, a person needed to cultivate the *habitus* or disposition of love through a lifetime of grace-assisted acts of love for God.[2]

But even though the gifts of grace acquired by Christ and given in the sacraments provided some reason for hope as the faithful of late-medieval Europe prepared themselves for the last day, Luther as a medieval Catholic pilgrim knew that he still had to face the scrutiny of the resurrected

1. Oswald Bayer, "Justification: Basis and Boundary of Theology," in *By Faith Alone: Essays in Honor of Gerhard O. Forde*, ed. Joseph A. Burgess and Marc Kolden (Grand Rapids: Eerdmans, 2004), 78, with reference to *LW* 45:59.

2. Steven Ozment, *The Age of Reform (1250–1550): An Intellectual and Religious History of Late Medieval and Reformation Europe* (New Haven: Yale University Press, 1980).

Christ as his judge. Unfortunately, the outcome of a life devoted to cultivating the *habitus* of love was anything but certain, a point captured poignantly by a German catechist on the eve of the Reformation. In *Mirror of a Christian Man*, a German priest named Dietrich Kolde lamented: "There are three things I know to be true that frequently make my heart heavy. The first troubles my spirit, because I have to die. The second troubles my heart more, because I do not know when. The third troubles me above all. I do not know where I will go."[3] The inevitable arrival of that day of wrath (*dies irae*, the Latin term used in popular literature) drove the monk Luther to despair because he realized that he could not face Christ as his ultimate judge and survive, no matter how hard he tried to live a holy life. And yet, as students of the Reformation know, Luther experienced a dramatic reversal. A shift in existence from sin to liberation is the story of the life and theology of Martin Luther.[4] He arrived at the point where he could joyfully pray for its appearance: "Come, dear last day." So what brought about his change of heart?

The Righteousness of God

Luther knew that the concept of God's righteousness meant that God acts in character in a way that is consistent with his nature. But Luther had been taught that the "righteousness of God" referred primarily (if not exclusively) to God's fairness or justice executed when he judges those who failed to live up to his expectations and rewards those who lived holy lives. The German word *rechtfertigen*, "to justify or render righteous," in sixteenth-century German thought meant "to do justice to," to inflict judicial punishment on those who had done wrong. It meant to execute the law's demands. It was used forensically, as an act carried out by speaking, the pronouncement of a judge.[5] This narrow definition as an expression of the performance of justice is rooted in the Hebrew Scriptures and the ancient philosophers who used it to define *epieikeia*, "fairness or equity." Thus, in his earlier years as a monk, Luther understood Romans 1:17 only in terms of the active righteousness that God demands from us. Looking back some years later, he recalled that the phrase "the righteousness of God" had stood in his way. "For I hated that word 'righteousness of God,' which, according to the use and custom of

---

3. Denis Janz, *Three Reformation Catechisms: Catholic, Anabaptist, Lutheran* (New York: Mellen, 1982), 127.

4. Bayer, "Justification," 81.

5. Werner Elert, "Deutschrechtliche Züge in Luthers Rechtfertigungslehre," in *Ein Lehrer der Kirche: Kirchlich-theologische Aufsätze und Vorträge von Werner Elert*, ed. Max Keller-Hüschemenger (Berlin: Lutherisches Verlagshaus, 1967), 29–31.

all the teachers, I had been taught to understand philosophically regarding the formal or active righteousness, as they called it, with which God is righteous and punishes the unrighteous sinner."[6] As a result,

> I did not love, yes, I hated the righteous God who punishes sinners, and secretly, if not blasphemously, certainly murmuring greatly, I was angry with God, and said, "As if, indeed, it is not enough, that miserable sinners eternally lost through original sin, are crushed by every kind of calamity by the law of the Decalogue, without having God add pain to pain by the Gospel and also by the Gospel threatening us with his righteousness and wrath!"[7]

In light of that, Luther viewed the gospel not as a different kind of righteousness than that set forth in Moses. The gospel simply set higher standards for achieving righteousness than Moses. "I regarded both [types of righteousness] as one thing and said that there was no difference between Christ and Moses except time and perfection."[8]

But Luther's reformation breakthrough occurred when he realized that with the phrase "The just shall live by faith" (Rom. 1:17), the gospel reveals a different kind of righteousness, a righteousness that is not demanded from us by God, but a righteousness that God bestows on us. "I learned to distinguish between the righteousness of the law and the righteousness of the gospel."[9] "There I began to understand that the righteousness of God is that by which the righteous [person] lives by a gift of God, namely by faith, and this is the meaning: the righteousness of God is revealed in the gospel, namely, the passive righteousness with which merciful God justifies us by faith, as it is written, 'He who through faith is righteous shall live.' Here I felt that I was altogether born again and had entered paradise itself through open gates."[10]

At this point, Luther discovered that Christ's death made manifest an everlasting mercy and love lying at the core of God's being. He expressed this succinctly in his Large Catechism: "We could never come to recognize the Father's favor and grace were it not for the Lord Christ, who is a mirror of the Father's heart. Apart from him we see nothing but an angry and terrible judge confronting us on the Last Day."[11] In other

6. Preface to first volume of the 1545 Wittenberg edition of his Latin works, *LW* 34:336; *WA* 54:185.12–20.

7. "Preface to Latin Works," *LW* 34:366; *WA* 54:185–86.

8. *WA TR* 5:210.6–7, #5518.

9. Luther expresses this distinction with striking clarity in his Great Confession of 1528: "For to be holy [*heilig*] and to be saved [*selig*] are two entirely different things. We are saved through Christ alone; but we become holy both through this faith and through these divine foundations and orders" (*LW* 37:365; *WA* 26:505.18–21).

10. "Preface to Latin Works," *LW* 34:337; *WA* 54:186.16.

11. Large Catechism, Creed, conclusion, 65; *Book of Concord*, 440; *BSLK*, 660.

words, the righteousness of God did not consist of God's demands as a judge, but of God's gift of salvation as a Father. This meant that when God punishes (even though he is just to do so), he acts in a way that is in some sense alien to him (*opus alienum*); and when God saves, he is acting in a way that is proper and appropriate to his very essence (*opus proprium*). God acted in character by freely assuming full responsibility for restoring his human creatures to their original righteousness, apart from any deserving activity on their part. This meant that salvation was not an arbitrary plan or capricious decision of a fickle God. Instead, God acted rightly (righteously) when he freely and unconditionally bound himself to reclaim the very creatures who had rejected him.[12]

Thus, when God acted to save his human creatures, he acted in a way that was consistent and congruent with his work as Creator when he created all things through the Word. Luther came to see that in creating heaven and earth out of nothing (*ex nihilo*), God established the relationship between himself and his human creatures as that of unconstrained giver to absolute receiver. For he had taken responsibility for the origin of everything that exists, including caring for his people. The Small Catechism draws Luther's characteristic language for justification into the article on creation when it elegantly states: I was created by "sheer divine goodness and mercy" and "without any merit or worthiness in me."[13] God created the world for Adam and Eve before they even existed. They simply inherited and received the world as a gift from God. Similarly, Adam and Eve were not given a probationary period in which to demonstrate that they were worthy of their humanity. It could not be earned. It was a gift passively received. Although they could not become righteous by keeping God's commands, they could become sinners, an abiding mystery beyond human grasp. The Creator continued to show his disposition of love and mercy to his human creatures in the preservation of creation. Here Luther learned from his instructors in the Ockhamist school of late-medieval theology that while God could do anything he wanted according to his absolute power (*potentia absoluta*), he had pledged himself to act in accord with his promises, namely, his "ordained" or "ordered" power (*potentia ordinata*).[14] In other words, God does not act in an arbitrary or capricious way. "What a kind, fine God he is! Nothing but sweetness and goodness—he feeds us, preserves us, nourishes us."[15]

---

12. Paul Althaus, *The Theology of Martin Luther*, trans. Robert C. Schultz (Philadelphia: Fortress, 1966), 182.

13. Small Catechism, Creed, *Book of Concord*, 354; *BSLK*, 510.

14. Heiko A. Oberman, *The Harvest of Medieval Theology: Gabriel Biel and Late Medieval Nominalism* (Cambridge: Harvard University Press, 1963), 30–47.

15. "Genesis Lectures 1535–1545" (on Gen. 1:9–13), *WA* 24:39.23–25.

This act of unconstrained generosity through God's creation determines human identity and self-perception. In his catechetical writings Luther argued that the first article of the Apostles' Creed describes "who you are, whence you came, whence came heaven and earth. You are God's creation, his handiwork, his workmanship."[16] In brief, the article on creation teaches people to confess, "I am a creature."[17] In many of his writings, Luther rejoiced in his creatureliness. It is a great honor to be called a creature. "It is a costly, great thing, so it is yet here a much higher and greater thing to be God's work and creature."[18] Although the world may seek honor in power and riches, the fact of the matter is that there is no higher title than to be called a creature of God. "How much more lordly is it, that God says to me: you shall be my creature and be the best creature, although the others also are good."[19]

This confession distinguishes God's human creatures from his nonhuman creation since human creatures alone are able to perceive their Creator and recognize themselves as creatures.[20] "No other creatures recognize the Creator nor know him, nor know where they come from, that have been created."[21] At the core of that recognition lies the realization that God freely created humans, who live by faith. They know that they and the course of their lives do not belong to themselves.[22] In brief, we are to perceive ourselves as creatures, and we are to recognize God as the exclusive giver of our lives and the whole context of created reality. Thus Luther argued, "I must learn to see myself as a creature of God and as one who receives everything from him and can thank him: 'If you know this, you will be a greater doctor than all the doctors of the university!'"[23] Faith lies at the core of human existence.

To Know Christ Is to Know His Benefits

According to the Reformation narrative of the gospel, God restored us to the fullness of our humanity—restored our righteousness—by sending his Son not only to make known the essence of God but also to restore

16. "Personal Prayer Book, 1522," *LW* 43:210; *WA* 38:373.20–21.

17. Albrecht Peters, *Kommentar zu Luthers Katechismen*, ed. Gottfried Seebass, 5 vols. (Göttingen: Vandenhoeck & Ruprecht, 1990–94), 2:57.

18. *WA* 45:15.1–2.

19. *WA* 45:16.1–3.

20. Michael Beintker, "Das Schöpfercredo in Luthers Kleinem Katechismus," *Neue Zeitschrift für Religionsphilosophie* 31 (1989): 12.

21. *WA* 42:xxi.30.

22. Beintker, "Schöpfercredo," 16.

23. Katechismuspredigten (1528), *WA* 30.1:88.22–24. See Beintker, "Schöpfercredo," 11.

what it means to be human. Because he understood the "image of God" to be grounded in true trust in God, Luther believed that sinners had lost that image even though sinners could to some extent live outwardly moral lives. Thus, Christ became incarnate in order to be the human being that God intended us to be when he created us, one who lives in complete dependence on the Father. In addition, as a human being he was "full of love, mercy, grace, humility, patience, wisdom, light, and everything good. His whole being was dedicated to serving everyone and harming no one."[24] Thus, the righteousness that God restores to human beings is not a righteousness that belongs intrinsically to his divine nature, but a righteousness that Christ acquires for us as the second Adam, to use Paul's image from Romans 5:12–21. Thus, Luther's followers stressed that while Christ was "both God and a human being in one inseparable person, he was thus as little under the law—since he was Lord of the law—as he was obligated to suffer and die for himself."[25] But his submission to the Father led him freely to place himself under the law and live a life in complete conformity to the law, thereby becoming the flawless substitute for sinners. Every event that occurred in his life laid the basis for his restoration of human righteousness through his death and resurrection. Luther's disciples stressed that the total obedience of the whole Christ (as God and man) to the path chosen for him by the Father is our righteousness.[26] As such, the righteousness that we receive is an "alien" righteousness, a righteousness that is acquired by someone else and belongs to someone else. It is given to us from outside of us. As Luther expressed it, "Above this life I have another righteousness, another life, which is Christ."[27]

However, it was the passive obedience of Christ, namely, his suffering and death, that received special prominence in the writings of the reformers. Luther expressed this core conviction of Christianity in the Smalcald Articles (1537): "Jesus Christ, our God and Lord, 'was handed over to death for our trespasses and was raised for our justification' (Rom. 4:25)."[28] On the cross he took our sins on himself as if they were his very own. In Luther's characteristically vivid language, he observed that in dying, Christ is not acting for his own person. "Now he is not the Son of God born of the Virgin. But he is a sinner, who has and bears the sins of Paul, the former blasphemer, persecutor, and assaulter; of Peter

24. "Genesis Lectures, 1535–1545" (on Gen. 1:24–27), WA 24:49.23–51.8.

25. Formula of Concord III.15, Book of Concord, 564; BSLK, 918–19.

26. They hold this over against the sixteenth-century reformer Andreas Osiander (and those who today advocate the equation of Luther's understanding of justification with the Eastern Orthodox view of salvation by theosis).

27. "Lectures on Galatians, 1531–1535," LW 26:9; WA 40.1:48.17–20.

28. Book of Concord, 301; BSLK, 415.

who denied Christ; of David, who was an adulterer and a murderer, and who caused the Gentiles to blaspheme the name of the Lord [Rom. 2:21–24]."[29]

Jesus Christ took the sins of human beings on his own body, not in the sense that he committed them, but he took our sins on himself in order to make satisfaction for them. As he eloquently expressed it in his Small Catechism, Christ "redeemed us lost and condemned creatures . . . purchased and won us from sin, death, and the power of the devil not with gold or silver, but with his holy precious blood and innocent suffering and death." Here one must be careful about dogmatizing atonement theories, for this satisfaction was no buyout or payoff. It was execution.[30] The law collected the wages of sin by condemning and executing him. The cross is where God carried out his judgment. There "God rendered his verdict upon sin; it is evil, and it must be destroyed."[31] In other words, Christ endured the final eschatological judgment that human beings, by their sin, fully deserved. Luther likened Christ's innocent death to an umbrella protecting us against the heat of God's wrath.[32] Along the same line of thought, one of Melanchthon's favorite titles for Christ is that of propitiator or atoning sacrifice. Like a lightning rod, Christ attracted, absorbed, and dissipated the wrath of God that had been stored up and was waiting for us on the last day. And so with Christ's death the law's claim and judgment on God's children died.

By raising Christ from the dead, God vindicated him as our righteousness. Commenting on the passage, "He arose for our justification" (Rom. 4:25), Luther declared that Christ's "victory is a victory over the law, sin, our flesh, the world, the devil, death, hell and all evils; and this victory of his he has given to us. Even though these tyrants, our enemies, accuse us and terrify us, they cannot drive us into despair or condemn us. For Christ, whom God the Father raised from the dead, is Victor over them, and he is our righteousness."[33] As the risen Christ, he continues to act as the mediator and intercessor for Christians from now until his return. The reformers especially emphasized this point in their polemic against the cult of saints. Christians no longer needed any recourse to the saints either as mediators of salvation or for intercession. "Christ has gone to the Father, not as a Judge but as one who has been made for us wisdom, righteousness, sanctification and redemption from God

29. "Lectures on Galatians, 1531–1535," LW 26:277; WA 40.1:433.26–31.

30. Robert Kolb, "God Kills to Make Alive: Romans 6 and Luther's Understanding of Justification (1535)," Lutheran Quarterly 12 (1998): 46.

31. Robert Kolb, "Luther's Theology of the Cross," Lutheran Quarterly 16 (2002): 454.

32. "Lectures on Galatians, 1531–1535," LW 26:153; WA 40.1:263.33–264.16.

33. "Lectures on Galatians, 1531–1535," LW 26:21–22; WA 40.1:65.12–17.

(1 Cor. 1:30); in short, . . . he is our High Priest, interceding for us and reigning over us and in us through grace."[34]

To summarize, by his death Christ swept the house clean of all sin; by his life he then refurnishes it with his own righteousness. For this reason, the Lutheran Confessions untiringly reiterate the point that we are righteous because of Christ (*propter Christum*).

The Word Bestows the Benefits (Righteousness) of Christ

As they inquired into how we receive the righteousness of Christ, the reformers made a critical distinction between Christ obtaining salvation for us two thousand years ago and Christ delivering salvation to us centuries later. Here Luther's strong theology of the Word steps into the foreground: "Although the work took place on the cross and the forgiveness of sins has been acquired, yet it cannot come to me in any other way than through the word."[35] For Luther, then, a Christian who desires to receive the forgiveness of sins cannot run to the cross, for there forgiveness is not yet imparted to us. Nor can we count on receiving it by keeping the memory of the suffering of Christ alive in our minds. Instead, we must go to the Word that imparts, gives, proffers, and delivers the forgiveness of sins that has been purchased on the cross.[36] Christ bestows his righteousness on God's human creatures through the Spirit, who brings it to us in the gospel. Luther saw in his opponents, both the medieval theologians as well as the more radical elements of the Reformation such as the Anabaptists, a tendency to deal with God apart from the Word. In the former instance, the church claimed a revelation of God to its hierarchy; in the latter instance, they saw it as an inner voice within each Christian. These examples attested for Luther that the chronic refusal to deal with God through the Word "clings to Adam and his children from the beginning to the end of the world—fed and spread among them as poison by the old dragon."[37]

What we must not underestimate in the thought of Luther and Melanchthon is how the concept of "promise" is central to their understanding of the gospel and their definition of faith. While "good news" provides an etymological translation of *euangelion* (gospel), it runs the risk of being viewed primarily as information about yesterday's events. Like a newspaper, it deals with past events, in this case, the past events of Jesus's

34. "Lectures on Galatians, 1531–1535," *LW* 26:8; *WA* 40.1:47.16–21.

35. Large Catechism, Lord's Supper, 31, *Book of Concord*, 469; *BSLK*, 713.

36. Herbert Girgensohn, *Teaching Luther's Catechism*, trans. John W. Doberstein (Philadelphia: Muhlenberg, 1959), 107.

37. Smalcald Articles (1537) III.viii.9, *Book of Concord*, 323; *BSLK*, 455–56.

earthly life. But when that happens, faith can be seen as little more than a form of intellectual activity, what the reformers criticized as historical faith. Such faith by itself cannot save since even the devils believe that Jesus died and rose. By itself, the biography of Jesus is not yet gospel. It becomes the gospel when it grasps the sinner with the promise that Christ lived, died, and rose "for you!" and "for me!" and "for us!"

The term "promise" highlights several things. First, the Bible is filled with promises. The promises of God highlight the unity of the Old and New Testaments better than the term good news. Second, the promise brings out the personal and relational character of God. God himself makes promises to us. Third, in the gospel God promises that he will receive us into the new age as fellow children and coheirs with Christ. The promise is a pledge and guarantee of God's favor in the eschaton. Finally, and most important for Luther, the promise is not an announcement that will be fulfilled only in the future; it is a creative word that takes immediate and present effect.[38] In the here and now it brings about the very thing that it announces about the future. It creates the reality that we are justified. It announces that we have gone through the eschatological judgment ahead of time.

The Word that freely justifies us is the same Word that first gave us physical life. Luther liked to say that God has his own grammar when he speaks. His words are not like our words, which we speak into thin air. Instead, God's words make things happen. Commenting on Psalm 2, Luther stated, "And when he speaks, the mountains tremble, kingdoms are scattered, then indeed the whole earth is moved."[39] God's Word says what it does and does what it says. Indeed, by his Word God calls into existence the things that do not exist (Rom. 4:17). When he said, "Let there be . . . ," he brought all things into existence (Gen. 1:3, 6, 9, 11, 14, 20, 24, 26). When God says "'Sun, shine,' the sun is there at once and shines."[40] Accordingly, the words of God are not full of hot air but are "things very great and wonderful, which we see with our eyes and feel with our hands." This means that human life—life as such—is a life that depends on God and God's Word. God's Word did not bring about all things only at the initial moment of creation, but embraced the entire subsequent creation. "For when God once said (Gen. 1:28): 'Be fruitful,' that Word continues to be effective down to this day and preserves nature in a miraculous way."[41] Luther believed that God already created us who live centuries later when his Word created the entire world (Gen. 1–2). Speaking about himself, Luther commented:

38. Bayer, *Living by Faith: Justification and Sanctification*, (Grand Rapids: Eerdmans, 2003), 51.
39. "Lecture on Psalm 2, 1532," *LW* 12:32–33; *WA* 40.2:230.20–231.28.
40. "Genesis Lectures, 1535–1545" *LW* 1:21–22; *WA* 42:17.
41. "Genesis Lectures, 1535–1545" *LW* 4:4; *WA* 43:138.36–41.

In God's sight I was begotten and multiplied immediately when the world began, because this Word, "and God said: 'Let us make man,'" created me too. Whatever God wanted to create, he created when he spoke. Not everything has come into view at once. Similarly, an arrow or a ball which is shot from a cannon (for it has greater speed) is sent to its target in a single moment, as if it were, and nevertheless it is shot through a definite space; so God, through his Word, extends his activity from the beginning of the world to its end.[42]

For this reason Luther can describe God's Word as being "without end"[43] and remaining effective "to this day."[44] For Luther, God's creative Word runs through the past, present, and future and binds them together.[45] In God's eyes all things are present to him at the same time. For Luther, just as "the Word of the Lord had defined reality in the act of creation," so "in the act of re-creation the Word of the Lord also defined the fundamental reality of the believer's existence."[46]

Thus, there is no conflict between being declared righteous and being made righteous. For years Lutherans have debated a well-known statement by Melanchthon: "'To be justified' means that out of unrighteous people righteous people are made or regenerated; it also means that they are pronounced or regarded as righteous. For Scripture speaks both ways."[47] This is no debate between "forensic" righteousness and "essential" righteousness. To put it this way, as Gerhard Forde remarked, is to pose false alternatives. He argues that "the absolutely forensic character of justification renders it effective—justification that actually kills and makes alive. It is to be sure, 'not only' forensic, but that is the case only because the more forensic it is, the more effective it is!"[48] Thus, justification is not a legal fiction. The word does what it says. When God declares a person to be righteous, that person is actually righteous. The Word has brought about a new reality. A new relationship has been established. Luther did not define the status of the believer "as if" one were righteous. The believer was not fundamentally a sinner for whom God "has purchased a ticket for heaven," where the sinner will finally lose that sinful identity while in this life the sinful identity remains primary. "For Luther the Word of the Lord had defined reality in the act of creation, and in the act of re-creation the Word of the Lord also defined the fundamental reality

42. "Genesis Lectures, 1535–1545," *LW* 1:75; *WA* 42:57.
43. "Genesis Lectures, 1535–1545," *LW* 1:75; *WA* 42:57.
44. "Genesis Lectures, 1535–1545," *LW* 1:21, 54; *WA* 42:16–17, 40.
45. "Genesis Lectures, 1535–1545," *LW* 1:76; *WA* 42:58.
46. Kolb, "God Kills," 51.
47. Apology of the Augsburg Confession IV.72, *Book of Concord*, 132; *BSLK*, 174.
48. Gerhard O. Forde, *Justification by Faith, a Matter of Death and Life* (1982; repr., Mifflintown, PA: Sigler, 1991), 36.

of the believer's existence."[49] In this Word, God created a relationship in which the new identity and status is determined by the Word.

With their understanding of the gospel as promise, the reformers provided a new understanding of the sacraments. By the mid-1520s Luther moved beyond an Augustinian-Platonic framework for the sacraments that viewed them as signs of a reality that lies elsewhere. He moved toward a view of God's Word in its sacramental form that brings the benefits of Christ into the world. In baptism we here and now undergo the death and resurrection that we will go through when Christ returns. Thus, baptism does not simply initiate us into a life of progressive dying and rising through repentance by which we slowly become emancipated from sin. "Paul teaches that baptism is not a sign but the garment of Christ, in fact, that Christ himself is our garment."[50] Holy absolution is God's eschatological word, his final word, spoken in the present. The Lord's Supper imparts the body and blood of Christ "for the forgiveness of sins," for pardon in the last judgment. Thus, it promises that we will participate in the eschatological banquet in the age to come. Whoever partakes of it already now sits at the table of the Lord and one day will be his guest in the future reign of God. Receiving with the mouth the body and blood of Christ brings to remembrance the death of Christ and arouses the anticipation of the coming of Christ. In the meantime, the reception of the body and blood of Christ is food for wayfarers, enabling them to wait for centuries or even millennia for Christ to return.

The declaration that we have been vindicated or justified does not come directly or immediately out of heaven to us. Instead, God delivers his promise to us through "another human person—in a very creaturely fashion."[51] God engages his people again through the relational dimension of life. God established the ministry of the Word. The reformers drew on the rationale of Paul in Romans 10 that in order for people to believe, they must hear the Word; but for them to hear the Word, it must be proclaimed to them, and in order that it may be proclaimed, God sends people to proclaim it. Thus another person, speaking in the name and on the commission of God, speaks this promise to me. Yet it is the speaking and acting of God. The reformers liked to quote the words of Christ to his followers: "He who hears you hears me" (Luke 10:16). "The moment we turn away from God's promises, we are left with ourselves and our judgment about ourselves."[52] This is to fall back into uncertainty. The Lord who came near to his chosen people in the person of Jesus Christ comes near to them through the words he has others of his chosen

49. Kolb, "God Kills," 51.
50. "Lectures on Galatians, 1531–1535," LW 26:353; WA 40.1:541.32–34.
51. Bayer, Living by Faith, 43.
52. Ibid., 44.

people speak to them. In this way he bestows passive righteousness. For he wants them to have the peace and joy that comes from being certain that he loves them and will remain their Father.

Righteous by the Joyous Exchange

A promise without faith accomplishes nothing. But faith without a promise has nothing to which it can cling. For Luther and Melanchthon, the promise of new life in Christ and faith in that same promise were corollaries. A promise by its very nature seeks a response. For example, when a young man makes a proposal of marriage to a young woman, his proposal seeks a positive response that joins their two futures together. A promise seeks to elicit the response of faith. Faith grasps the promise, and in this way the promise finds its realization and fulfillment. At the same time, Luther stressed that trusting the promise is not an accomplishment that we can claim for ourselves. On the contrary, faith is the work and gift of God, who justifies a person by giving faith to that one.[53] To that end the promise of the gospel itself creates and sustains that which it seeks: faith. In an analogous way we observe that in human relationships, speaking psychologically, those who are trustworthy elicit our trust; they do not command or compel it. People have confidence in savings bonds since they are backed by the full faith and credit of the United States government. It is much more the case with the promise of God. It is as unshakeable as God is, and so it is trust creating. The reformers themselves drew on the example of Abraham, who "realized that God keeps a promise on account of his faithfulness and not on account of works or merits."[54] In our case the promise is addressed to human rebels, who resist God's overtures at every turn. Through the promise, the Holy Spirit "courts" people; he seeks to melt away their resistance and win over their hearts. In a similar way young people speak about "falling in love." This expression contains an element that suggests we were not in control of the moment, that it just "happened" to us. We do not plan for it to happen. So also when the Holy Spirit ignites the spark of faith within us that grasps the promise.

As faith responds positively to the promise, it embraces this promise and clings to the one who made the promise. Here Luther likened faith to a wedding ring by which the Christian becomes joined to Christ in marriage. Luther declares, "Christ and the soul become one flesh" (Eph. 5:31–32). Commenting on Galatians 2:20, he writes, "Faith must be taught

53. Althaus, *Theology of Luther*, 231.
54. Apology of the Augsburg Confession IV.58, *Book of Concord*, 129; *BSLK*, 171.

correctly, namely, that by it you are so cemented to Christ and he and you are as one person, which cannot be separated but remains attached to him forever and declares, 'I am as Christ.' And in turn Christ says: 'I am as that sinner who is attached to me, and I to him. For by faith we are joined together into one flesh and one bone.'"[55] Christ is not only the "object" of faith but is himself present in faith. "The believing heart holds fast to Christ just as the setting of a ring grips the jewel: we have Christ in faith."[56] Faith does not leave Christ outside as if he were merely someone to think about or believe in, but embraces him, saying, "He is my beloved, and I am His."[57]

By creating faith and joining us to Christ, the Word of God effects what Luther would call a "wonderful" or "joyous exchange" (fröhlicher Wechsel)! In developing the marriage metaphor, Luther drew on German law to develop the idea of an exchange that takes place between Christ and the believer. German law distinguished between that which belonged to a person, was that person's own (proprium), and that which one possessed or used (as in "Possession is nine-tenths of the law"). He pointed out that in marriage everything that properly belonged to the groom now comes into the possession of the bride, and everything that properly belonged to the bride now becomes the possession of the groom. This union effects an exchange. So also with Christ and the Christian. "It follows that everything [each has] is [thereafter] held in common, the good as well as the evil. The believing soul can boast of and glory in whatever Christ has as though it were its own, and whatever the soul has Christ claims as his own."[58] Everything that belonged to Christ now belongs to me, and everything that belonged to me now belongs to Christ. So in the promise Christ declared, "Your sin is mine, and my innocence is yours." By receiving the promise, faith hides nothing and holds nothing back from Christ. It replies to Christ, "My sin lies on you, and your innocence and blessedness now belong to me."[59] The Christian is thus joined to Christ by a faith that clings to the Word and now accepts that Christ is totally responsible for us. This means "our sins are now not ours but Christ's, and Christ's righteousness is not Christ's but ours."[60] Only in faith are Christ and a human being so joined together, so made one, that in God's judgment the human person participates in Christ's righteousness.[61]

55. "Lectures on Galatians, 1531–1535," LW 26:168; WA 40.1:285.12–27.
56. Althaus, Theology of Luther, 231.
57. "Theses on Faith and Law, 1535," thesis 22, LW 34:110.
58. "The Freedom of a Christian, 1520," LW 31:351; WA 7:54.32–38.
59. Althaus, Theology of Luther, 213.
60. "Explanations of the Ninety-five Theses, 1518," LW 31:189–91; WA 1:593.3–38.
61. Althaus, Theology of Luther, 231.

For Luther, the good news of this happy exchange was that a person was not required (indeed inasmuch as one was enslaved to sin) to purify oneself in order to become a worthy bride for Christ. Instead, Christ binds himself to a sinful creature. Luther drew on the example of Hosea, whom God told to marry a prostitute to illustrate that in word and faith one who is holy joined himself to those who are unholy. As a sinner Luther rejoiced that the rich and divine bridegroom Christ "marries this poor, wicked harlot, redeems her from all her evil, and adorns her with all his goodness." This means that her sins cannot now destroy her since they are laid on Christ and swallowed up by him. As a result she has the righteousness of Christ her husband, which she may boast is her own and which she can confidently display alongside "her sins in the face of death and hell."[62] In the joyous exchange, the believer gains clarity and certainty that God is no fiction and that the promise made "to all who believe" is not a lie.[63]

In other words the gospel does not require a person to become internally "like" God or ontologically "like" God in order to be united with him. In the case of an "internal" association of the believer and God, a person is not required first to become "like Christ" by being transformed psychologically so as to become a person who has a perfect and undivided love for God in order to be worthy of his love. Indeed, Roman Catholic theologians of the day saw Luther's teaching of a joyous exchange of Christ's righteousness for human sinfulness, which takes place through faith, as blasphemous. In 1526 Jacob Hochstraten, the Dominican inquisitor of Cologne, summarized the traditional Catholic teaching on the subject as he ridiculed Luther's concept of the joyous exchange, in which the holy Christ unites himself to the sinful creature and thus eradicates our sin by making it his own and replacing it in us with his own righteousness:

> What else do those who boast of such a base spectacle do than make the soul . . . a prostitute and an adulteress, who knowingly and wittingly connives to deceive her husband [Christ] and, daily committing fornication upon fornication and adultery upon adultery, makes the most chaste of men a pimp? As if Christ does not take the trouble . . . to choose . . . a pure and honorable lover! As if Christ requires from her only belief and trust and has no interest in her righteousness and the other virtues! As if a certain mingling of righteousness with iniquity and of Christ with Belial were possible![64]

62. "The Freedom of a Christian, 1520," *LW* 31:352; *WA* 7:355.24–31.
63. Stephen E. Ozment, *A Mighty Fortress: A New History of the German People* (New York: Harper Collins, 2004), 85.
64. Quoted by Ozment, *Mighty Fortress*, 84.

Hochstraten lamented that Luther listed no preconditions for the spiritual marriage of the soul with Christ except that a person believes that Christ will bestow on him or her all that Christ promises. He complained that Luther did not speak about the mutual love by which the soul loves Christ. Luther said nothing about keeping the commandments, to the keeper of which eternal life is both promised and owed. After all, in Hochstraten's view the key to union with God was to become more and more like God by acquiring the virtues Christ himself had exhibited.

In the case of the "ontological" association of God and the believer, the person disappears into God by being absorbed into God's divine being, so as virtually to lose one's individual identity as a human creature. Luther's cementing together of Christ and the sinner does not blur the distinction between the Creator and the creature. But in the early 1550s the Lutheran reformer of the city of Nuremberg, Andreas Osiander, taught an ontological transformation of a person by contending that the believer is united with the divine nature of Christ. Osiander maintained that the essential righteousness of Christ's divine nature, his righteousness as the Second Person of the Trinity, becomes the believer's righteousness before God. By being united to Christ, sinners are transformed by his eternal divine righteousness, which swallows up our righteousness (as a drop of milk in the ocean), thereby transforming us into pure brides. In this way, Christ joins himself to a pure bride. The obedience of Christ and the death of Christ were in the end of little consequence in Osiander's exposition of justification. Some recent explanations of Luther's doctrine of justification sometimes veer in Osiander's direction by interpreting a few of his statements in a way that brings him into accord with an Eastern Orthodox view of salvation by "divinization," also called *theōsis* or *theopoiēsis*. These views ignore the radically different metaphysical base of Luther's understanding and that of the Eastern church, and they ignore Luther's understanding of the dynamic, re-creative nature of God's Word.[65]

Luther opposed both the view of salvation by psychological transformation and the view of salvation by ontological transformation (both of which make sense only in a Platonic, spiritualizing frame of reference). He held that the verdict of justification does not come at the beginning or end of a movement (toward becoming increasingly righteous); instead, it establishes an entirely new situation. The joyous exchange is thus not

---

65. For a summary of this view see Tuoma Mannermaa, *Christ Present in Faith: Luther's View of Justification*, ed. Kirsi Stjena (Minneapolis: Fortress, 2005). For critiques of this view, see Klaus Schwarzwäller, "Verantwortung des Glaubens: Freiheit und Liebe nach der Dekalogauslegung Martin Luthers," in *Freiheit als Liebe bei/Freedom as Love in Martin Luther*, ed. Dennis D. Bielfeldt and Klaus Schwarzwäller (Frankfurt: Lang, 1995), 146–48; and Reinhard Flogaus, *Theosis bei Palamas und Luther* (Göttingen: Vandenhoeck & Ruprecht, 1997).

a substantial exchange but a relational exchange. It puts me in a different set of relationships, which are the critical things, whether it means substantial change or not.[66] Luther held that the Christian is a person who, to use his famous dictum, is *simul justus et peccator* (simultaneously righteous and sinful).[67] The Christian is righteous by God's re-creative pronouncement and the response of faith in Christ (whose righteous obedience is reckoned to the believer) and sinful by virtue of one's fallen human psychological disposition and imperfect performance (as a fallen human being).[68] In his usual way, Luther expressed it succinctly and elegantly: "Though I am a sinner in myself, I am not a sinner in Christ."[69] Or to put it another way, "In myself outside of Christ, I am a sinner; in Christ outside of myself, I am not a sinner."[70]

Luther's *simul justus et peccator* means that in this life a person is a sinner in the eyes of the law, the world, and oneself, while at the same time completely a saint in the eyes of God on account of Christ. We should not take Luther's *simul* to mean that a person is partially a sinner and partially righteous, as if one could quantify it in terms of percentages. That would be to think of the Christian in terms of oneself, in terms of a person's progress upward on a spiritual continuum, whereby one's sinfulness gradually diminishes as one grows in righteousness either psychologically or ontologically. But Luther does not consider the human person substantially, in terms of some "empirically verifiable endowment in the creature."[71] He views the human person relationally and holistically. Thus for him, imputed righteousness "as a divine judgment brings with it the *simul justus et peccator* as *total* states."[72] The Christian is simultaneously completely and totally righteous in the eyes of God, even as the believer is completely and totally sinful when considered in and of oneself. This double character of a *totus-totus* existence remains through all of life up to the very moment Christ raises us from the dead. Because we are both—completely and simultaneously—until death, there is a constant psychological movement between the two poles.

A person who accepts God's gracious judgment "takes the risk of living before God on no other basis than that righteousness of Christ which

---

66. Althaus, *Theology of Luther*, 213.

67. "Galatians Commentary, 1535," *LW* 26:232; *WA* 40.1:369.13–25.

68. Ozment, *History of the German People*, 85.

69. "Commentary on Psalm 51," *LW* 12:311; *WA* 40.2:327.30–35.

70. "The Private Mass and the Consecration of Priests, 1533," *LW* 38:158; *WA* 38:205 .25–31.

71. Gerhard O. Forde, "Forensic Justification and the Christian Life: Triumph or Tragedy?" in *A More Radical Gospel: Essays on Eschatology, Authority, Atonement, and Ecumenism*, ed. Mark C. Mattes and Steven D. Paulson (Grand Rapids: Eerdmans, 2004), 116.

72. Ibid., 119.

God's mercy imputes to him."[73] There is no basis in oneself for living in confidence and joy before God. A person cannot try to find oneself, to find one's humanity within oneself. Those who turn their attention inward and on their own personal experience will find "only anxiety, mortal sin, damnation and unbelief (this last is crucial, because it is the source of all the others)."[74] For Luther, this is what it means for a Christian to suffer assault and self-accusation, namely, *Anfechtung*. It is the recurrent "experience of being attacked by an awareness of how offensive I am to God, a consciousness of sin and devil." The believer must refuse to put faith in empirical experience and instead look at Christ delivered in the Word. Just as the promises made between a bride and groom on their wedding day are made in order to elicit a trust that orients their entire being toward one another as they look to the future, so God's promise elicits a daring, joyous, and unconditional trust in him that orients our entire being toward him with regard to our present and our future. To that end, Luther urged, "Let us learn, therefore, in every temptation to transfer sin, death, the curse, and all the evils that oppress us from ourselves to Christ, and on the other hand, to transfer righteousness, life, and blessing from him to us."[75] For Luther, as for his mentor Paul, there is now no condemnation for those who are in Christ Jesus (Rom. 8:1). Thus, anyone who believes in Jesus will not have to face the last judgment with any doubt as to the outcome.

In the meantime, living only on the basis of Christ's righteousness involves the recognition that God's judgment contradicts the judgment that others make about us, as well as the judgment we render on ourselves. Daily life—the home, workplace, community, society—provides the context for an unending series of performance evaluations in which our capabilities and competencies are under constant critique. In these settings and relationships, we are forced to consider how others see us and judge us. We also have to live with the image that we have of ourselves as we enter the world around us and see how we are doing in comparison to those around us with respect to education, promotions, finances, popularity, and social mobility. Such daily audits of our own self-evaluation and the daily audit of how others evaluate us will continue until death. "Nevertheless, the balance sheet does not have the first and last say about my existence." The passive righteousness of faith ultimately frees us "from being determined now and finally by such an audit." It "frees me from pronouncing final judgment on myself." The passive righteousness of faith also frees me from what others say about me, for

---

73. Althaus, *Theology of Luther*, 230.
74. Phillip Cary, "Why Luther Is Not Quite Protestant: The Logic of Faith in a Sacramental Promise," *Pro ecclesia* 14 (2005): 472.
75. "Lectures on Galatians, 1531–1535," *LW* 26:292; *WA* 40.1:454.27–33.

what they say is not the "final judgment, but is always provisional."[76] For faith believes God's gracious judgment despite all empirical evidence to the contrary. In other words, we cling to the promise regardless of how many times instant replays of our weaknesses and failures flash before our eyes.

Similarly, as faith looks to the future, it grapples with the fragile character of life. The crippling effects of sin and evil on body and soul remain evident everywhere. We see countless examples of horror within the world and calamities within our lives that call into question the final verdict of justification in Christ and the promise of the new creation. These events must not have the final word. Luther responded, "You must close your eyes and shut off all your senses and not want to know or hear anything but that which God's Word says." Thus, when events in life call into question our identity and status as children of God, the Christian must reply, "But you are the kind of God that does not examine how pious or how evil a person has been if that person looks only to your goodness and trusts."[77] This is how the two kinds of righteousness function within the life of the Christian. Christians can only cling to the God revealed in the promise of Christ even though he is hidden behind the tragedies of life and the atrocities of history.[78] The story of Abraham proved to be a favorite of the reformers for Christians to imitate. God had promised Abraham and Sarah that they would be given a child in their advanced years. Yet Abraham "did not allow himself to be pulled away from it [the promise], even though he saw that he was unclean and unworthy." He believed the promise because God keeps a promise on account of his faithfulness and not on account of our works or merits.[79]

Faith thus constitutes the core of our very being and existence before God. As Oswald Bayer puts it, "Faith is not something attached *to* the human person. My very being is faith, that is, my trusting that life and what is necessary for life is given to me."[80] Faith lets God be God and lets humans be human. It accepts God's claim on our lives. It lets God do his proper work and be the Giver that he is.[81] Faith accepts that God

---

76. Bayer, "Justification," 84–85.

77. "Genesis Lectures, 1535–1545" (on Gen. 7:1), WA 24:184.10–29.

78. On the Lament Psalms, see Ingvar Floysvik, *When God Becomes My Enemy* (St. Louis: Concordia, 1997).

79. Apology of the Augsburg Confession IV, *Book of Concord*, 129, in a passage from the second edition not given in *BSLK*.

80. Bayer, "Justification," 70.

81. See Philip S. Watson, *Let God Be God! An Interpretation of the Theology of Martin Luther* (Philadelphia: Muhlenberg, 1947), who develops this theme throughout his book. Gerhard O. Forde comments, "God insists on being related to us as the giver of the gift" (*On Being a Theologian of the Cross: Reflections on Luther's Heidelberg Disputation, 1518* [Grand Rapids: Eerdmans, 1997], 26).

determines our understanding of all reality once again as at creation: he lets us call things what they are according to his created will as well as in their fallen state (which was the subject of Luther's original use of the "calling things what they are" language in the Heidelberg Disputation, that is, viewing reality as God sees it).[82] By contrast, just as in many cultures one dishonors the giver by refusing his gifts, so unbelief dishonors God by denying his promise and refusing his gifts. Unbelief constitutes a personal rejection of the giver. In the blindness of unbelief the human being wants to claim ultimate responsibility for oneself. Unbelief does not let God be God; it does not let God be the generous giver of all good things. Through faith Christ becomes once again Lord and the acknowledged focal point of all living in such a way that frees us to focus on our neighbor. Faith allows God to do his work in us.

82. "Heidelberg Disputation, 1518," thesis 21, LW 31:40; WA 1:354.21–22.

3

THE SHAPE OF
HUMAN PERFORMANCE

Righteousness is of many kinds. There is political righteousness, with which
the emperor, the princes of the world, philosophers, and lawyers have to
deal. There is also a ceremonial righteousness, which human traditions
teach, as for example, the traditions of the pope and other such traditions.
Parents and teachers may teach this kind of righteousness without danger
because they do not attribute to it any power to make satisfaction for sin,
to please God, and to earn grace; but they teach that these ceremonies are
necessary only for moral discipline and for certain observances. There is,
in addition to these, yet another righteousness, the righteousness of the
Law or of the Decalogue.

Luther, "Lectures on Galatians, 1531–1535"

In continuity with the early church, Luther confessed that God had built
a vertical bridge to his human creatures in the incarnation and work of
Jesus Christ. Luther's insight into the gospel made it clear that the bridge
between God and the world goes in only one direction: directly into the
depth of human sin and brokenness. Our daily activities, religious or
nonreligious, do nothing to establish, reestablish, promote, preserve, or
perfect our relationship with God. Christ's righteousness makes us secure

at our core before God.[1] Thus, before God we live a "receptive" life and experience a passive righteousness. But at the same time Luther saw that the counterpart to such passiveness before God is our active, energetic engagement with the world. Over the years people have not always sufficiently appreciated this point. This is unfortunate since Luther's reformatory contribution to the church lay not only in rediscovering our passive righteousness before God. It consisted equally in his recognition that the one who clothed him in the righteousness of Christ is the same one who created him for life in this world. Thus, as Luther developed his teaching on justification in the 1520s, he also explored and extolled the creaturely life and our worldly righteousness within God's creation.[2] The Creator has created human beings in his image for a life of activity, in which they exercise the dominion he has given them in this world alongside all other people. With regard to the nature of the work and excellence with which human activities are carried out (assuming they are in accordance with God's will), there is no difference between those of Christians and non-Christians. The distinction simply refers to the fact that Christians carry out their activity in faith and that it flows from faith.

In regard to the active righteousness of human life, Luther stressed that we have been created not only for a relationship with God but also for relationships with each other. Commenting on Genesis 44:17, he observed, "We have not been created for a solitary life, to be separated from the communal society of human beings."[3] In other words, it is not good for the human person to be alone (Gen. 2:18). "The solitary life leads the human being into desperation; one needs another over against oneself. The human needs conversation."[4] As social creatures, we have been fashioned by God to live in a social web of mutually constitutive relationships, in which we not only receive life and support from others but also contribute to the life and well-being of others. Other people (parents, teachers, employers, and others) will judge us by how well we carry out our creaturely responsibilities—"which is not at all unimportant for their neighbor's well-being."[5] For this reason, Luther could

1. Mark C. Mattes and Ronald R. Darge, *Imaging the Journey* (Minneapolis: Lutheran University Press, 2006), 88.

2. As early as 1519 Luther spoke of three kinds of righteousness, distinguishing the righteousness of faith, the righteousness of works performed by a Christian, and the righteousness of works performed by non-Christians.

3. "Genesis Lectures, 1535–1545" (on Gen. 44:17), *LW* 7:366; *WA* 44:573.15–16.

4. Johannes Schwanke, "Luther on Creation," in *Harvesting Martin Luther's Reflections on Theology, Ethics, and the Church*, ed. Timothy J. Wengert (Grand Rapids: Eerdmans, 2003), 88.

5. Marc Kolden, "Earthly Vocation as Corollary of Justification by Faith," in *By Faith Alone: Essays on Justification in Honor of Gerhard O. Forde*, ed. Joseph A. Burgess and Marc Kolden (Grand Rapids: Eerdmans, 2004), 281–82.

actually state that in our human relationships the law justifies people on earth[6] inasmuch as the law defines our responsibilities (even though the law does not justify in the eyes of God). His statement makes the point that human activity is needed for the well-being of the human community in this world. Finding such righteousness in the eyes of our neighbor within the variety of situations in life in which we live may well come with its own rewards or benefits. For example, it may determine whether or not we get promotions, have a positive self-image, and the like. But inasmuch as we are dealing with secondary relationships, such evaluations cannot touch (or replace) the core of a Christian's being, which is determined by our passive righteousness of faith.

Luther's Robust Theology of Creation

Luther's conviction that God created the world, and that the world he created is good, provides the presupposition for human engagement with the world. Luther develops two aspects of creation rather extensively. First, Luther stresses the ongoing creative work (*creatio continua*) of God within the world and counts it as the necessary foundation for life in this world.[7] Second, in his creative activity God has designed us to "live as good and faithful creatures on this earth (in relation to the natural and social world that God is continually creating, preserving, and renewing)."[8] God gave human beings the privilege of exercising dominion over his creation: he gave them the responsibility of managing the goods of creation for the well-being of one's neighbor. In giving human beings that responsibility, God also holds them accountable for their management of creation. This accountability is not rendered only on the last day before God; it is also mediated through others.

These two aspects of Luther's understanding of creation come together in his reminder that God carries out his work by enlisting human beings as instruments of his creative activity for the good of his creation. Both human creatures and nonhuman creatures function as masks of God (Luther used the Latin term *larvae Dei*), behind which he remains the creative agent of life. These creatures are the instruments by which he provides and preserves life. Luther describes creatures as "the hands, channels, and means through which God bestows all blessings. For example, he gives to the mother breasts and milk for her infant or gives

6. "Lectures on Galatians, 1531–1535," *LW* 26:117; *WA* 40.1:209.
7. Kolden, "Earthly Vocation," 270.
8. Colin E. Gunton, *The Triune Creator: A Historical and Systematic Study* (Grand Rapids: Eerdmans, 1998), 208.

grain and all sorts of fruits from the earth for sustenance—things that no creature could produce by itself."[9] God is continually at work in the generation of new life, in the growing of trees and grain, in the rain and rivers, the sun and warmth, in human work with the soil and animals, creating and governing social and economic life.

Sin and human evil have not prevented God's ongoing work within creation. So effective is God's activity as Creator that the nonhuman creation continues to bring forth its bounty in spite of ecological destruction perpetrated by human beings. Moreover, in spite of their rejection of God with the fall into sin, people continue to function as God's instruments for the good of creation, even if they do so unwittingly and unwillingly: farmers, carpenters, all "who handle creation's wares, carry God's gifts to their neighbors, even if their purpose is not always to serve."[10] Luther was even willing to grant that at times the godless "fulfill the second table of the Decalogue so brilliantly that they 'indeed at times appear holier than Christians.'"[11] Although all people have God-given roles within life, only those called by God will understand that these roles are places where God has called them to serve in specific ways; only believers will see themselves as coworkers with God on earth.

According to Luther's understanding of human vocation, God carries out his creating work by summoning us to action through the gifts and needs of our neighbor to a life of constant activity and work. "Just look at your tools—at your needle or thimble, your beer barrel, your goods, your scales or yardstick or measure"; they are all crying out to you, "Friend, use me in your relations with your neighbor just as you want your neighbor to use his property in his relations to you."[12] After all, this is the reason for which God has given us the gifts of creation, to be used in service to others.

In a similar fashion Luther labeled the needs of our neighbors as God's call for us to serve. Thus, a child's need for food and clothing functions as a call from God for a mother and father to give aid. Even following the fall into sin, that summons remained, but it became what Gustaf Wingren referred to as an "unrecognized demand" that "pressures" human beings to act in a way that benefits their neighbor.[13] This means that even if non-Christians do not recognize God's call, they nevertheless discover that the needs of others are difficult

9. Large Catechism, First Commandment, 26, *Book of Concord*, 389; *BSLK*, 566.

10. Gustaf Wingren, *Luther on Vocation*, trans. Carl C. Rasmussen (Philadelphia: Muhlenberg, 1957), 9.

11. "On the Councils and the Church, 1539," *LW* 41:167; *WA* 50:643.27–29.

12. "The Sermon on the Mount," *LW* 21:23; *WA* 32:316.6–15.

13. Gustaf Wingren, *Creation and Law*, trans. Ross Mackenzie (Edinburgh: Oliver & Boyd, 1961), 57–69.

to ignore (e.g., a crying baby that needs its diaper changed) as these needs appeal to our conscience and compel us to act. In some cases their needs even compel us to act contrary to our own desires, perhaps even to our own disappointment. The needs of a sick child may result in cancelling the parents' dinner plans. This "unrecognized demand" is experienced when we encounter the expectations of others in our many relationships (e.g., as husbands, wives, parents, citizens, employees, employers, and so forth). So just as creation itself continues to yield food for the world in spite of the human insatiable appetite for sin and the resultant destruction of the environment, God guides human activity in the world for the sake of preserving and protecting the human community.

By enlisting our active engagement within the world, God makes us coworkers or partners in his ongoing work of sustaining the human community within the world and preserving creation's resources. This is not to say that human beings can ever hope to achieve a utopian society or to save the world. The utopian dreams of the late nineteenth century were shattered by the horrors of the twentieth century. The world continues to groan as it awaits the full revelation of its redemption (Rom. 8:23) when Christ returns. Sin continues to nibble and gnaw at life from inside and outside ourselves. Though we cannot explain it, progress toward the good is too often eroded through our own failure to pay attention or through the maliciousness or carelessness of others.

In the meantime, however, the coordination of divine and human activity in creation stabilizes life in the world in the same way that an emergency medical technician (EMT) arriving on the scene of an accident stabilizes an accident victim. The goal of an EMT is to keep patients alive until they can be taken to the emergency room of the hospital, where their wounds can be tended and eventually healed. By analogy, human righteousness serves life in this world (according to the first article of the Apostles' Creed, on creation) so that people may be brought to Christ (the creed's second article, on redemption), who deals with sin once and for all, and may live as God's children (the creed's third article, on sanctification). Beyond this stabilization, believers work to attain justice and improve the temporal welfare of their neighbors. Through their lives and through the "civil righteousness" of those outside the faith, the world may become somewhat better for some and for a time. But Christians know that their struggle on behalf of justice and the welfare of all human beings and all of creation will never end, for sin and evil continue to intrude in the midst of their best efforts. But rather than being discouraged by this recurrence of evil and the undermining of the good, believers simply proceed with love and service, assisting as God has called us to assist with the care of his creation.

Creaturely Walks of Life

Luther believed that the social web of mutually constitutive relationships in which people carry out their work is not a matter of arbitrary social construction. With other reformers, Luther believed that when God created human beings for community with each other, he placed them and bound them together in comprehensive spheres or structures of life (*genera vitae*), which might be called created orders[14] or walks of life.[15] The reformers drew on and adapted medieval social theory to describe these created spheres of human activity in terms of three "estates" or "situations." In the Middle Ages the three orders were those who fought and governed (princes and dukes), those who taught and prayed (monks and priests), and those who worked the fields or fashioned the goods that provided for the physical needs of all (peasants and artisans). Although Luther dealt with the topic of estates in a variety of places, he provided a nice summary of the matter in his treatment of the fourth commandment in the Large Catechism. There he organized these created structures of life around four groups of "fathers." These groups included, first of all, biological parents, or fathers and mothers by blood. This involves the order of marriage and family life (*domus*), which also encompasses our relationships as grandparents, parents, children, spouses, siblings, and the like. The second includes fathers and mothers of households in their roles as employers (*patres et matres familias*).[16] This order involves economic life (*oeconomia*), which includes not only our place as workers but also our role as consumers, creditors, debtors, investors, and the like. The third includes fathers of the nation (*patres patriae*)[17] and focuses on magistrates and princes, or those with responsibilities for public order and public service. In our day, this order addresses the public life of citizenship and voluntary associations (*civitas/politia*). Finally, Luther

14. See Oswald Bayer, *Living by Faith: Justification and Sanctification* (Grand Rapids: Eerdmans, 2003), 61. See also Werner Elert, *The Structure of Lutheranism*, vol. 1 (St. Louis: Concordia, 1962), esp. 405–62; and Reinhard Schwarz, "Luthers Lehre von den drei Standen und die drei Dimensionen der Ethik," *Luther-Jahrbuch* 45 (1978): 15–34.

15. Various authors have used a variety of terms for this concept: "orders of creation" (Dietrich Bonhoeffer, *Ethics*, trans. N. H. Smith [New York: Touchstone, 1995], 204–10), "natural orders" (George W. Forell, *Faith Active in Love: An Investigation of the Principles Underlying Luther's Social Ethics* [Minneapolis: Augsburg, 1954], 112–55), "places of responsibility" (Robert Benne, *Ordinary Saints: An Introduction to the Christian Life* [Minneapolis: Fortress, 1988], 69–83), "Situations" (Robert Kolb, "God Calling, 'Take Care of My People': Luther's Concept of Vocation in the Augsburg Confession and Its Apology," *Concordia Journal* 8 [1982]: 5).

16. "Ten Sermons, 1528," *LW* 51:148–49; Large Catechism, Ten Commandments, 143–49, *Book of Concord*, 406–7; *BSLK*, 597–98.

17. "Ten Sermons, 1528," *LW* 51:149; Large Catechism, Ten Commandments, 150–51, *Book of Concord*, 407; *BSLK*, 598–99.

indicates that one should include a fourth estate: spiritual fathers such as pastors and priests.[18] The religious life (*ecclesia*) deals with religious communities comprised of pastors and parishioners.[19]

Of the four orders of life in which people find themselves, Luther argued that the family had been the least appreciated and most disparaged in his day. From late antiquity through the late Middle Ages, many theologians believed that God's command for men and women to multiply and fill the earth had been fulfilled and thus no longer applied to everyone.[20] Issues of overpopulation and insufficient food supply had been a concern reaching back to the time of Augustine of Hippo, who lived in the waning years of the Roman Empire. In addition, the church's attitude toward the family remained reserved, even suspicious, and was based on Jesus's warning, "Whoever loves father and mother more than me is not worthy of me" (Matt. 11:37). From such theologians' point of view "the claims of kin competed with the claims of God."[21] By contrast, the reformers argued against the monastic life, in which Luther himself once lived, on the grounds that the union of male and female is a matter of natural law and divine right and thus is immutable.[22]

Luther extolled marriage and family life (*domus*) as the foundational order that God established "before all others as the first of all institutions." He identified three purposes for marriage. First, God created man and woman "to be true to each other."[23] In creating them "differently (as is evident)," he "implanted in each the desire and urge for the other."[24] And so in marriage, "God brings us into relation with one who is different from us but who also reflects back to us something of the truth of our own nature."[25] It is not good to be alone and not have another person to call us out of ourselves to serve or to learn from. Here a person learns what it means to serve and love the good of another. Second, God bound

18. Large Catechism, Ten Commandments, 103–60, *Book of Concord*, 400–408; *BSLK*, 586–602.

19. Luther regarded religious life with the household to be fundamental in creation as a result of God's address to human creatures that results in worship. Here we think especially of church/religious community as an institution or order. See Oswald Bayer, "'I Believe That God Has Created Me with All That Exists': An Example of Catechetical-Systematics," *Lutheran Quarterly* 8 (1994): 129–61.

20. Apology of the Augsburg Confession XXIII.8, *Book of Concord*, 249; *BSLK*, 335.

21. David Herlihy, *Medieval Households* (Cambridge, MA: Harvard University Press, 1985), 114.

22. Apology of the Augsburg Confession XXIII.7–13, *Book of Concord*, 249–50; *BSLK*, 334–36.

23. Large Catechism, Ten Commandments, 207, *Book of Concord*, 414; *BSLK*, 612.

24. "The Estate of Marriage, 1522," *LW* 45:18; *WA* 10.2:276.9–20.

25. Gilbert Meilaender, "The Venture of Marriage," in *The Two Cities of God: The Church's Responsibility for the Earthly City*, ed. Carl E. Braaten and Robert W. Jenson (Grand Rapids: Eerdmans, 1997), 119.

man and woman together in order "to be fruitful, to beget children, and to nurture and bring them up to the glory of God."[26] The God who calls us out of our "isolation into union of mutual love ordains that it should turn outward in order that human life may be sustained and friendship increased."[27] For Luther, the home was "no introspective, private sphere, unmindful of society, but the cradle of citizenship, extending its values and example into the world around it. The habits and character developed within families became the virtues that shaped entire lands."[28] Third, Luther noted that after the fall into sin, marriage serves another purpose for those who have not received the extraordinary gift of the single life (1 Cor. 7:7). Marriage helps to curtail the "incessant ragings of secret passions, unchaste thoughts, and evil desires" that would proceed "unrestrained and unimpeded [1 Cor. 7:2, 36]."[29] It thus has a healing function whereby it guards against infidelity.

After identifying the family as the foundational and first order of human life, Luther placed the other orders, especially government and the church, in the service of the family. This, too, represented a major shift in perspective. Throughout the Middle Ages, commentators debated which was higher: civil authority or spiritual authority. For hundreds of years this debate played out in the ongoing power struggle between emperors and popes. Luther, however, saw all other authorities as deriving their authority from the office of the parent—and not the other way around.[30] As such, the other walks of life serve as assistants and helpers of parents. "For all other authority is derived and developed out of the authority of parents. Where a father is unable by himself to bring up his child, he calls upon a schoolmaster to teach him; if he is too weak, he seeks the help of friends and neighbors; if he dies, he confers and delegates his responsibility and authority to others appointed for the purpose. In addition, he has to have servants—menservants and maidservants—under him in order to manage the household."[31]

In the second order of human life, God created us for work and so gave Adam and Eve a garden to tend. This sphere of human activity involves economic life (*oeconomia*). In Luther's day, it included the family farm in an agrarian-driven economy, or the family shop in which a trade was practiced, with hired hands and servants. It also included everything

26. Large Catechism, Ten Commandments, 207, *Book of Concord*, 414; *BSLK*, 612.
27. Meilaender, "Venture," 119.
28. Steven Ozment, *When Fathers Ruled: Family Life in Reformation Europe* (Cambridge, MA: Harvard University Press, 1983), 9.
29. Large Catechism, Ten Commandments, 216, *Book of Concord*, 415; *BSLK*, 614.
30. Large Catechism, Ten Commandments, 141, *Book of Concord*, 405; *BSLK*, 596.
31. Large Catechism, Ten Commandments, 142, *Book of Concord*, 405–6; *BSLK*, 596–97.

that happened in the market, stores, butcher shops, wine and beer cellars, workshops, and wherever business was transacted and money was exchanged for goods and services.[32] The economic life of a community includes the production and consumption of goods and services for the well-being of the whole. Thus it embraces not only our place as workers but also our role as consumers, creditors, debtors, investors, and the like. By means of the workplace and the marketplace, God provides us with the goods and services necessary to sustain our physical life and community. Through these, God provides food and nourishment for the body, clothing for warmth and protection of the body, healthcare and medicine to heal illnesses and diseases, houses as shelter against the elements, and all my goods.

The economic sphere provides places for service in at least two ways. First, within the workplace there is the relationship between employers and employees. The company, bank, or hospital addresses the needs of its employees by providing them with a reasonable salary, working conditions, and benefits. The workers in turn address the needs of the employer by providing an honest day's labor so as to make their employer sustainable within the economy. Second, there is the place of service between the business or company and the public that receives the products produced. Businesses and hospitals and stores provide goods and services that meet the needs of the public in the form of food, housing, furnishings, transportation, medical care, loans and investments, and so forth. Conversely, the consumers' purchase and use of such things through prompt payment, not stealing, contributes to the health of the company and also to the well-being of their own families through health, education, home, and so forth.[33]

The third order within the structure of human life addresses temporal government. In his earlier years, Luther tended to treat this order as a postlapsarian necessity. But in his later years he recognized the human need for organization in society. And so, against some Anabaptists of the sixteenth century, the Lutheran reformers stressed that "legitimate civil ordinances are good creations of God and divine ordinances."[34] Christians

---

32. Large Catechism, Ten Commandments, 224, *Book of Concord*, 416; *BSLK*, 616.

33. Luther provided instruction for the proper conduct of economic matters in the seventh commandment. There he urged employers to provide an appropriate salary for the work they require as well as for employees to render an honest day's work for an honest day's wage. He also warned against those who turn the free public market into nothing but a carrion pit and a robber's den. Among other things, this means that merchants should not cheat their customers through "defective merchandise, false weights and measures, and counterfeit coins" or different forms of crafty deals. On Luther's view of economic life from the standpoint of the sin of greed, see Ricardo Rieth, *"Habsucht" bei Martin Luther: Ökonomisches und theologisches Denken* (Weimar: Böhlau, 1996).

34. Apology of the Augsburg Confession XVI.1, *Book of Concord*, 231; *BSLK*, 307.

could serve as princes, judges, and even soldiers. Good government (politicians and citizenship) protects the peace, punishes crime, promotes the common good, and supports the church, family, and other institutions. In the twenty-first century we would expand this to include the public life of citizenship and voluntary associations (*civitas/politia*). This order also includes voluntary roles, such as coaches and athletes, volunteers in all areas of public service, and other aspects of life, such as friends simply doing things together. In his treatment of the fourth commandment, Luther points out that through civic rulers, as through parents, "God gives us food, house and home, protection and security, and he preserves us through them."[35] Where peace exists, we have "our bodies and lives, wives and children, houses and homes, all our members—hands, feet, eyes—and all our health and liberty."[36] Conversely, where "dissension, strife, and war prevail, there daily bread is already taken away or reduced."[37]

Luther gives considerable attention in his writings to the topic of a prince's responsibilities. Overall, Luther identified at least three central responsibilities of temporal governments. First, temporal rulers must secure justice for those who fear God. Rulers are to provide the conditions under which God's Word can flourish within their lands. Second, government authorities need to help the poor, the orphans, and the widows find justice and thereby further their cause. This virtue includes tasks that range from establishing good laws and customs so that people live together peacefully, to endowing hospitals and filling community chests. Finally, rulers should protect and guard their people against violence and crime. For all these reasons, Luther in explaining the fourth petition of the Lord's Prayer suggested that princes ought to emblazon on their coat of arms a loaf of bread instead of a lion in order to remind everyone that their office is one of providing peace and protection, without which bread could not be baked or eaten in peace.[38]

The fourth order of life, the religious life (*ecclesia*), deals with external religious communities, congregations consisting of pastors and parishioners. Luther argued that we could consider religious life within the context of creation for two reasons. First, as creatures we were designed to trust God for his gifts. Second, God gave Adam his Word that he was to proclaim to Eve and formed a community within creaturely life dedicated to hearing the Word and praising God together. In the New Testament the church was called into existence in order to preach the Word, administer

35. Large Catechism, Ten Commandments, 150, *Book of Concord*, 407; *BSLK*, 598–99.

36. "Psalm 82," *LW* 13:55; *WA* 31.1:203.

37. Large Catechism, Lord's Prayer, 74, *Book of Concord*, 450; *BSLK*, 680.

38. Large Catechism, Lord's Prayer, 75, *Book of Concord*, 450–51; *BSLK*, 680.

the sacraments, and exercise Christian discipline.[39] Furthermore, the church, as a human community, needs rules and guidelines for its practice of life together. As it takes form in the world, the congregation of God's people functions as an institution that needs structures and governance. Even apart from Christianity, the traces of this walk of life remain even though people do not reflect and do not serve the true God (for example, people found alternate religious communities or observe rituals to ensure good things happen to them). Although Adam and Eve fell into sin by being pulled away from God's Word, the human religious impulse was not destroyed. Instead, it became distorted so that humans invented religions to replace the true knowledge of God that they had lost. Thus, when considering religious life within the realm of active righteousness, within the world, we are dealing particularly with what might be called ceremonial righteousness. Those who live according to the traditions, practices, and precepts of the church or their religious community may well be called "good" or "active" members of the community. God calls them to live consistently with teachings and practices of their religion so that others can recognize their piety as good for the wider community.

Luther's positive view of creation led him to heap praises on ordinary activities carried out within creaturely walks of life, praises that people had formerly heaped on the spiritual orders of the monastic or clerical life. In the Small Catechism, he referred to these walks of life as "holy orders," the very term people in the Middle Ages had used for clerical and monastic estates. In light of the passive righteousness of faith, human activity in one God-ordained walk of life is no better or more holy in the eyes of God than works carried out in another creaturely walk of life (as long as it does not involve sin, such as stealing, prostitution, and other such vices). This does not mean that there are no differences between the different walks of life established by God, or that all of them make an equal contribution to the wider society. Even though God has charged each of these four structured communities to discharge complementary tasks for the good of creation, Luther made marriage the foundational order, based on its contribution to society. Along the same line of thought, Melanchthon suggested that the field of military affairs surpasses agriculture (preserving peace makes it possible to farm) and eloquence surpasses architecture (as used in political speeches to promote policies for the public good).[40]

We also should not take Luther's praise of the various walks of life to imply that they are to be seen in purely static terms, as some scholars have at times suggested. It would be a misunderstanding to interpret

39. Augsburg Confession, XXVIII.21, *Book of Concord*, 94; *BSLK*, 123–24.
40. Apology of the Augsburg Confession XXIII.38, *Book of Concord*, 253; *BSLK*, 340.

his understanding of vocation in such a way that it does nothing more than tell people to be content where they are and not to aspire to another calling. Although Luther did not live in a society with many opportunities for moving up the social ladder from one station in life to another, his own experience led him to recognize that vocations do change with time and circumstance. To be sure, this happens simply in the course of human development. A child has a calling to obey parents when young and take care of them when old. When the child grows up and marries, that child now acquires a new vocation as a spouse and perhaps eventually as a parent. Moreover, a person often lives in several walks of life at the same time; for example, a person may simultaneously be a father, husband, employee, taxpayer, citizen, and church member. At different stages of life, believers strike a different balance among these callings.

In addition, Luther came from an early-modern European family that itself had experienced and fostered its own upward mobility. His father left the farm to become a successful smelter. Luther himself had been sent as the first ever in his family to the university in hopes that he would win a place in the governmental structures of some princedom or city. His own rebellion against his father's plans moved him from the faculty of law to a life in the monastery. Luther knew that God can direct lives in such a way that vocational change takes place. So in our day, Luther's understanding of vocation would not view as inappropriate the aspiration to seek a better job or a promotion as long as one does not turn that new job or promotion into an idol (as evidenced when a person feels that life is no longer worth living if one does not attain it), but instead views it as an avenue for better serving God and neighbor. For God's callings to his people are not ends in themselves. They are instruments of his providential care of his creation; they are expressions of our humanity that reveal something about the God who has fashioned us in his own image.

Divine Law and Human Reason

The tasks required to meet my neighbor's need and the responsibilities entailed in formal roles such as being a parent or an employee are given substance and form by the law that God wove into the very fabric of creation itself—most commonly known as natural law or the law of creation.[41] As law, its authority is derived from its congruence with God's

41. Gustaf Aulén, *The Faith of the Christian Church*, trans. Erich H. Wahlstrom and G. Everett Arden (Philadelphia: Muhlenberg, 1948), 189: "The idea of *lex naturae* has often appeared as a substitute for the *lex creationis*, or *lex creatoris*, of Christian faith. *Lex naturae*, the Law of nature, could be described as a rationalized and secularized variety of *lex creationis*. The foundation of both is a universal Law. The difference between them can

design of creation. It describes the grain of the universe and serves the universal good. For this reason the phrase "law of creation" may be preferable to "natural law," which in our time "has come to mean a law which 'Mother Nature' imposes, one which is impersonally 'natural' to what we are or have evolved to be at this stage of nature's unfolding."[42]

Because it is grounded in creation, this law of creation is no secret. In some sense it is universally accessible and applicable. The mind can grasp its rightness for human life. For this reason natural law provides a vital point of contact for conversation about morals and works between Christians and non-Christians. Hence, Christians can appeal to what is right by arguing from natural law without specifically citing the Bible. And so Luther contended that "natural law and natural reason" are the "source from which all written law has come and been issued."[43] Thus, one can speak of natural law as "universal common sense of the human race,"[44] a common moral ground underlying the traditional moralities of East and West, be they Platonic, Aristotelian, Stoic, Christian, or Confucian.[45] Due to fallen reason, these philosophical and ethical systems can only approximate the outward regulations of natural law. They cannot understand the law in its true function as a servant of the Creator. With Aristotle, for example, law does not entail an "ought" as much as a "right." Furthermore, due to sin, the specifics of natural law are not always easily defined since they are entangled in human evasions, denials, and subterfuges.

The dimming of natural law in the human mind does not mean that it has no value for preserving the human community. At the least, natural law deals with the "ineradicable minimums of creatureliness."[46] As such, Melanchthon contended that it provides a minimal framework for managing our relationships with God, other human beings, and the goods of creation. Melanchthon identified three basic requirements that natural law impresses on us. First, "God ought to be revered." Second, "because we are born into a network of social relationships, no one should injure

---

be defined in this way, that *lex naturae* is a metaphysical conception, while *lex creationis* is a religious concept, originating in the relation to God and inseparably connected with faith in God as 'Creator.'"

42. Robert Kolb, *Teaching God's Children His Teaching: A Guide for the Study of Luther's Catechism* (Hutchinson, MN: Crown, 1992), 2.

43. "Psalm 101," *LW* 13:161; *WA* 51:212.14–25.

44. J. Budziszewski, *What We Can't Not Know: A Guide* (Dallas: Spence, 2003), 15; see p. 14 for a list of things that the natural law is not. See also his earlier work, *Written on the Heart: The Case for Natural Law* (Downers Grove, IL: InterVarsity, 1997).

45. C. S. Lewis, *The Abolition of Man* (New York: Harper Collins, 2001), 18. Lewis borrowed the word "Tao" from Confucianism to describe the natural law that underlies all of these traditional moralities. Aristotle spoke of "first principles of practical reason."

46. James Arne Nestingen, "Preaching the Catechism," *Word and World* 10 (1990): 36.

another." Third, "human society demands that we use all things for the common good."[47] Although the specifics of the law of creation are difficult to define with any precision, the reformers contended that the effects of its transgression are readily apparent and observable.[48] Individual human life and the larger human community cannot survive the constant violation of its norms. For example, coveting rarely leads to contentment. More often it leads to dissatisfaction with what one has. Marriages fall apart when spouses despise, demean, and abuse one another. People cannot remain friends when they lie to each other. Businesses do not thrive if they cheat their customers or produce shoddy goods. For these reasons, some have suggested that we can also describe the law of creation in terms of "orders of preservation," which restrain human beings from destroying the world and themselves with it.[49]

Due to human sinfulness, the reformers recognized the need for a written law of God to bring into bold relief once again what God had written on human hearts, a law that he spelled out in the Scriptures. Luther, in particular, believed that the law of creation finds its clearest expression in the Ten Commandments.[50] In one sense, Luther believed that the Decalogue belonged to the age of the old covenant and no longer applied to Christians since Christ was the fulfillment of the law. In another sense, however, he maintained that the Decalogue retained its validity for Christians because of its correspondence to natural law.[51] In other words, Luther believed that the Decalogue applied to Christians not because it appeared in the Bible but because it expressed the

47. See *The Loci Communes of Philip Melanchthon* (1521), trans. Charles Leander Hill (Boston: Meador, 1944), 113; *CR* 21:117–18. In his later *Loci*, Melanchthon expands the list: "I. Love God; II. Because we are born unto a kind of common society, injure no man but assist whomever you may with kindness; III. If it cannot be that no man is injured, let this be done in order that the smallest amount of people be injured by the removal of those who disturb the public peace. For this duty let magistrates be appointed, and punishments for the guilty be instituted; IV. Divide property for the safety of public peace. As to the rest, let some alleviate the wants of others through contracts" (Hill, *Loci Communes*, 116). The last point is redefined so as to embrace an openness to property rights.

48. Melanchthon acknowledged this in his 1521 *Loci communes*.

49. George W. Forell, *Ethics of Decision* (Philadelphia: Muhlenberg, 1955), 81.

50. Luther's view is detailed in "Against the Sabbatarians, 1538" (*LW* 47:65–98; *WA* 50:312–37) among other works. See also Wingren, *Creation and Law*, 123–73; and Charles P. Arand, "Luther on God behind the First Commandment," *Lutheran Quarterly* 8 (1994): 397–423.

51. Joseph Sittler states: "The Ten Commandments, as the Law of God, are a verbalization of the given structures of creation. They stand above all men, believers and nonbelievers alike, as an accurate transcription of the facts—that the world is of God, that ultimate relations among men and things are grounded in him. The Stoic-immanental concept of natural law with which many systems of philosophical ethics operate is not introduced here because it is not needed" (*The Structure of Christian Ethics* [Baton Rouge: Louisiana State University Press, 1958], 70).

law of creation: "It is inscribed and engraved in the hearts of all people from the foundation of the world [Rom. 2:15]."[52] Luther used the Ten Commandments, as found in Exodus and Deuteronomy, because when taken as a whole they are an "unsurpassed summary of the natural law."[53] As he put it, Moses fitted the law of creation "nicely into his laws in a more orderly and excellent manner than could have been done by anyone else."[54]

The law given at Sinai was not a new, never-before-known reality, but "a fuller particularization of how the community can take on its God-given creational responsibilities in view of new times and new places."[55] And so even though the Decalogue had been given to Israel, it in fact belongs to the whole world. This means that the Ten Commandments are not a heteronomously imposed set of rules. The Decalogue's force and authority derives from its ability to describe accurately the way things are. It delineates the shape of life as God created it. The Ten Commandments tell us what God has made us to be: "You are to be this rather than that."[56] Life begins, is lived, and ends under the force of the law, under the objective moral order. So Luther reads the Decalogue as describing life "from the bottom up, to get to the nonnegotiable requirements of the human condition," to explicate "the ineradicable minimums of creatureliness."[57] One could think of the Ten Commandments as an

52. Large Catechism, Creed, 67, *Book of Concord*, 440; *BSLK*, 661. This conviction remained constant throughout Luther's life. In his lectures on Exodus in 1525, he asserted that what Moses had written in the Ten Commandments "we feel naturally in our conscience" (*WA* 16:431.28–29). "I keep the commandments which Moses has given, not because Moses gave the commandments, but because they have been implanted in me by nature, and Moses agrees exactly with nature" (*LW* 35:168). Toward the end of his life, in his Second Disputation against the Antinomians, Luther again reiterated that the Decalogue "does not come from Moses; he is not the author but the interpreter and illustrator of the biblical commandments in the minds of all men" (*WA* 39.1:454.3, 15).

53. Ronald M. Hals, "Luther and the First Commandment: You Belong to Me," in *Interpreting Luther's Legacy: Essays in Honor of Edward C. Fendt*, ed. Fred W. Meuser and Stanley D. Schneider (Minneapolis: Augsburg, 1969), 3. Cf. Aarne Siirala, *Gottes Gebot bei Martin Luther: Eine Untersuchung der Theologie Luthers unter besonderer Berücksichtigung des ersten Hauptstückes im Grossen Katechismus* (Helsinki: Luther-Agricola Gesellschaft, 1956), 42–43.

54. "Against Sabbatarians—Letter to a Good Friend, 1538," *LW* 47:90; *WA* 50:330.12–13. Cf. "How Christians Should Regard Moses, 1525," *LW* 35:155–74; *WA* 16:363–93.

55. Terrence E. Fretheim, "The Reclamation of Creation: Redemption and Law in Exodus," *Interpretation* 45 (1991): 363. "At Sinai, Israel comes to know that it is the Creator God who issues these commands, and hence Israel is expected to obey them for the sake of the creation" (364). He makes the important point that the Exodus is not an event that creates the law.

56. Robert Jenson, *A Large Catechism* (New York: American Lutheran Publicity Bureau, 1991), 6–7.

57. Nestingen, "Preaching the Catechism," 36.

instruction manual for living in creation and using the gifts of creation for the purpose that God gave them.

Luther's conviction that the Ten Commandments summarize the law of creation finds particular expression in his treatment of the Decalogue within his catechetical writings.[58] Here Luther did not include or expound the entire prologue from Exodus 20 ("I am the LORD your God, who brought you out of the land of Egypt"). He argued that the first half of the verse, "I am the LORD your God," applies to everyone because God created the entire world, but the second half of the verse, "who brought you out of . . . Egypt," applied only to the Israelites. For in the course of human history, God led the Israelites and only the Israelites out of Egypt. This particular narrative served as the creed by which Israel recognized the identity of its God. Thus, when the Israelites crossed the Jordan River into Canaan and become dazzled by the glitter of the Canaanite gods, they were to ask themselves, "Did these gods lead us out of Egypt?" If the answer was "no," "then avoid them!" This portion of the verse was supplanted in Luther's thinking by the words of the Apostles' Creed, as a summary of God's saving work in Christ, who "suffered under Pontius Pilate, was crucified, dead, and buried," a summary by which the New Testament people know the identity of God. When Christians are tempted to follow another god, they need to ask whether or not that god has died for them. If not, then avoid it.

Similarly, Luther believed that the first commandment expressed natural law because faith is intrinsic to what it means to be human. Thus, the question posed by the first commandment is not, "Should you have a god?" Luther assumed that everyone has a god since no one could live without trust, which defined the core of human existence. The only question remaining is whether or not a person places his or her trust in the true God. During the 1520s Luther shifted his explanation of the third commandment from an emphasis on an inner spiritual rest, something of a "Sabbath rest of the soul," to one that was grounded in nature and focused on the body. Rest is a part of God's created design for his creatures. People simply cannot work twenty-four hours a day, seven days a week, 365 days a year. Thus, nature "teaches and demands that the common people should retire for a day to rest and be refreshed."[59] Luther also argued that since this day had been established for bodily rest, God did not fix the time when it should take place. "Nature also shows and teaches that one must *now and then* rest a day, so that man and

58. See Arand, "God behind the First Commandment."
59. Large Catechism, Ten Commandments, 83, *Book of Concord*, 397; *BSLK*, 581.

beast may be refreshed. . . . It is clear that he who does not need rest may break the Sabbath and rest *on some other day*, as nature allows."[60]

The law of creation as expressed in the Ten Commandments identifies the specific responsibilities entailed by the formal roles assigned to us by God within our various walks of life. It defines the form of human life (the "that-ness" of our responsibilities), but it does not fix the specific human activities by which we carry out those responsibilities.[61] Instead, the law serves "more like a general standard of measurement than a norm that predicts the will of God in all individual cases." That we cherish our spouse is one thing. How we cherish our spouse is another matter. So in our care of the world, the law must be tailored to the task. God has given human beings the freedom to decide how best to carry out those responsibilities. To that end God has equipped his creatures with intellect, reason, and imagination, as Luther confessed in explaining the first article of the creed: "I believe that God has . . . given me reason and all my senses."[62] These creaturely faculties mediate the law into our lives by identifying the specific activities entailed in our roles and by showing us how to carry them out.

For Luther, human beings have the God-given capacities for discerning the moral ordering of life and thus can ascertain with some degree of clarity what is best for daily human life. Reason's identification and definition of these activities may take the form of customs and traditions within families, guidelines and codes of ethics within the workplace, useful practices within the church, and positive laws within societies (as particular regulations for the administration of societies and countries).[63] The result of reason's mediation of the law will take different forms from society to society, culture to culture, and even family to family.[64] It will give rise to different political systems, different ways in which families function, different ways that individuals act, all within the fundamental structures and rules that God built into his creation.

Sometimes human beings learn to tailor the law for the common good through informal means such as personal experience, or they learn from

60. "Against the Heavenly Prophets, 1525," *LW* 40:98; *WA* 18:81.26–82.6; italics added.

61. Robert Kolb, "Christian Civic Responsibility in an Age of Judgment," *Concordia Journal* 19 (1993): 19.

62. Small Catechism, Creed, *Book of Concord*, 354; *BSLK*, 510.

63. Despite differences among actual legal codes, such codes are attempts to codify the law of God as it confronts humans "in the very structure of the world" (Forell, *Ethics of Decision*, 87).

64. Differences are mainly a matter of degree. "There is a tremendous difference between Pennsylvania Quakers and New Guinea headhunters—but the difference is rather in the scope of the prohibition than in the prohibition. Even the headhunters have Laws that prevent them from taking the lives of their fellows in the same tribe or village" (Forell, *Ethics of Decision*, 86–87).

the experience of previous generations, which has been handed down to them. In both cases, they cultivate wisdom or practical knowledge. The Wisdom literature in the Old Testament, such as Proverbs and Ecclesiastes, records observations about how life works based on the experience of its authors. Aside from the Scriptures, Luther pointed out, there are good sources in non-Christian literature to which one could turn. "How could one prepare a finer book on worldly heathen wisdom, than that ordinary, silly children's book called Aesop?"[65] People can also learn through more formally structured fields of research to identify tasks, activities, and goods for the good of the human community. In Luther's day people were giving renewed attention to the relationship of natural law and positive laws (the written laws of nations) in a variety of fields of study, including philosophy, law, and theology. Melanchthon mentioned a number of such disciplines in his day. Politics serves the welfare of society by enabling people to live together for the common good.[66] "Medicine serves health, meteorology serves navigation, civic virtues serve public tranquility."[67] Ethics assists statecraft and the construction of laws.[68] Rhetoric assists writing and oratory. Theology serves preaching and faith. The development of ecclesial traditions provides time for worship and prayer. In our day, the social sciences serve the mental and emotional well-being of people and assist in the building of healthy relationships. Fields of learning, such as nutrition and health fitness, contribute to the physical well-being of others. Every decade new fields continue to arise to assist people in living out productive lives, such as behavioral finance, which assists people in managing the goods of creation for the well-being of their family and community.

Consider the example of government leaders. In a sermon on Psalm 101 (1534/35), Luther observed that good and wise princes are as common as rare gemstones among the pebbles of the sand. And so he encouraged government officials to learn from the experience of the best of pagan rulers and thinkers. He pointed out that the pagan wisdom imperial Rome developed long before Constantine Christianized the empire was far superior to the silly and childish rules found in canon law, even though canon law was devised by those who were considered much holier.[69] Roman law had been developed by those who were endowed with exceptional intelligence and were experienced in dealing with social

65. "Psalm 101," *LW* 13:200; *WA* 51:243.31–33.

66. Apology of the Augsburg Confession IV.18, *Book of Concord*, 123; *BSLK*, 163.

67. Timothy J. Wengert, *Human Freedom, Christian Righteousness: Philip Melanchthon's Exegetical Dispute with Erasmus of Rotterdam* (Oxford: Oxford University Press, 1998), 15.

68. Ibid., 93.

69. On Psalm 101:5, *LW* 13:198–99; *WA* 51:242–43.

matters on a large scale. Thus, he advised that whoever wants to rule his land well and be learned in secular government should read Homer, Virgil, Demosthenes, Aristotle, Cicero, Livy, and others whom Luther called God's pagan "prophets" and "apostles" in secular affairs, even as Moses, Elijah, Isaiah, and others were his prophets in spiritual affairs. Rulers should also learn from the example of exemplary rulers (endowed with wisdom and courage) of worldly governments, such as Alexander the Great, Philip his father, Augustus, Trajan, and others, who were the Davids and Solomons of the pagans. One difference between pagan and Christian rulers consisted in the fact that the former attributed their success to the goddess Fortuna whereas Christian rulers recognized their success as a gift of God. Such divine direction is especially necessary in secular governments, for rulers like David and other God-fearing Christian princes serve God and govern the people.

The Ambiguity of Human Wisdom

Human beings will always experience a certain amount of ambiguity about how best to carry out the demands of the law, whether it is natural law or positive law. This lack of clarity cannot be removed simply by developing exhaustive sets of rules that cover every situation a person might ever encounter. In these areas we are dealing with what might be better or best courses of action. We are dealing in an area that involves decisions about what might be most appropriate and for which there may be several good options. We see different ways for a person to cherish a spouse, for parents to discipline their children, for a person to lend assistance during a disaster, for a person to serve the community. God has fashioned his human creatures with a rich complexity that enables us to accomplish goals in more than one way in many aspects of life. And so a husband has to make a decision about how he can best cherish his particular spouse. A person has to decide how best one can help the neighbor given one's resources, abilities, and time. Parents must decide how best to deal with the differences in their children. The difficulty of making such decisions is exacerbated by the sin and evil that infects all systems and roles, thus bringing about suffering through greed and incompetence. At times this makes it "very difficult to tell what is truly good for one's neighbor and for God's creation."[70] This sometimes gives rise to the desire that we be given tasks and works that are unambiguously good because we don't want to bear the responsibility for making decisions without knowing with certainty how they may play out in the future.

70. Kolden, "Earthly Vocation," 277.

Lacking a clear-cut, obvious answer for what we should do places us in a situation that calls for the use of wisdom (*sapientia* in Latin), a practical knowledge of the head and heart as distinct from *scientia*, a fixed body of theoretical knowledge. Luther also referred to this wisdom as *Gleichmut*, a word that translates the Greek *epieikeia* and the Latin *equitas*, a "technical term coined by Aristotle and used extensively by the Stoics in their ethical writings."[71] As Timothy Wengert has noted, *Gleichmut* can be translated as "equity," "fairness," or perhaps better yet, "reasonableness." In the third section of his famous tract *On Secular Authority*, Luther counseled his prince to render judgments by making use of common sense and being guided by love when applying the law in specific cases. "A right good judgment must not and cannot be spoken out of books but rather from common sense [*aussz freyem synn*], as if there were no lawbooks at all. But such a free judgment comes only from love and natural law, of which reason itself is full. From books come only strained and wavering judgments."[72] Here Luther encouraged a prince to avoid the easy route of applying lawbooks simplistically and in ways that do not take into account the specifics of the case or the outcome of his actions. "Rather than deriving our behavior from rigid principles, it must come from love—which means that we do not have the luxury of idolizing what we do."[73] Guided by love, such "wisdom" has to make an "educated guess" about the best course of action in many instances. This means that we will make mistakes: we just dare not worship them but must confess them and turn away from them.[74]

What such wisdom might look like can be seen in two situations involving marriage and the family during the sixteenth century. At the time of the Reformation, children often married when they were in their midteens if not earlier. Consequently, parents played a significant role in choosing their children's spouses. The Fourth Commandment required the obedience of children, but they often recoiled from the marriages that their parents arranged and instead entered into secret engagements. Could parents forbid such engagements? In 1524, Luther advised that marriage should be a family decision that respects the wishes of all the members of the family, especially those directly involved.[75] When parents were confronted with a marriage not acceptable to them, Luther

---

71. Timothy Wengert, "Gleichmut, Gewissen, Glaube, and Gemeinschaft: Luther's Ethical Practice," unpublished paper, August 2006.

72. *WA* 11:279.26–34; *LW* 45:128.

73. Wengert, "Gleichmut, Gewissen, Glaube, and Gemeinschaft."

74. Ibid.

75. "Parents Should Neither Compel Nor Hinder the Marriage of Their Children and Children Should Not Marry without the Consent of Their Parents," *LW* 45:385–93; *WA* 15:558–62.

advised that they state their objections frankly but permit the marriage to go on and thereby let the children experience their parents' wisdom. He counseled youth to follow their parents' wishes unless they were confronted by an "outrageous injustice" of a forced, planned marriage. Then they could turn to the local magistrates or relatives, or even flee to another land.[76]

Another good example occurred in 1535 and was "the kind of case that Wittenberg's theologians dealt with constantly, once the Reformation did away with the old episcopal family courts in the 1520s."[77] In this particular case a man asked his pastor for permission to marry his cousin. In fact, however, "the couple was already living together and had a child." When the pastor asked the faculty at Wittenberg for advice, it responded by acknowledging that while Scripture does not forbid such a marriage (witness the patriarchs!), traditionally this was not the sort of thing allowed in Germany. The professors suggested that the man be thrown into jail for three weeks and after that might marry his cousin. "This way, people will not follow his example, but the child and mother will have a father and husband."

Luther observed that the "noble gem called natural law and reason is a rare thing among the children of men."[78] Using our heads to figure out how best to carry out the responsibilities of our walks of life within creation will lead to different decisions by different people. The choices that we make will depend greatly on our particular creaturely gifts, abilities, and talents. Problems arise when everyone thinks that they equally and clearly perceive the best course of action to take in accord with natural law. When that happens, everyone thinks that they are as capable "of ruling and waging war as were David, Augustus, and Hannibal."[79] But all are not alike. God has given some people exceptional intelligence and courage so that whatever they decide turns out well. "In all walks of life there are some people more outstanding and skillful than others."[80] Some learn in a day what takes others several years.

Luther then identified two types of people. There are those who, due to their insight, intelligence, and wisdom, are able to think "outside the box" of written laws and codes. Then there are those who would do best by simply following directions and guidelines laid down by others. He suggested that we consider a rule requiring a person to eat two rolls and drink a small glass of wine with the meal. If a strong and well-conditioned

76. Steven Ozment, *Protestants: The Birth of a Revolution* (New York: Doubleday, 1992), 156.

77. Wengert, "Gleichmut, Gewissen, Glaube, and Gemeinschaft."

78. "Psalm 101," *LW* 13:161; *WA* 51:212.24–25.

79. "Psalm 101," *LW* 13:161; *WA* 51:212.14–17.

80. "Psalm 101," *LW* 13:157; *WA* 51:209.27–30.

person comes to the meal, he may consume three or four rolls along with a decanter of wine. Such a person needs more than the law stipulates. But if a weak and sickly person dines who can only consume one roll and no wine, then we must stipulate an amount according to his ability. Few fall into the category of those gifted with outstanding insight and wisdom. Most must remain disciples of those speechless teachers called books. Most must follow the advice of the best people who live in our midst until a healthy hero or exceptional person comes along who either changes the law or overrules it in such a way that everything prospers in the land. Luther stressed that this is not necessarily a bad thing because we are not all alike. "If a person is so weak that he cannot walk very well, then it is no shame for him not to be able to keep up with a strong person. It is to his credit that he lets himself be guided and led or that he walks with a cane until he arrives as best he can."[81]

The decisions people make when carrying out the responsibilities of their callings arise not only from their personal abilities, but also from their character or collection of virtues. Given the diversity of ways by which we serve our neighbor and the variety of gifts each person possesses, there are some things that remain constant. The way in which we carry out our particular responsibilities according to the unique gifts God has given us determines whether or not we are regarded righteous *coram mundo*. Am I a good parent? Am I honest and fair? Am I a person of character? Our gifts are used within a common framework. Melanchthon suggested that when it comes to cultivating the process of practicing virtues and social ethics, people could not do much better than to look to Aristotle's *Nichomachean Ethics* for guidance on acquiring virtue.[82] He proposed three steps. First, we must choose to act in a way that is deemed moral or ethical. We must want to be the best that we can be. This requires instruction regarding the standards of behavior and instruction on how to meet them. Second, practice makes perfect. The acquisition of righteousness requires the development of habits through repeated practice. Such practice shapes our behavior until it becomes "second nature," even instinctive. Third, righteousness is cumulative. A single act of righteousness does not make a person righteous any more than one act of bravery makes one a brave person. Random, isolated acts do not make a person a model citizen or a good husband. Instead, the achievement of this righteousness requires a lifetime of effort and progress.

These virtues, too, will vary in degree and quality from person to person. In the conclusion of his "Disputation on Faith and Love" (1531),

81. "Psalm 101," *LW* 13:162; *WA* 51:213.9–10.
82. Melanchthon employs what today is called "virtue ethics," but limits them to the cardinal rather than the theological virtues.

Melanchthon stated, "Aristotle rightly and wisely said that moderation in virtue is to be determined geometrically, not arithmetically."[83] Here Melanchthon appeals to Aristotle's well-known concept of the "golden mean." Virtuous actions avoid excess (which would be considered vice). Thus, when it comes to the emotions, which often impel us to action, Melanchthon cautioned, "too much fear, and too much daring, too much anger, and too much joy, cause injury."[84] And so courage is the mean between cowardice and recklessness. Yet the "golden mean" is not the same for everyone nor does it cover situations in which the total rejection of that which is wrong or the zealous adoption of the right is the godly thing to do. Virtues are relative to each person in one's particular calling. In practice this means that one cannot establish a fixed (one-size-fits-all) standard of virtue for everyone. In principle, a virtue is the same for all, but it exhibits differences in the way in which individuals practice or implement it in specific situations, according to their own personalities and the needs of their neighbors. "Temperance is not the same mean in a strong man and a weak man."[85] While we can highlight temperance as a mean, what constitutes temperance will differ from one person to another. With regard to generosity, we cannot establish a single sum that constitutes generosity for all people. It will be proportionate in such a way that when a prince gives generously and a pauper gives generously, it will constitute the same mean for both people.

The exercise of wisdom depends heavily on a person's abilities and virtues and thus less on whether or not that person is a Christian or non-Christian. "There is nothing particularly 'Christian' about either our actions or our roles; rather, they are human and creaturely (and in that sense are profoundly Christian). A believer will know that the call is from God, but the actions and responses may be the same for believers and unbelievers alike."[86] Within creation some people are better at certain things, whether or not they are believers. Some people have more resources or are more talented or better educated or more compassionate, and so they might be more effective at looking after the needs and providing solutions than others might be. Here a nonbeliever may accomplish just as much or more than a believer; and in one sense God

83. Temperance will be defined differently for different people. Some can only drink one beer before they become sleepy or dizzy. Others can consume two or three beers before experiencing the same effects. Melanchthon refers to this in his "Disputation on Faith and Love." See "Philip Melanchthon's Disputation: We Are Justified by Faith and Not by Love, 1531," trans. Charles P. Arand, in *Sources and Contexts of the Lutheran Confessions*, ed. Robert Kolb and James A. Nestingen (Philadelphia: Fortress, 2001), 141–43.

84. *CR* 16:211, "Ph. Mel. Ad ethicen et politicen spectantia et Dissertationes iis annexae, II. Ethicae doctrinae elementorum libri duo."

85. *CR* 16:212.

86. Kolden, "Earthly Vocation," 280.

does not care (if we may speak that way) because God's concern in terms of the creation is the good of the neighbor. Or, a believer may actually be more effective than a nonbeliever in doing good, but it may not be because of one's faith or Christian insight but because of the creaturely gifts and accomplishments with which one has been blessed.

In this sinful world we cannot attain perfection in carrying out our responsibilities. But I can be a good husband, if not a perfect husband. I can be a good employer, if not an ideal employer. God calls me to strive to bring his love in as complete a form as possible into my part of his world. A form of human righteousness can still be achieved in the eyes of the world even though the pursuit of active righteousness in this life remains severely impaired and impeded by sin. For this reason Melanchthon stated that within the world even civil righteousness, or truly responsible behavior, is rare. More often than not, the achievement of human righteousness now has to be compelled by the threat of punishment and penalties.

While the passive righteousness of faith constitutes the nature of our relationship to God, the active righteousness of faith constitutes and sustains our relationships with other members in the human community. The active righteousness of daily life as recovered by Luther carves out the necessary theological space to speak positively about life in this world and all that preserves our life—whether law, works, or human reason—in a way that does not compromise the passive righteousness of Christ. Moreover, it encourages the cultivation and use of resources that have been developed in various fields of study. When it comes to life in this present age, we should be able to speak of doing good works and carrying out tasks that are in accord with God's law in positive ways. At the same time Luther recognized that the pursuit of active righteousness in daily life as God intended cannot take place independently of passive righteousness. Indeed, active righteousness ultimately depends on passive righteousness! Conversely, our active righteousness provides the context for our need of passive righteousness. Those who seek to use active righteousness as the basis for their relationship with God will end up worn out and rendered empty *coram Deo*.

4

THE SUBVERSION OF
OUR HUMAN IDENTITY

In a Christian the law must not exceed its limits but should have dominion
only over the flesh, which is subjected to it and remains under it. When
this is the case, the law remains within its limits. But if it wants to ascend
into the conscience and exert its rule there, see to it that you are a good
dialectician and that you make the correct distinction. Give no more to the
law than it has coming, and say to it: "Law, you want to ascend into the
realm of conscience and rule there. You want to denounce its sin and take
away the joy of my heart, which I have through faith in Christ. You want
to plunge me into despair, in order that I may perish. You are exceeding
your jurisdiction. Stay within your limits, and exercise dominion over the
flesh. You shall not touch my conscience. For I am baptized."

Luther, "Lectures on Galatians, 1531–1535"

Luther's recovery of the gospel included the insight that the only way to
preserve the integrity of the passive righteousness of faith (and with it
the active righteousness of works) is to keep it distinct from our righteousness in relationship to other creatures (*coram mundo*). To be sure,
life within the created walks of life, law, works, and reason play indispensable roles in ordering and preserving our life together. God himself instituted such things. Therefore, outside of God they are the best

things to which people can devote themselves in this life. They build human community, cultivate virtue, contribute to the preservation of creation, and establish a person's identity *coram mundo*. But what we think, feel, and do have no place in establishing our standing with God. *Coram Deo* we must seek a righteousness that is *beyond* the law.[1] This is why the Scriptures stress what Melanchthon labeled "the excluding expressions": those words or phrases that exclude human contributions to our standing before God, such as faith justifies "apart" from works and "without" the law. In the same spirit, the Reformation insistence on the *"solas"*[2]—grace *alone*, faith *alone*, Scripture *alone*—function to exclude all human activity from having any salvific value that might be attached to it. The indispensable prerequisite for anyone who would be righteous in the eyes of God is that one must leave every form of human righteousness behind on earth. For Luther, this meant that a person must learn to "ignore the law and to live before God as though there were no law whatsoever."[3] Without doing so, the passive righteousness of faith cannot be preserved.

The Desire to Be More Than Human

Ignoring the law and keeping our active righteousness on earth (and out of heaven) is not easy. Nothing could be more counterintuitive for human beings after the fall into sin than to ignore the law with its demand that we take action. As Luther put it, human beings reason, "Surely faith is not enough; you *must* do works!"[4] This is because in the fall and after the fall, human beings deem faith to be insufficient for our life with God or with the gods that we have shaped in our own image, to our own liking. Luther identified the source of all sin as "unbelief and doubt and abandonment of the Word."[5] In his exposition of the first commandment in his Large Catechism, Luther provided some of his most insightful and trenchant theological insights into human nature and faith. There he observed that the ultimate question of the first commandment is not whether people will have faith. That is a given. Faith is intrinsic to human beings by their very nature as creatures. It is inherent in human

1. Apology of the Augsburg Confession IV.20, *Book of Concord*, 124; *BSLK*, 163–64.

2. It is true that these sixteenth-century reformers themselves did not use the phrase as such, but along with "Christ alone," it does describe key elements in their thought.

3. "Lectures on Galatians, 1531–1535," *LW* 26:6; *WA* 40.1:43. Luther develops this concept of true Christian freedom at a number of points in these lectures, for example, on Gal. 4:27, *LW* 26:442–49; *WA* 40.1:666–75.

4. *LW* 35:370; *WA* DB 7:8/9, 33–34, 34–35.

5. "Genesis Lectures, 1535–1545," *LW* 1:149; *WA* 42:112.20–22.

beings to center their lives around something or someone and from it seek meaning, security, or identity. The only question that needs to be answered is in what or in whom does a human being place one's trust. Any other option than God the Creator results in idolatry.

The loss of faith leaves us to ourselves with no one to rely on except ourselves. Self-reliance fills the void of God's promises. God originally created human beings to live from his gifts and to carry the wares of creation to their neighbors in joy, but when they became caught up in a vision of independence, self-sufficiency, and self-determination, they declared their independence from God. In so doing, they became *incapable* of receiving God's gifts with no strings attached, for in their desire for independence and self-sufficiency, they found charity (even if it is from God) too demeaning, unsatisfying, and even unreliable. Therefore, the human creature now cannot help but say "No, thank you" to God. In matters involving God, the human intellect is now blind and the will is so bound that it cannot do other than seek substitutes for God.[6] Unable and unwilling to live with God on his terms, humans found no one to rely on except themselves.[7]

So deeply rooted is this desire for self-reliance that even after God provided reconciliation in Christ, human beings still find it too risky to live by faith alone in the righteousness of Christ. To receive righteousness as a gift (by faith alone) takes away the illusion of control over our lives. Luther had a profound sense of this human tendency. "Thus, human reason cannot refrain from looking at active righteousness, that is, its own righteousness; nor can it shift its gaze to the passive, that is, Christian righteousness, but it simply rests in the active righteousness. So deeply is this evil rooted in us, and so completely have we acquired this unhappy habit!"[8] Human beings can only conceive of securing their lives in terms of what they need to accomplish by their own decisions and actions. Seventeenth-century theologians called this habit the opinion of the law (*opino legis*) in human hearts.

Now that each human being had to secure life for oneself, a person must desire that "whatever happens shall be to his own advantage."[9] Ernest Becker, an American cultural anthropologist, has nicely captured the egocentricity of human nature by recognizing that one of Sigmund Freud's lasting contributions was his discovery that each person "repeats

6. See Robert Kolb, *Bound Choice, Election, and Wittenberg Theological Method: From Martin Luther to the Formula of Concord* (Grand Rapids: Eerdmans, 2005).

7. Gerhard O. Forde, *On Being a Theologian of the Cross: Reflections on Luther's Heidelberg Disputation, 1518* (Grand Rapids: Eerdmans, 1997), 54.

8. "Lectures on Galatians, 1531–1535," *LW* 26:5; *WA* 40.1:42.11–16.

9. Gustaf Wingren, *Luther on Vocation*, trans. Carl C. Rasmussen (Philadelphia: Muhlenberg, 1957), 6.

the tragedy of the mythical Greek Narcissus: we are hopelessly absorbed with ourselves. If we care about anyone, it is usually ourselves first of all."[10] Becker recounted how Aristotle had also observed that humans call it "luck" when the arrow hits the person standing next to us instead of hitting us. "Twenty-five hundred years of history have not changed man's basic narcissism: most of the time, for most of us, this is still a workable definition of luck."[11] The tragedy of human destiny is such that every person "must desperately justify himself as an object of primary value in the universe; he must stand out, be a hero, make the biggest possible contribution to world life, show that he counts more than anything or anyone else."[12] This is not to say that human beings will not make sacrifices for others, engage in acts of generosity, or even lay down their lives for their country or cause. But a person has to believe that "what he is doing is truly heroic, timeless, and supremely meaningful."[13] To secure oneself, the human being now has to think of oneself "from beginning to end, as a doer and maker."[14] The human being has to become self-creating and self-constituting. We want to secure our future, shape our image, and determine our self-worth through human effort alone. Johann Gottlieb Fichte expressed the sentiment well: a human being is defined by one's activity, "you are here for action; your action, and your action alone, determines your worth."[15] The human being is what one makes of oneself.

Once human beings saw themselves as doers and makers, they had to construct theologies that enable them to place their trust in themselves and their works in order to be saved.[16] They find that putting their faith in the promises of God alone is too unsatisfying and too risky. It is like putting all their eggs in one basket. This is not to say that God cannot be involved or a part of the picture. But we want to minimize the risk, and so we want to keep one hand on the wheel, or have a backup system in place, to be a part of a cooperative partnership where we rely partly on God and partly on ourselves. This would allow us to exercise a certain amount of control over our own destiny. Luther called these attempts "theologies of glory," in which human deeds elicit and thus predict (at least in part)

10. Ernest Becker, *The Denial of Death* (New York: Simon & Schuster, 1973), 2.
11. Ibid.
12. Ibid., 4.
13. Ibid., 6.
14. Oswald Bayer, "Justification: Basis and Boundary of Theology," in *By Faith Alone: Essays in Honor of Gerhard O. Forde*, ed. Joseph A. Burgess and Marc Kolden (Grand Rapids: Eerdmans, 2004), 72.
15. Johann Gottlieb Fichte, *The Vocation of Man*, ed. R. Chisholm (New York: Liberal Arts Press, 1956), 84.
16. Gerhard O. Forde, *Where God Meets Man: Luther's Down-to-Earth Approach to the Gospel* (Minneapolis: Augsburg, 1991), 24.

God's deeds.[17] Over the course of Christian history, the amount of coopera-
tion and the value such theologies placed on human righteousness have
ranged from Pelagian systems, which put full responsibility on ourselves;
to semi-Pelagian systems, which coordinate God's grace and human effort;
to synergistic systems, which see our role in salvation as minimal but still
give human beings a part to play, however infinitesimal it may be.[18] But
in every instance the pattern remains the same. In the end, life with God
depends on the role the human creature chooses to play. "Therefore when
faith has been lost, there follow unbelief and idolatry, which transfer the
glory of God to works."[19] Those whom Luther labels "theologians of glory"
create a God in their own image and a picture of the human creature
after their own longings. Unfortunately, neither the image of God nor the
picture of the human being ever corresponds to reality.[20]

In general, every theology of self-glorification exhibits three characteristics. First, theologies of glory must write a new script for God on the basis
of human observations about the world around them. Human reason must
penetrate nature and history in order to perceive the invisible things of
God. From these observations and experiences, human beings can draw
universal conclusions about God, thereby putting human epistemology
in charge of divine revelation. But in the blindness of their minds they
"exchanged the truth of God for a lie [Rom. 1:26]." They rewrite God's
job description! The new job description for God incorporates human
performance into it. Theologians of glory want assurance that God acts
in predictable ways. They rewrite the contract in such a way that if we
live up to our end of the bargain, God must live up to his. By controlling
my actions, I can in some way determine what God does, we think. In
this way we try to take control of our own future, for through controlling
what we do, we anticipate what God should do in response. God becomes
someone we can manage. He has become domesticated. This new job description for God applies whether one clings to the true God manifested
in creation or to idols totally fashioned by human hearts.[21] In the process
of constructing our own theologies, we refuse to let God be God.

17. Adolph Koeberle, *Quest for Holiness: A Biblical, Historical, and Systematic Investigation* (New York: Harper, 1936), 447.

18. "Pelagianism" is the belief that the sinful human being can attain salvation with
the help of little or no divine grace. "Semi-Pelagianism" attributes more significance to
God's grace in the process of salvation but gives the contribution of human performance
a significant role in the salvation of sinners. "Synergism" teaches that sinners are saved
by grace alone but must make themselves eligible for the free gift of salvation by opening
their minds and hearts to the Holy Spirit.

19. "Genesis Lectures, 1535–1545," *LW* 1:149; *WA* 42:112.26–28.

20. Robert Kolb, "Luther on Theology of the Cross," *Lutheran Quarterly* 16 (2002): 448.

21. Luther and Calvin concurred that the human heart has become a veritable factory
of idols (*fabrica idolorum*).

In addition to redefining God's job description, theologies of glory have to devise a new script for human beings, their capacities, and their relationship to God. In particular, theologies of glory enlarge the importance and magnificence of human accomplishments in order to capture God's favor. If God's job is to reward our works, then our activities and works must be of such a nature that they bring God's favor or blessing on us. What kind of activities do human beings assume necessary to perform or think they ought to perform? Regardless of what sort of work we carry out, that activity must above all else be directed to God and be performed for God, whether directly or indirectly. When our "good" works are aimed at achieving righteousness before God, we tend to place a premium on the development of what might be called "religious" or "spiritual" activities rather than "earthly" works since ultimately we intend to be doing them for God directly rather than for the creature/creation.[22] Unlike the ambiguity that exists in the choices we make on a daily basis for serving fellow creatures (Should I do this or that? What is the right decision?), the works we imagine we need to be able to please or satisfy God must be unambiguously clear. In the sixteenth century, spiritual activities like pilgrimages, attending shrines, cultivating devotional habits including prayer, and the like often focused on the worthiness or quality of the performance of the works as well as the worthiness or holiness of that person before God rather than focusing on the good they accomplish here on earth in meeting the actual needs of one's neighbors. Not only do my activities often trespass on God's grace in my relationship with the other person, but my active righteousness also becomes distorted: we force human works to serve purposes other than those for which God intended them.

As a corollary, and perhaps as an unintended consequence, of rewriting our relationship with God, patterns of works righteousness invariably lead to a new relationship with my neighbor. Becker lamented, "It is one of the meaner aspects of narcissism that we feel that practically everyone is expendable except ourselves. We should feel prepared, as Emerson once put it, to re-create the whole world out of ourselves even if no one else existed."[23] On one hand, Becker pointed out, that thought frightens us because we do not know how we would survive without others. On the other hand, there lies deep within us the belief that we could survive alone if we just trust ourselves. Thus, supplementing or supplanting passive righteousness with active righteousness *coram Deo* also has a significant impact on our human relationships. As a result of the fall

22. Marc Kolden, "Earthly Vocation as a Corollary of Justification by Faith," in Burgess and Kolden, *By Faith Alone*, 277.
23. Becker, *Denial*, 2.

into sin, our aid for neighbors is more often than not constrained by the need to take care of self within both dimensions of life. As a result, the works I do for God are first and foremost those that benefit me. We serve others to the extent that such benevolence improves our chances of cultivating the favor of God.

Works done on the premise of becoming righteous before God are ultimately works done not for one's neighbor but for the glory and salvation of self.[24] Our neighbor's needs then become little more than means to an end. They cannot and are not carried out simply for the good of neighbor or because they are the right thing to do regardless of the benefit we may gain from them. Whatever benefit they give the neighbor is collateral, like "icing on the cake." In the process, the neighbor either becomes instrumentalized as a means to an end or devalued as of little use. In the attempt to secure my future, I cannot carry my service to my neighbor, and thereby I deprive my neighbor of the Creator's gifts. Theologies of glory thus create a situation where a person does only the bare minimum required to meet the need of one's neighbor.

Theologies of Human Self-Glorification

In the attempt to become "like God," human beings have struggled over the centuries with the need to force God's Word into a cooperative schema that enhances the value of human works. Human beings did not eliminate God from their theologies of glory, for they could not evade their creatureliness. They could not live unaided, or conduct their lives without centering them on something or someone that provided them security, identity, and meaning. For the most part they still saw a need for God or at least for the divine in some semipersonal or impersonal form. They realized that they needed to connect with something Ultimate or with God in order to transcend their human finitude. But if one god failed to live up to their expectations, they did not hesitate to find a replacement. After all, as both Luther and Calvin observed, the human heart is a veritable factory of idols (*fabrica idolorum*). Although we are accustomed to thinking of non-Christian religions as idolatrous, Christianity itself has not been immune to the perennial human temptation to redefine God's job description and thus his very person. Both Christians and non-Christians engage in the construction of theologies of glory. In every case, we sinners adopted a schema of works by which we could deal with God and build a relationship with God on our own terms.

24. Forde, *Theologian of the Cross*, 105.

Within the feudal society of the late Middle Ages, Luther had been taught to think of God as one who acted like a king or lord. He was perceived as a stern and judging God who expected unconditional obedience and would not hesitate to knock heads if need be in order to compel immediate compliance. The aim of dealing with such a God was to escape his judgment and with it the prospect of hell. With that objective in mind, some medieval theologians and preachers (for Luther, above all, Gabriel Biel) constructed a system that accorded human beings the ability to placate God and identified the types of works required to do so. These theologians and preachers contended that God handed out temporal rewards for the works God requires (*praecepta*) of all people, but that he rewards eternal life more quickly to those who, with the assistance of grace, carry out the far-more-demanding works required by the gospel (*consilia evangelica*).[25] To be sure, Christ acquired grace for us, but these leaders defined such grace as something like a booster shot or a form of spiritual steroids. As such, grace helped the Christian pilgrim to follow God's will more easily and more readily and thus attain righteousness before God.

The church multiplied the number of works required by the gospel and increased the difficulty of performing them for the spiritual elite in the monasteries, while making it easier for laity to meet a minimum standard that puts them on the path toward heaven. The former included devoting one's entire life to God through monastic practices, such as keeping vows of obedience, poverty, and chastity. For those who wished to attain perfection in this life (as opposed to finishing the task in purgatory), the most efficient route lay in the pursuit of the holy life within monasticism. These vows required that one separate oneself from the world in order to dedicate one's life entirely to God as an ascetic or a monk or nun. But these works of striving for salvation took attention away from serving the needs of one's neighbor. My neighbor becomes devalued when I relegate to the background "worldly" works for neighbor so I can pursue more spiritual or religious self-chosen works in order to achieve righteousness before God. At times it was even argued that society needed the poor; otherwise there would be no one to whom we could give alms and thereby acquire merit for salvation.

Although people in the Middle Ages saw God as demanding more than we could humanly accomplish, people in the twenty-first century have

25. Human reason cannot discern the depth of the demands of God's law, particularly those of the first commandment. Reason deals with the senses and external actions, not the inner heart (Apology of the Augsburg Confession IV.134, *Book of Concord*, 141; *BSLK*, 186). Thus Luther can state, "We do nothing even when we do much; we do not fulfill the law even when we fulfill it" ("Lectures on Galatians, 1531–1535," *LW* 26:8; *WA* 40.1:46.25–28).

constructed a picture of God that has moved in a different direction. Today postmodernity seeks to make God "nice," affirming, supporting, and uplifting the individual. They see God less as a king or lord and more as a friend or therapist. This requires that God be less demanding, more tolerant, and especially nonjudgmental about the wayward behavior of his human creatures. Today it is often more offensive to affirm God's wrath than to affirm his love. It is not uncommon to hear about any intimation of God's wrath in the statement "God would never do that," or "I would never believe in a God that would do that." This "God-Lite" grows out of a society that affirms a therapeutic individualism and an egalitarian inclusiveness. In such a culture, God is seen as one who is willing to overlook my shortcomings because my good intentions are present.

Such an approach to God plays down his love for his creatures as he designed them and diminishes human moral standards. Too often it focuses largely or exclusively on feeling good about self. In other words, *not much* is expected of us other than taking care of ourselves. Bad behavior is removed from the category of sin and put in the category of activities that demand the understanding of others. When sin is addressed, it is considered in terms of vulnerabilities and weaknesses that have to do more with how sin affects the individual than how it offends God or even how it harms one's neighbor. God knows that people will treat each other unjustly on occasion, it is said, but he also understands their human frailties. Therefore, he does not punish them; he ignores them.[26] Christ is viewed as one who assists us along the journey of our lives by providing us with the grace and strength needed to become righteous. At times, Christ might be seen as a name for the power of God that I need in order to achieve personal happiness or to reach the fulfillment of my human potential rather than as the person he is. Within all of this, the religious seeker may be advised to follow prescribed steps for spiritual living in order to obtain God's blessing. The works we do are directed at ourselves and aimed at building self-esteem or self-confidence to make us feel good about ourselves. Yet one's neighbor is still instrumentalized, though in a different way than in the Middle Ages. Now I help others because it makes me feel good about myself, which means that anything I do for them I really do for myself.

In neo-Gnosticism we see an increasingly common example of what Luther called a "theology of glory," a means by which we add to our own glory by finding our own way to God.[27] Gnosticism can be described as a worldview that believes there exists a single source from which flows all

26. Alan Wolfe, *The Transformation of American Religion: How We Actually Live Our Faith* (New York: Free Press, 2003), 163.
27. A. R. Victor Raj, *The Hindu Connection: Roots of the New Age* (St. Louis: Concordia, 1995).

spiritual energy into the universe. This spiritual energy courses through all things, including every human being. All we need to do is tap into it or release it from within us into our lives. The goal is a form of communion with God that involves the complete submersion, absorption, disappearance, and dissolution of a person's individuality into the divine oneness. Gnostic or neognostic worldviews, today sometimes labeled "New Age," define salvation in terms of a special spiritual insight and ecstatic union with God. They may liken union with God to a single drop of water that is absorbed into the infinite ocean or to a flickering flame that loses itself in the original fire. Brahamanism and Vedantism in India, for instance, hold that the goal of human reflection and effort is to deliver the soul from its transmigrations and absorb it into Brahma forever. The ancient Greek philosopher Plotinus insisted that the goal of human life was to realize its mystical return of the soul to the Ultimate and Absolute by freeing itself from the sensuous world by using successive steps of purification. Whereas ancient Gnosticism sought to liberate the "spiritual" within us through a secret knowledge delivered by Christ or some other revealer, neo-Gnosticism seeks to liberate the inner self through self-knowledge and self-expression. It places a strong emphasis on the autonomous self and the "emptiness" of the soul in modern culture. The fundamental problem of human existence is not that we are fallen but that we are incomplete. What keeps one from God is lack of true knowing, a lack of self-knowledge. The inner self needs to respond to the warmth of God within us. Thus, to know ourselves at the deepest level is to know God. To know self is to love God. Self-loving is the way to experience God's grace. Yet excessive concentration on our own inner spiritual situation and strengths can lead to indifference and apathy toward the neighbor.

Luther also recognized that people may substitute another human being's approval for the approval of God, or seek affirmation and security in material goods. The human heart makes many idols, but Luther refers to mammon (an expression for material wealth, especially ill-gotten gains or money) as the most common idol on earth. Those who lack it lust to acquire it. Those who have it fear losing it. Materialism is nothing new, but it takes the form of neomaterialism. What is new about it in contemporary Western society is the widespread phenomenon of prosperity. A special and sometimes acute form of material self-indulgence may be associated with the inner spiritual pilgrimage of neo-Gnosticism. In times past, most people trusted wealth as a way of gaining for themselves a sense of physical security. Relatively few had more than they needed to satisfy their bodily needs. Today, however, many in the Western world (or the northern hemisphere) suffer little want and have much more than they need for food, shelter, and clothing. Therefore, they seek other things from material goods. They now seek intangible benefits from the tangible. Thus, neo-Gnosticism thrives in a consumerist culture by using the material world in order to pamper the inner self, and then discarding it when it no longer satisfies and is therefore easily thrown away. Many people use relationships for the same purpose, only to discard them. Contemporary "Mammonites" seek security, happiness, fulfillment, and pleasure in the acquisition of material goods. In the past, only a few could indulge in this way (Luther occasionally referred to the contemporary banking family of Augsburg, Germany, the Fuggers). Today such indulgence is widespread.

To obtain these benefits, people devote much of their time to acquiring as much money as they can, not for physical needs, but for the "spiritual" satisfaction that they think it can bring. As the money comes in, they purchase things they hope will provide them with identity, image, self-confidence, and the like. Their style of living increases, and with it their expectations. The stuff they acquire satisfies for a short while, but then it leaves them empty and wanting more. This then feeds another cycle in which they have to serve mammon by working to obtain ever-increasing amounts of it in order to finance the ever-greater expectations of a particular lifestyle. In this way it proves to be a cruel god that ever promises but never fully satisfies. Christianized forms can be found in "name it and claim it" theologies, which suggest that if the believer's faith is strong enough, God will somehow feel himself compelled to comply with faith's demand, as well as mantralike approaches such as the prayer of Jabez (1 Chron. 4:10). Such a lifestyle has a profound effect on our relationships with our neighbor. Neighbors are valued particularly if they can help us acquire possessions for ourselves. In a culture of consumerism, we buy things not only to pamper our inner self but also to lift ourselves above those who cannot afford them.

In recent years there has been a rise or rediscovery of neopaganism that engages in various forms of worshiping or reverencing the earth, as did the ancient Druids, or the spirits within the earth, as did some Native Americans. Neopaganism is not a reproduction of every aspect of every ancient form of paganism. In general, concern about global warming and human destruction of the environment have prompted many to take an interest in worshiping the earth as mother goddess in the hope that if we see the earth in divine and personal terms then we will rethink how we act toward nature. Some have taken an increased interest in Gaia (the Greek goddess of the earth), treating the earth as a living organism if not a living being. Our relationship to the earth is described as intimate and unbreakable: human beings were born out of the womb of a goddess and were nursed at the breasts of a goddess. This means that we too are in some sense divine in that we share in the DNA of the earth goddess.

In this view, the activities that cultivate our connection to mother earth are of such a nature as to be devoted primarily to serving the earth, even if it is at the expense of the human use of it. Some may even regard human beings as aliens who do not belong in nature. Reverence for the earth as an end itself replaces an instrumental use of the earth. Thus, adherents of this view engage in various activities oriented toward "saving the earth." One's spirituality is nurtured through meditation and contemplation of nature or feeling at one with nature. More radical forms include Wiccan communities and performing ritual dances and practices aimed at connecting us with the spiritual forces that permeate the natural world.

In every society, Christians have confronted the challenges of other ideologies and worldviews. North American Christians have become accustomed to living in a culture in which biblical values, the "Judeo-Christian heritage," formed the common points of departure for public discourse and religious thinking. But in our time, the age of the "Judeo-Christian heritage" may be coming to an end. Believers today meet people who simply have never learned to think in biblical categories and who are quite unaware of the basic elements of the Christian tradition and heritage. Some people are simply indifferent toward the Christian faith; others are aggressively hostile. Some confront us in the course of daily conversation; others determine what is delivered by the public media, which convey information and form attitudes toward life in our culture. In such a world, the struggle of the Christian amid normal daily engagement with the world involves clearly seeing what differences it makes when we presuppose that God exists and has revealed himself in Jesus Christ. Our struggle to remain faithful to God involves integrating the conviction that our identity springs from him alone and that our performance and accomplishment in life follows his design and structure. This means that we must resist attitudes conveying gnostic, materialistic, or pagan views of the world as they try to take root in our minds and hearts (2 Cor. 10:2–6; 11:4). It means that we must repeat and renew the call of the gospel every day in our lives.

The Inevitability of Human Self-Destruction

The temptation to define ourselves and lodge our identity in our own performance remains "natural" for those struggling against sinful desires, whether these desires are mixed with gnostic, materialist, and pagan ideas or not. Given the perennial human desire to create a schema of works for justifying oneself and making sense of life, how did Luther suggest that human beings be brought to the point that they can experience and retain the passive righteousness of faith? It begins by experiencing firsthand the futility of human endeavors and the tyranny of the law.

For Luther, the flaw in all human schemata of works lies in the fundamental misunderstanding that the law does not bestow life (only God does); it evaluates life.[28] When human creatures ask themselves, "Have I done enough?" "Have I arrived?" the law gives only one answer: "Try harder!" Whether we measure ourselves by the law God has given or some law we have constructed for ourselves, we find ourselves coming up short. The law does not deliver on what we want it to do, thus prompting us to try all the harder. We either cannot satisfy the requirements expected of us, or when we do, the idols we create cannot deliver on their promises! This means that no matter how hard we try to live according to the law, we will find ourselves coming up short—a point that the law makes abundantly clear to us. A classical Lutheran expression declares, "The law always accuses" (lex semper accusat). It constantly reminds us of our shortcomings. People attribute to the law the power to bestow life when the law only evaluates life and confronts us with the judgment of God. Luther called this accusing activity the "chief function" of the law, not that it was part of God's original design, but since we are never without sin, we are never without the accusation of the law. The harder we try, the more our limitations and failings confront us. So even though human performance may advance us on the road of human righteousness, it does not advance us along the path of righteousness coram Deo. The law simply cannot and does not deliver on its promises. Those promises prove to be illusions because the law and human activity were never designed for the purpose of achieving salvation. It is like using a hammer to saw a plank of wood; it does not work.

In the end, the law proves not only unattainable (especially in terms of producing the attitudes and dispositions required by the first commandment) but also untamable. Here again, human beings persistently misunderstand the purpose and function of God's law. They eventually discover that human works not only are completely useless for acquiring righteousness coram Deo but also actually make things worse when we rely on them. Luther brings out this point in an apparent paradox in the first thesis of his Heidelberg Disputation: "The law of God, the most salutary doctrine of life, cannot advance humans on their way to righteousness, but rather hinders them."[29] In every case the law accomplishes the opposite of what we hope. "The law does not work the love of God, it works wrath; it does not give life . . . , it kills; it does not bless, it curses; it does not comfort, it

28. Kolb, "Theology of the Cross," 448.
29. Forde, Theologian of the Cross, 23.

accuses; it does not grant mercy, it judges. In sum, it condemns everything not in Christ."[30] It does not provide a means for winning God's favor.

Luther points out that the Scriptures are filled with warnings that the wrath of God is being revealed from heaven (Rom. 1:18) and that God will hold the entire world accountable before him (3:19–20). This realization of facing the final judgment of God and being held accountable nearly drove Luther to despair as a monk. At times Luther describes the office or work of the law in vivid language. For example, he likens the law as it reveals the wrath of God to a "thunderbolt," by means of which God "destroys both the open sinner and the false saint and allows no one to be right but drives the whole lot of them into terror and despair." For Luther, the "open sinners" were those who did not care what God expected or mandated. They were going to live a life of active and open rebellion against God. The "false saints" were those who believed that they had kept the law, lived exemplary lives, and were otherwise above reproach. But for both people, the law of God "is the hammer of which Jeremiah speaks: 'My word is a hammer that breaks a rock in pieces' (Jer. 23:29)."[31]

However, people today no longer experience the law of God since Immanuel Kant elevated the individual as a moral agent and rejected all claims to moral authority external to the self. This rejection of external authorities elevated the individual as a moral agent to a position of complete autonomy. Thus, moral decision making became radically individualistic. Moral direction is said to arise from within the individual through some principle resident within that person. Kant's third practical principle stated, "The will of every rational being as a will . . . makes universal law." "The will is therefore not merely subject to the law."[32] Instead, it makes the law for itself. Kant thereby initiated a division between fact or reality and value, with the former assigned to the sphere of natural science and the latter relegated to the subjective sphere of feelings. Though not Kant's intention, morality became a matter of choosing values appropriate to each person.

Since Kant, Western culture (and much of Protestantism) has developed a neuralgia against all forms of legalism, which is defined as the imposition of an external and transtemporally valid legal code. In his essay "The Me Decade and the Third Great Awakening," American journalist Tom Wolfe wrote that at the heart of the new religious consciousness lies "an axiom first propounded by the Gnostic Christians some eighteen hundred years ago: namely, that at the apex of every human soul there

---

30. "Heidelberg Disputation, 1518," thesis 23, *LW* 31:41; *WA* 1:354.25–26.

31. Smalcald Articles (1537) III.iii.2, *Book of Concord*, 312; *BSLK*, 436–37.

32. *Kant's Critique of Practical Reason and Other Works on the Theory of Ethics*, trans. Thomas Kingsmill Abbott (London: Longmans, Green, 1954), 59, 114–19.

exists a spark of the light of God."[33] This principle, more than any other, guides the human being, and anything that interferes with its operation comes between that person and God.

The trajectory provided by Kant's ethics found popular expression in Joseph Fletcher's situation ethics in the 1960s. He wrote that "situationism" is "the crystal precipitated in Christian ethics by our era's widespread reaction against legalism."[34] Fletcher reframed Kant's moral imperative (Do your duty) in Christian terms as "Do the loving thing." Where Kant focused on reason or the will as the inner moral principle of human beings, Christians were left to emphasize the inner working of the Holy Spirit for moral guidance. God deals with us personally and directly rather than through an external medium, Fletcher intimated. Every believer can know the will of God through one's faith in Christ. "Emotivism" became the criterion for moral action. Alasdair MacIntyre defines "emotivism" as "the doctrine that all evaluative judgments or more specifically all moral judgments are *nothing but* expressions of preference, expressions of attitude or feeling, insofar as they are moral or evaluative in character."[35] A well-known song in the 1960s put it well: "It can't be wrong if it feels so right!" Obedience, then, is rendered not to the law of God but only to the will of God at any particular moment. "We are set free to do what we want, as long as we have a 'good will' (are motivated by the 'gospel') and thereby intend 'something good' in what we do."[36]

In the end some forms of Protestant theology often undermined the passive righteousness of faith *coram Deo* by removing the basis for God's accusation. The anomian understanding of the gospel among many mainline Protestants resulted not only in the loss of an active righteousness of works normed by the law, but also, ironically, in a watering down of the very gospel they sought to guard from all forms of moralism and legalism. Without a clear articulation of the law of God, the love of God becomes little more than benign benevolence or apathetic tolerance of human misbehavior. That God loves us therefore means he lets us do what we want. H. Richard Niebuhr's characterization of the American Protestant gospel in 1937 still holds today: "A God without wrath brought men without sin into a kingdom without judgment

33. Quoted in Philip Lee, *Against the Protestant Gnostics* (New York: Oxford University Press, 1987), 197.

34. Joseph Fletcher, *Moral Responsibility* (Philadelphia: Westminster, 1967), 27.

35. Alasdair C. MacIntyre, *After Virtue: A Study in Moral Theory*, 2nd ed. (Notre Dame, IN: University of Notre Dame Press, 1984), 11–12.

36. Reinhard Hütter, "The Twofold Center of Lutheran Ethics: Christian Freedom and God's Commandments," in *The Promise of Lutheran Ethics*, ed. Karen L. Bloomquist and John R. Stumm (Minneapolis: Fortress, 1998), 36.

through the ministrations of a Christ without a cross."[37] Around the same time, Dietrich Bonhoeffer, in his book *The Cost of Discipleship*, accused the church of his day of offering a cheap grace: "Cheap grace is the preaching of forgiveness without requiring repentance, baptism without Church discipline, Communion without confession, absolution without personal confession."[38] Grace, Bonhoeffer pointed out, is both completely free, rather than cheap, and costly. It cost Christ his life; it costs the sinner his or her very existence as sinner; it costs the believer the burden, pain, and deprivation of bearing the cross of Christ in order to love the neighbor.

But even when people would have the law fit rather loosely around them as children of the Enlightenment, they cannot live without structure or standards. Gerhard Forde correctly observed that antinomianism is really the only impossible heresy.[39] If people reject God's law, they will simply replace it with one of their own making. In the end, if human beings see themselves as makers and doers, they will find themselves having to carry the entire world on their shoulders like the mythical Atlas holding up the world on his back. They will experience the crushing burden of saving the world, making sense of their lives, playing substitute for God in whatever ways they choose.

Some say that the Christian message presumes that people recognize their own sinfulness, and for this reason most people in Western cultures, who do not recognize their own sinfulness, cannot understand what Jesus Christ should mean for their lives. While it may be true that many minimize what they personally do wrong, the fact remains that life does not flow smoothly. Everyone experiences disruptions and disappointments in life. The law of God is not only an agent of his accusation. As his plan for what human life is to be, his law serves as a diagnostic instrument. It does so when we perpetrate violations of his design for daily life, and it does so when others perpetrate such violations against us. God's law speaks to victims as well as to those who practice injustice and exploit their neighbors. It reminds victims that they and their false gods are insufficient managers and governors of life, inadequate to protect and preserve the good life. Most people thus experience the burden of the law through the pressures of everyday life apart from feelings of guilt and shame. Also, victims of wrongdoing seek to regain mastery of life when it seems threatened by other people, by "the system," by failing health or wealth.

37. H. Richard Niebuhr, *The Kingdom of God in America* (New York: Harper & Brothers, 1937), 193
38. Dietrich Bonhoeffer, *Cost of Discipleship*, trans. R. H. Fuller and I. Booth, 6th ed. (New York: SCM, 1959), 180.
39. Gerhard Forde, "Law and Sexual Behavior," *Lutheran Quarterly* 9 (1995): 18.

Without adding self-invented spiritual activities to the list of requirements, the law is heavy enough for those who simply try to live out their daily lives for the good of neighbor according to God's design. Such activities will constantly encounter judgment within creation. Among other things, the schema of works confronts us with our reluctance and resistance to tend to the responsibilities of our callings. Human beings encounter resentment within their hearts for having to help an aged parent or infirm spouse because it deprives them of pursuing their own desires and pleasures. Parents encounter the burden of the law as they try to meet the expectations placed on them by society or themselves to involve their children in club sports, music programs, and other extracurricular activities so they can get into the good universities. One good example of this phenomenon is the harried mother who feels inadequate because she cannot accomplish and do for her family all that she feels she is expected to do. Human beings also constantly encounter God's curse on the earth as we battle creation's resistance to yield its bounty, sicknesses and diseases, and the daily trials and tribulations of life. In all of these instances, we experience guilt *coram Deo*. We encounter God's judgment in the hardness of life that wears us down until it eventually results in death.

Guilt and judgment *coram Deo* always occur within the world because our relationship with God is inseparable from our relationships with neighbors or the things of creation. The requirements to look after neighbor will force one to encounter a lack of trust and faith within the heart. Willingly giving to my neighbor requires that I simultaneously rely on God to look after my needs. But the interconnection of these three relationships is not always clear. "The foremost office or power of the law is that it reveals inherited sin and its fruits. It shows human beings into what utter depths their nature has fallen and how completely corrupt it is."[40] When Luther and his colleagues spoke about the law revealing original sin, they nearly always had in view sins related to the first commandment. They readily affirmed that reason can to some extent recognize the sins of the second table of the law, those that involve harming our neighbor, matters involving adultery, stealing, and lying, or similar sins. But human reason does not comprehend the depth of our corrupted nature, including those things involving unbelief, false belief, idolatry, being without the fear of God, presumption, despair, blindness, and not knowing God.[41] The depth of our inherited nature must be believed on the basis of the revelation of Scripture. Although the law is experienced in daily life, it must also be proclaimed in order to expose the false idols that we create for ourselves and the disappointment they bring.

40. Smalcald Articles III.ii.4, *Book of Concord*, 312; *BSLK*, 436.
41. Smalcald Articles III.i.2, *Book of Concord*, 310; *BSLK*, 434.

When the law crushes, people end up oscillating between the pole of despair and the pole of hypocrisy. Human beings cannot break out of the cycle. The only way to break out of it is to recover our humanity through the birth from above that takes place by way of death and resurrection.

The Rebirth of the Human Creature

Not only is the attempt to transcend our human creatureliness by becoming "like God" doomed to failure on the grounds that the creature cannot become the Creator; human efforts to recover the core of creatureliness in terms of faith are also doomed to failure because of the human fall into sin. By themselves, human beings simply cannot let go of their desire to be "like God." Luther quarreled with Erasmus on this very point: he contended that his learned correspondent essentially believed that human beings need no more than reform, renovation, and remodeling, which they themselves could accomplish through a process of self-improvement. For Luther, a more radical solution was required than what was offered by the theologians of his day. He argued that humans do not need to be reformed but rather regenerated. Luther put it bluntly in describing the repentance he believed must take place each day in a believer's life: "You must all become something different from what you are now and act in a different way, no matter who you are and what you do."[42] Gerhard Forde expressed it well: "No repairs, no improvements, no optimistic encouragements are possible. Just straight talk: 'You must be born anew.' Sinners must die (Rom. 6:23a)—either eternally or baptismally."[43] A person must undergo the rebirth that takes place through repentance. Two quite different assumptions regarding the extent of sin's damage to the human person lay behind the respective solutions.

Much of medieval theology maintained that the damage of sin was extensive but not completely debilitating. Working with a human model inherited from Aristotle, thinkers had divided the person into a taxonomy of component parts. From top to bottom, the human person was viewed as consisting of reason, will, passions, and bodily movements. The higher faculties like reason and will linked us to the image of God. The lower faculties like emotions and bodily locomotion linked us to the animal world. This did not mean that our passions were sinful, but there was a sense that they were unruly and needed to be controlled, for they tended to attach us to this world. Ideally, the human person functioned in such a way that reason provides information to the will,

42. Smalcald Articles III.iii.3, *Book of Concord*, 312–13; *BSLK*, 437.
43. Forde, *Theologian of the Cross*, 97.

which then made choices or decisions that kept the passions in check. Before the fall, God had given Adam and Eve a gift of stabilizing grace, a kind of spiritual steroid, to help them maintain the working balance of the human parts. The fall into sin and loss of grace damaged the human race by bringing about disorder within the human being: human reason became darkened (but not blinded) and the human will was weakened (but not rendered impotent). Having lost their balance, the passions now informed the decisions of the will as much if not more than did reason.

Several implications flowed from such a view of the human condition before and after the fall. First, the taxonomy of the human creature meant that people considered sin primarily in terms of individual activities voluntarily carried out. Emotions were neither good nor bad unless carried out in actions. If it was not a conscious or voluntary act, it was not a sin. Second, since sin did not completely damage human reason and will, late medieval thinkers argued that, theoretically, human beings could still love God with all their heart. But with the loss of grace, it had become terribly difficult if not impossible to do so. Third, this model assumes that human beings want to do the right thing. What prevents them from doing so is that they lack the right information. Provide the right information, and they will make good and informed decisions. They just need a little assistance. The gospel story gave human reason the information or knowledge of God that it needed, while sacramental grace enabled the human will to love God more easily. With some adaptations, this medieval model still remains the operative model for many Christians, particularly those who believe that non-Christians are capable of making a decision for Jesus or having the strength to give their hearts to Jesus. In other words, conversion and rebirth become matters of human reformation that make us the subject of the final chapter of the gospel story. "I chose Jesus." "I gave my heart to Christ." "I decided to follow him."

By contrast, Luther's understanding of faith as constituting the core of human and creaturely existence led him to consider the human person relationally and holistically rather than in terms of a set of qualities, capacities, or possessions that need to work harmoniously together. In Luther's eyes, this meant that a person is either completely turned toward God or completely turned away from God. In the desire to become "like God," human beings turned away from God and thereby lost the ability to know God as he is, to trust him, and to love him.

Having to work with the medieval categories and descriptions of the human person that he inherited in order to communicate with his opponents, Luther insisted that as a result of the fall, human reason was blinded (not merely darkened) and the human will was rendered impotent (not merely weakened) with regard to the affairs of God. Conversely, the human person remained addicted to sin (one looks good outwardly, but can't live without sin). In light of the two kinds of righteousness, Luther maintained that humans still retained some reason and choice with regard to the matters involving life in this world (the things under our dominion) that made it possible for civil righteousness to occur for the sake of preserving the world. He even praised it as a good gift from God in his explanation of the first article of the Apostles' Creed. But with regard to our relationship with God, the human being was completely bound and enslaved to sin. Thus in his explanation of the third article of the creed, Luther confesses, "I *believe that by my own understanding or strength* I cannot believe in Jesus Christ my Lord or come to him, *but instead the Holy Spirit has called me* by the Gospel" (emphasis added).[44]

The implications of Luther's thought were far reaching. First, he did not consider sin primarily in terms of actions that we chose to carry out as a result of an informed decision. First and foremost, sin was the lack of faith. So deep and pervasive is the corruption that human beings cannot discover it or perceive it by any native ability. People may experience the effects of sin through pressures and trials of life. They can recognize sins but cannot see the root sin. One must acknowledge it on the basis of God's revelation. Second, apart from the Holy Spirit, the human will could only flee God, hate God, and fight God. We *cannot* by our own reason or effort believe in Jesus Christ or come to him. Third, what is needed is rebirth, not information. The only way for the sinner to stop struggling against God is for the sinner to be struck down and killed (to become dead to sin). The only way for the sinner to believe in Jesus Christ is to be raised again from the dead. God must accomplish both events in the life of a person. At this point the classical Lutheran distinction between law and gospel (as exemplified in works by C. F. W. Walther and Werner Elert)[45] hits its stride in order to bring about a new birth through repentance. Both Luther and Melanchthon stressed that when it comes to justifying sinners, law and gospel are two works of God by which he kills in order to make alive. The law crushes and accuses so that we might empty our hands and give up on ourselves and so that the gospel might enter to revive us with the gifts of Christ. The gospel arouses faith in the righteousness of Christ that is bestowed on us.

In Luther's view, the final chapter of the gospel narrative still places us as the objects of God's action. Faith talks in terms of what God has

44. *Book of Concord*, 355; *BSLK*, 511.
45. See note 1 of chap. 1 above.

done to us and for us. Prepositional phrases were important for Luther, particularly the phrase *pro me* (for me). No longer am I the doer of the action (I decide, I chose, I commit) and the subject of the narrative, as humans were when they wanted to become like God. Instead, I recover my place as the object of the story regarding God's involvement and activity within the world. In his explanation of the catechism, Luther thus teaches children "faith talk." We are never the (acting) subject of the gospel narrative; we are the object of the gospel narrative. Luther brings this out in his explanation of the three articles of the Apostles' Creed. In the first article he confesses: "God has made me, . . . given me my body and soul, . . . given me clothing and shoes, . . . richly and daily provides [for] me, . . . defends me and protects me." In the second article: God has "redeemed me . . . won me . . . that I belong to him." And in the third article: "The Spirit called me, enlightened me, sanctified and kept me . . . will raise me . . . and give eternal life to me."[46]

Rebirth suggests a one-way street. This does not mean that the Christian or faith is inactive as it is ignited. When a baby emerges from its mother's womb, it enters the world kicking and crying, but in no way assisting with the birth or contributing to the birth. The mother alone—through rhythmic breathing, hard work, and pushing—gives birth to the child. In Bo Giertz's novel *The Hammer of God*, a young pastor declares, "I have given Him [Christ] my heart!" An older and wiser Rector replies, "One does not choose a Redeemer for oneself, you understand, nor give one's heart to Him. The heart is a rusty old can on a junk heap. A fine birthday gift, indeed! But a wonderful Lord passes by and has mercy on the wretched tin can, sticks His walking cane through it and rescues it from the junk pile and takes it home with Him. That is how it is."[47] Because the human person cannot give birth to self but only passively receives birth, others are involved. In his Small Catechism, Luther says that the Spirit brings me to faith even as he has gathered the entire Christian church. We do not come to faith in isolation from other believers. They bring us to the baptismal font or place the Word within our hearts. Pushing the birth metaphor, Luther in his Large Catechism insists that the one holy Christian church is "the mother that begets and bears every Christian through the Word of God, which the Holy Spirit reveals and proclaims, through which he illuminates and inflames hearts so that they grasp and accept it, cling to it, and persevere in it."[48] In other words, it is intrinsic to its very nature that the church bears children through the Word.

46. *Book of Concord*, 355-56.
47. Bo Giertz, *Hammer of God*, 2nd ed. (Minneapolis: Fortress, 2005), 147.
48. Large Catechism, Creed, 42, *Book of Concord*, 436; *BSLK*, 655.

Christian Life as Daily Repentance

According to Luther, being put to death by the law and raised by the gospel is not a onetime occurrence within the world this side of eternity. On the contrary, it provides the rhythm of the entire Christian life. Here we come to the direct implications of Luther's theology of baptism. In discussing the significance of baptism in the life of the Christian, Luther in his catechism affirms that baptism signifies "that the old creature in us with all sins and evil desires is to be drowned and die through daily contrition and repentance, and on the other hand that daily a new person is to come forth and rise up to live before God in righteousness and purity forever."[49] In his Large Catechism he states that the effect of baptism "is nothing else than the slaying of the old Adam and the resurrection of the new creature, both of which must continue in us our whole life long."[50] Thus, Luther believed, the human creature who has received the passive righteousness of faith wages an ongoing struggle against the sinful nature's tendency to make its own idols. This struggle must be understood within the context of two observations.

First, Luther's rendering of Romans 6:4 extrapolates from the biblical statement. Where Paul stated that we were "buried into death," Luther states that we were "buried in death" in order to express God's baptismal action as both a onetime act and a continuing state of being. Peters summarizes Luther's mature understanding: "Our whole humanity is given over into death once and for all—in body, soul, and spirit—not only in the moment of our baptism but [also] in the sacrament's eschatological reality, with the result that we have secured participation in the life won by Christ's resurrection already here on earth for all eternity." This means that "our participation not only in Christ's death but also in his resurrection makes us certain that, in our daily dying as the old person and in our daily rising as the new person in Christ, the goal of our eschatological hope is present in a hidden manner. This new creature who daily reemerges is already here and now identical with that person who will stand for all eternity before God's throne."[51]

To be sure, from God's point of view the baptismal righteousness of a Christian is full and complete. At the same time it is a righteousness that must be given ever anew in the struggle against the sin that remains, "a struggle called repentance." In the first of the Ninety-five Theses,[52] Luther's famous statement that the whole of the Christian life is a life of

---

49. Small Catechism, Baptism, 12, *Book of Concord*, 360; *BSLK*, 516.

50. Large Catechism, Baptism, 65, *Book of Concord*, 465; *BSLK*, 704–5.

51. Albrecht Peters, *Kommentar zu Luthers Katechismen*, ed. Gottfried Seebass, 5 vols. (Göttingen: Vandenhoeck & Ruprecht, 1990–94), 4:100, 103.

52. "Lectures on Galatians, 1531–1535," *LW* 26:170; *WA* 40.1:288.15–16.

repentance "never receded in importance in his understanding of daily life."[53] Here he addresses the ongoing reality of sin within the Christian life as well as the lifelong struggle with Satan. The Christian is engaged in an internal warfare between the old creature (sinful flesh) and the new creature (life in the Spirit). Luther describes the old creature as "irascible, spiteful, envious, unchaste, greedy, lazy, proud—yes—and unbelieving; it is beset with all vices and by nature has nothing good in it." This old creature must daily decrease until it is destroyed. Left unchecked, it simply gets worse with each passing year.[54] In his baptismal booklet, Luther describes this in vivid imagery by warning that through baptism we hang around the child's neck a "mighty, lifelong enemy" named Satan.[55] This daily dying and rising of the believer remained a major topic as Luther sketched his agenda for the proposed papal council to be held in Mantua in 1537.

Second, the daily repetition of baptism through dying and rising does not take place through artificial "mortifications of the flesh," such as fasting, or becoming a monk in the desert to devote oneself to conquering the flesh. Instead, it takes place within full view of the world, where Christians live out their callings. More specifically, with respect to their standing before God, the daily dying and rising of which Luther speaks occurs through confession and absolution. Repentance is an earnest attack on the old creature and an entering into new life.[56] In light of the passive righteousness of faith, confession is no longer something that we do for God while trying to render the appropriate recompense to God for our sins (that would be to deny the work of Christ). Instead, by the activity of confessing sins, Christians empty their hands of their sins. It is a way of carrying out the blessed exchange. In confessing their sins, Christians may say, "Lord, I don't want to hang on to my sins anymore. You take them. Get them out of my sight." Only when their hands and hearts are empty are they in a position to receive the benefits of Christ. For Luther, it would be more appropriate to speak of private absolution than private confession since the entire focus of confession has shifted from the human activity of confessing to the divine activity of forgiving. Intense and exhaustive soul searching is abandoned. Upon confession, the confessor absolves. Period.

The sins that one confesses focus on the first commandment and the human addiction to idolatry. But this always takes place within the world since the only things that humans can deify are elements of creation,

53. Robert Kolb, "God Kills to Make Alive: Romans 6 and Luther's Understanding of Justification (1535)," *Lutheran Quarterly* 12 (1998): 51.

54. Large Catechism, Baptism, 68–70, *Book of Concord*, 465; *BSLK*, 705.

55. Small Catechism, 1529, Baptismal Booklet, 3, *Book of Concord*, 372; *BSLK*, 536.

56. Large Catechism, Baptism, 75, *Book of Concord*, 466; *BSLK*, 706.

including their own thoughts, possessions, or other people. When we deify anything within creation we cannot use it to serve our neighbor. In his Brief Form of Confession, Luther thus encourages Christians to "reflect on your walk of life in light of the Ten Commandments: whether you are father, mother, son, daughter, master, mistress, servant; whether you have been disobedient, unfaithful, lazy; whether you have harmed anyone by word or deed; whether you have stolen, neglected, wasted, or injured anything."[57] Confessing involves admitting that we have not been living as God designed us to live. Luther then proceeds to give several examples of what such a confession might look like from within the various walks of life in which we find ourselves. In this way the dying and rising that took place in baptism takes place on a daily basis until a Christian breathes one's final breath. At that moment, baptism finds its culmination in the death and bodily resurrection that occurs when Christ returns.

To preserve the passive righteousness of faith, the reformers insisted that one must turn a deaf ear to the law's demands and accusations and cling only to the gospel, which shows that God has provided another way for us to obtain righteousness: by faith in Christ. Righteousness *coram Deo* "means to do nothing, to hear nothing, and to know nothing about the Law or about works but to know and believe only this: that Christ has gone to the Father and is now invisible."[58] Moreover, it assures us that this has always been God's answer to the human predicament. The passive righteousness of faith comforts the conscience and makes the heart glad.

---

57. Small Catechism, Confession and Absolution, 20, *Book of Concord*, 360; *BSLK*, 517.
58. "Lectures on Galatians, 1531–1535," *LW* 26:8; *WA* 40.1:47.15–18.

5

THE DYNAMIC OF FAITH

When I have this [passive] righteousness within me, I descend from heaven like the rain that makes the earth fertile. That is, I come forth into another kingdom and I perform good works whenever the opportunity arises. If I am a minister of the Word, I preach, I comfort the saddened, and I administer the sacraments. If I am a father, I rule my household and family, I train my children in piety and honesty. If I am a magistrate, I perform the office that I have received by divine command. If I am a servant, I faithfully tend to my master's affairs. In short, whoever knows for sure that Christ is his righteousness not only cheerfully and gladly works in his calling but also submits himself for the sake of love to magistrates, also their wicked laws, and to everything else in this present life—even, if need be, to burden and danger. For he knows that God wants this and that this obedience pleases him.

Luther, "Lectures on Galatians, 1531–1535"

Weak on Sanctified Living?

Luther's insight that works are not needed for justification before God soon elicited the question "What are they good for?" Why are they needed at all? Luther's catchphrases "faith alone" and "freedom of the Christian" raised alarms that a Lutheran antinomianism would undermine the social order of the empire and foster anarchy. Indeed, Roman Catholic opponents claimed that the German Peasants' Revolt of 1525 gave those charges strong credence even though serious peasant rebellion had rocked several areas within Germany in the previous quarter century. In addition, a student of Luther, Johann Agricola, argued in 1527 that the law no longer applies to Christians since they are freed from the law. The law belongs in the courthouse, not in the church. In other words, the law must be proclaimed to non-Christians, not to Christians.[1]

As a response to the conflict between Agricola and Melanchthon, Luther wrote the Large Catechism (1529), in which he devoted nearly half of the entire text to giving a positive exposition of the Ten Commandments. A year later, Luther's followers found themselves called to Augsburg by Emperor Charles V in order to explain why they had changed a variety of traditional practices within the Protestant lands. Nearly ten years after Luther had stood before the emperor at Worms, the Protestant princes presented to the emperor the Augsburg Confession, in which they explained, "Our people are falsely accused of prohibiting good works."[2] Melanchthon's masterpiece on the doctrine of justification, found in the Apology of the Augsburg Confession, devotes over two hundred paragraphs to the subject of faith and good works. The Lutherans needed to defend themselves against the charge that their rejection of works as a basis for righteousness before God rendered good works unnecessary, irrelevant, unimportant, and even detrimental; their defense continued throughout the sixteenth century.

Reflecting this criticism of Lutheranism, Carter Lindberg has asked, "Do Lutherans shout justification but whisper sanctification?" He answered with a decisive "no!"[3] Nonetheless, heirs of Luther today still hear the accusation that they remain paranoid that any talk about works will immediately be interpreted as works righteousness, so that it is safer to say nothing at all. Indeed, in the view of some, talk about moral progress "actually draws us away from a trusting faith in Christ's atoning sacrifice on our behalf."[4] In other words, the argument runs, since Christ is the end of the law, doing good works does not apply to Christians. At times, this has led to the charge that "Lutherans are lazy."[5] To be sure, certain Lutheran uses of the distinction between law

1. For an account of this controversy, see Timothy J. Wengert, *Law and Gospel: Philip Melanchthon's Debate with John Agricola of Eisleben over Poenitentia* (Grand Rapids: Baker Academic, 1997), 77–210.

2. Augsburg Confession XX.1, *Book of Concord*, 52; *BSLK*, 75.

3. Carter Lindberg, "Do Lutherans Shout Justification but Whisper Sanctification?" *Lutheran Quarterly* 13 (1999): 1–20.

4. David P. Gushee, "The Struggle to Love," *Christianity Today* 47 (2003): 76.

5. Marc Kolden, "Earthly Vocation as a Corollary of Justification by Faith," in *By Faith Alone: Essays on Justification in Honor of Gerhard O. Forde*, ed. Joseph A. Burgess and Marc Kolden (Grand Rapids: Eerdmans, 2004), 286.

and gospel have given some preachers pause about exhorting people to good works since the law always accuses (*lex semper accusat*) people of being sinners in the eyes of God. In such cases, Luther's saying is transformed into the "law only accuses" (*lex sola accusat*). Then the law will be seen in purely negative terms, without positive value for the Christian life. In this dichotomy the gospel triumphs over the curse of the law and the wrath of God (the law condemns, the gospel acquits). A caricature of the Lutheran position can be expressed about the different ways in which Christians teach the Ten Commandments. "In the Middle Ages it was said, 'God wouldn't have given us the Commandments if we couldn't keep them, so keep them.' Lutherans say, 'God gave us the Ten Commandments to show us that we couldn't keep them, so don't bother trying!'" This obviously misrepresents Luther's view of Christian living.

Part of the problem with the perception that Luther's followers do not emphasize good works or sanctification may lie in what they think the Christian life should look like. If we answer the question "What does the Christian life look like?" by drawing a sharp line of distinction between what the Christian life should look like and what the upright non-Christian life should look like, then it may appear to all outward appearances that Lutherans are weak on sanctification. Or if one answers these questions by drawing out specific prescriptions for living that apply only to Christians, then it may appear that Lutherans have little to say about the activities of the Christian life. But for Luther there is only one pattern for being human, designed by God, and it is possible to conform to outward standards of behavior in relation to other human beings even apart from faith in the Creator.

Certainly, the passive righteousness of faith does not eliminate the need for active involvement in the world; it does not call for retreat from the world, as Luther's own life demonstrated. Nor does the passive righteousness of faith require that we seek perfection within this world or impose a new agenda on it. Both of these approaches seek to lift us above our neighbor and end up disparaging the world. In one sense, for Luther the Christian life is distinctive in that Christians do not live for the purpose of glorifying themselves or justifying themselves (in any case, we cannot see motivations). But in another sense, the Christian life looks quite ordinary and mundane with regard to the activities that are carried out. Christian life is human life, as God designed it for all his human creatures. It lives by God's word of forgiveness in trust toward him, and it carries out the tasks he has commanded for praising and serving him and for loving and caring for other creatures.

Faith Brings a New Life

Luther's identification of the two kinds of righteousness brought about a fundamental and radical theological reinterpretation of the place that works play within the Christian life. The fact that active righteousness does not contribute to our life with God or righteousness *coram Deo*, however, does not mean that active righteousness is of no importance or value. On the contrary, the distinction between the two kinds of righteousness stresses that we seek to live in both dimensions of our humanity, trusting God and loving others, but for different purposes. Faith makes us righteous in the eyes of God. Good works serve a different purpose. Pastors are to urge Christians with a stipulation: "Help your neighbor, not because it saves you, but because it is good for your neighbor and because it is the way in which God intends humanity to be enjoyed." This does not mean that passive righteousness is restricted to our relationship with God, as if the world were merely secular or our relationship with God took place in isolation from the world. Luther made a strong connection between them in such a way that the active righteousness of works is the corollary of the passive righteousness of faith. Once we recover our core identity *coram Deo* (as children and heirs), we can embrace our roles and responsibilities *coram mundo* (as parents, citizens, neighbors) and carry out the tasks they entail. As Luther put it, "A person is justified without works—although he does not remain without works when he has been justified."[6]

One of Luther's most well-known comments on the relationship between the passive righteousness of faith and the active righteousness of works is found in his preface to the epistle to the Romans, a statement also cited in the Lutheran Formula of Concord. It highlights the natural connection between faith and good works:

> Faith, however, is a divine work in us which changes us and makes us to be born anew of God, John 1[:12–13]. It kills the old Adam and makes us altogether different men, in heart and spirit and mind and powers; and it brings with it the Holy Spirit. O it is a living, busy, active, mighty thing, this faith. It is impossible for it not to be doing good works incessantly. It does not ask whether good works are to be done, but before the question is asked, it has already done them, and is constantly doing them. Whoever does not do such works, however, is an unbeliever. He gropes and looks around for faith and good works, but knows neither what faith is nor what good works are. Yet he talks and talks, with many words, about faith and good works.
>
> Faith is a living, daring confidence in God's grace, so sure and certain that the believer would stake his life on it a thousand times. This knowledge of and confidence in God's grace makes men glad and bold and happy in

6. "Preface to the Epistle to the Romans, 1546," *LW* 35:374; *WA* DB 7:16.17–19.

dealing with God and with all creatures. And this is the work which the Holy Spirit performs in faith. Because of it, without compulsion, a person is ready and glad to do good to everyone, to serve everyone, to suffer everything, out of love and praise to God who has shown him his grace. Thus it is impossible to separate works from faith, quite as impossible as to separate heat and light from fire.[7]

To drive home the connection of faith and works, Luther frequently drew on the biblical image of a good tree that produces good fruit. A tree that is healthy cannot do anything other than what comes naturally. The tree cannot do anything other than produce good fruit. For Luther, this meant that those who have the passive righteousness of faith do good works. Luther sought to make several points by means of this analogy.

First, faith gives the Christian a new orientation and new spiritual impulses. The Holy Spirit gives us a new orientation that is less egocentric and more exocentric, oriented toward other people, precisely because it is christocentric. Faith alone can free us from preoccupation with matters involving our identity, meaning, and security so that we can concentrate on the world around us, which God has placed under our dominion, for our serving and caring, not according to the model of the Gentiles but of Christ himself (Mark 10:42–45). In his treatise *On Good Works* (1520), Luther states, "Good works do not make a good person. A good person makes good works." The first half of Luther's statement highlights the point that doing good works does not enhance our standing in the eyes of God. The second half makes the same point as his analogy of the good tree: a good person produces good works. With our relationship to God secure, we can now focus on rehabilitating and looking after our relationships with each other. The person who is saved "can leave the question of self-enhancement both before humans and God behind, enter freely into the world, and do the good that appears good to do."[8] Hence, I do good works, such as looking after my family, serving the community, and feeding the poor, not because they improve my standing with others (or out of guilt), but because they make for a happy household, support public life, and fill stomachs. It is the right thing to do. But with faith the Holy Spirit enables Christians to do these things willingly and gladly rather than from compulsion or coercion.

Second, everything that a human creature does in faith as a child of God that is not contrary to his will is a good work (Rom. 14:23). Every

7. "Preface to the Epistle to the Romans, 1546," *LW* 35:370–71; *WA* DB 7:10.6–23, 11.6–23; cf. *Book of Concord*, 576; *BSLK*, 941.
8. Gerhard O. Forde, "Luther's Ethics," in *A More Radical Gospel: Essays on Eschatology, Authority, Atonement, and Ecumenism*, ed. Mark C. Mattes and Stephen D. Paulson (Grand Rapaids: Eerdmans, 2004), 146.

human activity—getting up in the morning, brushing one's teeth, eating breakfast, feeding the dogs, going to work, balancing the checkbook, washing the dishes, or raking the leaves—is a good work in the eyes of God. What makes a work good is not how well the work is performed or the nature of the work. What makes it good in the eyes of God is that it is done because of a trust that acknowledges God as God and clings to him. When a mother declares her child's finger painting to be priceless, she does so not on the basis of its intrinsic quality or because she had it appraised by experts. She praises it because of who painted it—her child! So it is with God regarding the works of a believer. Conversely, even though a work may look good in the eyes of the world, it is not necessarily a God-pleasing good work unless it is the work of a good or righteous person. In the eyes of the world the Christian life does not look particularly glamorous. Melanchthon illustrated this with a story of Saint Anthony, the "founder" of the hermitic form of monasticism, who asked God to show him what progress he was making in his life of sanctification. As a basis for comparison, God showed him a shoemaker in the city of Alexandria. When Anthony went to have a look, he did not see or hear anything special other than that the man prayed in the morning for the whole city and then "paid attention to his business."[9] What was the point of the story? One walk of life is no better than another for attaining righteousness before God. One walk of life does not render a person more holy or more perfect than another. Thus, whatever your God-ordained vocation, attend to it! Having said that, Melanchthon was willing to rank the various walks of life (and the works they require) not in terms of their ability to make us holy but only in terms of their contribution to the well-being of the human community.[10]

Faith Embraces the World as God's Creation

If the creature of faith no longer does good works for the purpose of self-improvement or enhancing one's standing with God, but instead for the sake of others, it means that an entirely different arena is opened up in which our active righteousness finds its proper place: within creation. Faith in the God who justifies is at the same time faith in the God who created the world. Thus, faith embraces the world as God's good creation. "Our new relationship to God creates a new relationship to

9. Apology of the Augsburg Confession XXVII.38, *Book of Concord*, 283–84; *BSLK*, 389.

10. Apology of the Augsburg Confession XXIII.38–40, *Book of Concord*, 253; *BSLK*, 340–41.

the world."[11] The passive righteousness of faith returns us to creation. The concept of the passive righteousness of faith in Christ eliminates all of our works from consideration when thinking of how we can justify our lives to God, using them to secure our relationship with him. This concept relocates these works in the world God created for human beings in the first place; they belong there for the sake of others, for the common good. Here the Lutheran doctrine of justification expresses itself in a robust doctrine of vocation that the Christian embraces as one reenters creation. Carter Lindberg has suggested that Luther brought about something of a Copernican revolution by the way he "lifted secular life out of the inferiority assigned it by the medieval church."[12]

As believers return to creation, they encounter some harsh realities. The Creator's sovereignty is disputed on every front by the devil, the world, and their own desires, which reject God's lordship and design. Believers find themselves surrounded by sin, evil, death, and decay. Christians find their faith under constant assault by events suggesting that God is not in control. Drawing false conclusions from a false correlation of evil and God's intention toward his creatures, some Christians throughout history have concluded that the world is too corrupt a place in which to live, much less in which to work out their sanctification. Creation and our responsibilities in creation are not good enough to attain true holiness. According to this view of life, creation is no more than our stepping-stone to the life hereafter. Once I am saved, I can begin saying good-bye to this world. It ceases to be of strong interest or concern to me. Thus, Christians are tempted to live only as aliens or strangers in this world, pilgrims who are making the journey through this life. Such a belief argues that it is necessary to retreat from the world. Thus, the enticement of a creation-denying, world-fleeing, self-depriving spirituality has confronted Christians of every age.[13] "We are always on our way somewhere else, to an idealist heaven where there is no change or decay or flesh or sex or children and all that, or to a utopia, to Solla Salloo, where they never have any troubles, or at least very few."[14] While Christians do discipline their lives and avoid excessive indulgences, ever ready to make sacrifices for others, they confess that this world belongs to their Father and their family. Therefore, they feel free to use his created gifts in ways that please him.

For critique, Luther singled out the monks who thought they should flee the corrupt and empty world and thereby serve God. Christian monks

---

11. Oswald Bayer, *Living by Faith: Justification and Sanctification* (Grand Rapids: Eerdmans, 2003), 27.

12. Carter Lindberg, "Do Lutherans Shout Justification but Whisper Sanctification?" *Lutheran Quarterly* 13 (1999): 109.

13. Kolden, "Earthly Vocation," 282.

14. Forde, "Luther's Ethics," 150.

were not the first or the only ones to flee the world. The reclusive life also appeared among Buddhists, Stoics, Neoplatonists, and Gnostics, though Christian monastics flee the world for other reasons than these groups held. For instance, the gnostic view of life is shaped by the myth of the exiled soul, which found its highest expression among the Gnostics during the second century. Through some precosmic misadventure on the part of a demiurge, the soul splintered off from the divine, lost its way, and eventually became trapped in a material body within a world of death and decay. Now living in exile, it lies slumbering, unaware that its true destiny is to return to its origin in the spiritual realms above. Its awakening takes place by the acquisition of a new or secret knowledge that reveals to the soul its immortal destiny. In this story the physical world is regarded as evil, being itself the result of a precosmic fall by a divine demiurge. Thus, the human body is seen as a tomb imprisoning the soul, which is freed upon the death of the body. The resurrection of the body must be rejected. In the meantime, the appropriate behavior for one who has acquired this secret knowledge is to devote oneself either to purging the body of its lusts or to licentious living because the Gnostics held that the body's actions cannot affect the soul.

Such ideas were indeed floating through the public square in North Africa when Christian monasticism originated in the desert of Egypt and came into its own in the fourth century.[15] People who wanted to take their Christianity seriously reacted against the lax standards of Christian living (a consequence of Constantine's Christianizing of the empire) by going out into the desert to pursue a life of perfection. Justification for the life of solitude was found in the Gospels, beginning with the example of John the Baptizer, who lived in the wilderness. Furthermore, they contended that Christ wanted his followers to be perfect, to which end he had given certain evangelical counsels of poverty (Go and sell all that you have!), chastity (Abstain from sex!), and obedience (Prove your humility by submission!). By adhering to these counsels, one could pursue a life of perfection. Obeying the counsels required that a person free oneself from any attachment to created things through the conquest of sensuality and human desires.[16] External practices like fasting, sleep deprivation, and other forms of bodily mortification were weapons in that struggle for self-conquest. Only the continual mortification or killing of natural appetites and the

15. Christian monasticism developed in two directions. Some adopted the eremitical life of the solitaries, made famous by St. Anthony (c. 270), living in caves and huts apart from each other. But far more adopted cenobitic life within an organized community of monks and nuns, as developed by St. Pachomius (c. 292–346).

16. Clifford H. Lawrence, *Medieval Monasticism: Forms of Religious Life in Western Europe in the Middle Ages* (New York: Longman, 1984), 3.

progressive mortification of the mind within a life of solitude could free the mind for contemplation of God. Thus, monks accepted the challenge of total surrender to Christ by separating themselves from the world and living a life in solitude apart from society.

Augustine of Hippo gave a theological justification for retreat from the world. Thus, as an Augustinian monk, Luther's theology and life had been shaped by a Christian worldview that was combined with an Augustinian Neoplatonic devaluation of the world. Heaven, the world to come, is my home, and it is the destination to which I travel. The worldly and material possess no inherent dignity, let alone spiritual significance. To dedicate oneself totally to God on the pilgrimage through this world, a person does not want to become too attached or to settle down lest they become distracted from their true destination. Sin had brought about disorder in the human faculties so that rather than having one's actions guided by reason informing the will, now the sensual appetites more often than not controlled the will. The world might be used for our needs as we journey toward heaven, but it should not be enjoyed for its own sake. The world was viewed as a hierarchy of the supernatural and the natural, in which the natural was subordinate to a higher "spiritual" order as a *status perfectionis* nearer to God. The behavior by which we pursue a life of purification, according to medieval monastic thinking, requires those who wish to be holiest to follow not only the *praecepta* (a medieval term for God's commandments) incumbent upon every human being, but also the *consilia evangelica* (in medieval monastic theology, the special evangelical counsels given by Christ in the Sermon on the Mount), attainable by only a few.[17] To accomplish this, many in Luther's day left family and other societal obligations to live behind cloistered walls. Luther battled what he saw as a similar phenomenon among some Anabaptists of his time. They sought to restore the practices of the New Testament church by means of a commitment to individual holiness of conduct. Their aversion to temporal governments, under which they often experienced persecution (as well as their concern to love the enemy by not bearing the sword), led to their conviction that Christians could not serve as rulers, soldiers, or carry out other forms of civic duties. Some of them even practiced a community of goods in their rejection of the ownership of private property. Parallel movements have arisen amid the excesses of contemporary North American society as well.[18]

17. Oswald Bayer, "'I Believe That God Has Created Me with All That Exists': An Example of Catechetical-Systematics," *Lutheran Quarterly* 8 (1994): 137. See Thomas Aquinas, *Summa theologiae* (New York: McGraw Hill, 1964), 1/2, Q.108, 14.

18. Mark Ellingsen, *The Evangelical Movement: Growth, Impact, Controversy, Dialog* (Minneapolis: Augsburg, 1988), 278–80.

In the twenty-first century, even though monasticism is rarely viewed as a viable option, dividing life into a sacred sphere and a secular sphere continues to persist. Such a division brings with it, however, two quite different temptations. First, such a division will always create the possibility that Christians may regard one realm of existence as superior to another, as happened in the Middle Ages when many elevated the realm of grace (*regnum gratiae*) over the realm of nature (*regnum naturae*). Practically speaking, this happens when Christians regard questions related to salvation as the only really important matters that deserve their attention. Christians then focus their spiritual existence in such a way that they think of themselves as only "resident aliens" in this world and citizens of the heavenly world, rather than being and living as citizens in both worlds. Then they will be tempted either to abandon or to give up on life in a secular sphere that is "going to hell in a handbasket," preferring instead to wait for the life to come.

Second, such a bifurcation of reality allows for secular existence to claim autonomy for itself from the spiritual sphere. For the last two hundred years, contemporary life in the Western world has increasingly given rise to a compartmentalization of life: faith is part of our spiritual life, but it has little or nothing to do with our public lives, our lives within human society. Some have insisted that God and faith are not to be part of public conversation, prompting talk of a "naked public square" or suggesting that God has become little more than a hobby for people. Western life has thus relegated and confined the spiritual to the realm of the private life of each individual. Such a division of life creates a dilemma for Christians, who find themselves living a divided and conflicted existence in which the two spheres are pitted against each other and have no relation with each other.

Luther's concept of the two kinds of righteousness deprives Christians of the option of living in one or the other world. Christians cannot regard one realm of existence as inferior to the other; both belong to God. "Belonging wholly to Christ, [the Christian] stands at the same time wholly in the world."[19] To retreat from the world as it lies under bondage to sin and evil is to surrender to sin and to abandon the world as God's creation. On the contrary, Luther realized that like Christ, Christians are sent into the world to become deeply involved in daily life. There they find that this physical world of creation is our home even though it needs purging, renovation, and restoration. Therefore, Christians respond to the fallen world (even as Christ did) not by flight into Christian colonies but "by standing tall, rolling up one's sleeves, and saying, 'I am not going

19. Dietrich Bonhoeffer, *Ethics*, trans. N. H. Smith (New York: Macmillan, 1955), 198.

anywhere; this world has been bought by Christ and his [work], and I am going to serve by living life as he intended it to be.'"[20] Thus, Luther's understanding of the two kinds of righteousness not only maintains a distinction between the two but also creates a new relationship between them. In particular, the two kinds of righteousness open up the world as God's good creation so that Christians can live unreservedly in the world,[21] where good works are done for neighbor and for the good of creation.

Faith Embraces Everyday Creaturely Activities

In returning us to creation, faith frees us from "the perennial human tendency to devalue what is close at hand and seek to do something extraordinary," so that we can instead embrace the ordinary, everyday activities of daily living.[22] Luther experienced firsthand how easy it is for us to judge our God-given responsibilities according to our own feelings rather than according to his Word. Against the backdrop of monasticism's exaltation of celibacy, Luther observed that without faith the "clever harlot," our natural reason (which the pagans followed in trying to be most clever), takes a look at married life. She turns up her nose and says,

> Alas, must I rock the baby, wash its diapers, make its bed, smell its stench, stay up nights with it, take care of it when it cries, heal its rashes and sores, and on top of that care for my wife, provide for her, labor at my trade, take care of this and take care of that, do this and do that, endure this and endure that, and whatever else of bitterness and drudgery married life involves? What, should I make such a prisoner of myself? O you poor, wretched fellow, have you taken a wife? Fie, fie upon such wretchedness and bitterness! It is better to remain free and lead a peaceful, carefree life; I will become a priest or a nun and compel my children to do likewise.[23]

Luther's criticisms here applied to the entire medieval understanding of vocational (religious) vows, whereby people did not want to fulfill

---

20. Robert Rosin, "Christians and Culture: Finding Place in Clio's Mansions," in *Christ and Culture: The Church in a Post-Christian(?) America*, Concordia Seminary Monograph Series (St. Louis: Concordia, 1995), 69.

21. Bonhoeffer, *Ethics*, 193.

22. Kolden, "Earthly Vocation," 289.

23. "The Estate of Marriage, 1522," *LW* 45:39; *WA* 10.2:295.16–26. Eisleben pastor Caspar Gütell, a disciple of Luther, wrote: "For this reason they say: 'It would be nice to get married, but how will I live? I have nothing; if I take a wife things will really get tight. And marriage brings with it many new troubles and cares and requires much effort and work. The wife complains or gets sick; the children wail and scream, this one demanding something to drink, another something to eat'" (quoted in Steven Ozment, *When Fathers Ruled: Family Life in Reformation Europe* [Cambridge, MA: Harvard University Press, 1983], 4–5).

ordinary and mundane God-given tasks of everyday life. In his Large Catechism, Luther particularly singles out the Carthusian order as the object of his wrath.[24] Their renowned isolation and rigorous monastic practices did little else than disparage the true works of God carried out in the context of everyday life. They thought their religious tasks would please God and make them holy. In the process, this conviction led them to neglect the tasks at hand.

In his preface to Ecclesiastes, Luther points out that faith enables the Christian to see that "all God's creatures are good (Gen. 1:31 and 1 Tim. 4:4), and that a person should be pleased with his spouse and enjoy life with her." Faith opens the Christian's eyes "to look upon all these insignificant, distasteful, and despised duties in the Spirit, and [to be] aware that they are all adorned with divine approval as with the costliest gold and jewels."[25] Thus, faith embraces the most menial activities, for God's Word has given them his stamp of approval. These are the very things he wants us to do. For this reason Luther constantly chose ordinary activities from daily life as examples of a Christian's return to creation and embrace of vocation. These included such activities as the father washing smelly diapers, the maid sweeping the floor, the mother cooking supper, and the baker making good bread. Of all the activities found in daily life, none was extolled more than marriage and family. In contrast to medieval assumptions that "maligned marriage and parenthood, Luther exalted the family in all its dimensions and utterly without qualification."[26] While still unmarried, Luther wrote, "When a father goes ahead and washes diapers or performs some other menial task for his child, and someone ridicules him as an effeminate fool, . . . God with all his angels and creatures is smiling."[27] As Steven Ozment put it, "Never has the art of parenting been more highly praised and

24. The Carthusian order was founded by Saint Bruno and six companions who sought to escape increasing urbanization and the temptation of academic pride at the University of Paris by founding rural communities. They reached the height of their expansion between the fourteenth and sixteenth centuries. Much of this growth took place in Germany. Part of their rigorous monastic observances resulted from their strenuous efforts to avoid outside contacts. On this, see Dennis D. Martin, *Fifteenth-Century Carthusian Reform: The World of Nicholas Kempf* (Leiden: Brill, 1992). Steven Ozment provides a succinct description: "The Carthusians attached special importance to silence, manual labor, and the strict suppression of sexual desire. They continued to practice self-flagellation after Pope Clement VI forbade flagellant processions in 1349" (Steven Ozment, *The Age of Reform (1250–1550): An Intellectual and Religious History of Late Medieval and Reformation Europe* [New Haven: Yale University Press, 1980], 87).

25. "The Estate of Marriage, 1522," *LW* 45:39; *WA* 10.2:206.

26. Steven Ozment, *Protestants: The Birth of a Revolution* (New York: Doubleday, 1992), 165.

27. "The Estate of Marriage, 1522," *LW* 45:40; *WA* 10.2:207.

parental authority more wholeheartedly supported than in Reformation Europe."[28]

As Christians reenter creation, they find that they are now in a position to properly carry out the first Great Commission, to exercise dominion over the earth by serving it and preserving it (Gen. 1:26). They take up their vocations as places of service to others, where they can live as human beings according to God's design. Within the home, husbands and wives need not see marriage as a straitjacket that keeps them from seeking multiple lovers but instead view it as an arena in which faith is exercised and faithful love is best expressed. Parents need not see children as a means for personal fulfillment or as intolerable burdens. Similarly, grown successful children need not be ashamed of their parent's lowly background or refuse to care for them when feeble. In the economic walks of life, Christians receive their income and work with thanks, always seeking to render honest labor. They need not view government as intrinsically evil or corrupt. Instead, they will appreciate (if not always agree with) the important role that it plays in addressing the needs of the wider society. As citizens they gladly carry out their civic responsibilities, including paying taxes, volunteering, and running for office. They also find ways to become involved in church and its activities and to support their pastors and other servants of the Word of God in their midst.

Within and through their vocations, Christians carry out the second Great Commission of sharing the gospel. From within the midst of creation (as Luther confessed in his explanations of the first article of the Apostles' Creed, which is on creation), they deliver the gift of redemption, which sows into the first creation the seeds of the new creation. Just as they provide the specific arena for carrying out the first Great Commission, they also provide the particular "mission assignment" for each person within the larger task of taking the gospel to the entire world. Within our various walks of life, God calls us to action through our neighbors' needs, both physical and spiritual. Parents are responsible for teaching the gospel to their children rather than giving in to the fear that they shouldn't impose their beliefs on their children. For this reason Luther wrote his Small Catechism. Because the spheres in which we live are limited in scope (not every person can go on an evangelism crusade like Billy Graham), these mission assignments need not overwhelm the individual, thereby paralyzing one from springing into action. Within them we are given freedom to figure out how and when we carry out these tasks.

Within their vocations, Christians embrace the law, not because it compels them to act, but because it helps them channel their new

28. Ozment, *When Fathers Ruled*, 132.

Spirit-given energies and impulses into the world. Christians embrace what God wants them to do in contrast to the pursuit of self-chosen works. With the psalmist, Christians can find delight in the law now that they are no longer under its curse (Ps. 1:2). As Luther puts it in his Small Catechism, "God promises grace and every blessing, therefore we should love and trust him and willingly do all that he commands."[29] Thus, Christians go beyond fulfilling the bare minima of the law as prescribed by the prohibitions. Those minima require that we not kill or steal, for such things lead to the destruction of the human community. In the Small Catechism, Luther's explanations of the commandments summon Christians to go above and beyond the "call of duty." Out of fear of God they avoid killing their neighbor, but out of faith in God they help and befriend their neighbor in every time of need. They are no longer content to avoid falling into adultery but want to love and cherish their spouses in every way possible. As Christians make use of the law, they can also leaven the law so that it is not used or applied legalistically.

Christians recover their freedom to find how to mediate the law in their lives. While reason is blind and the will lies in bondage to sin when it comes to spiritual matters *coram Deo*, reason still has some ability and freedom in matters *coram mundo*.[30] Thus, as Christians go about their work with God in the world, they use reason and their sanctified common sense in the development of all aspects of culture, which embraces "anything people create as they freely interact with their natural environment and each other."[31] They are not limited to identifying and adhering only to "biblical principles" for building their relationships with one another, as if the world did not belong to God or had not been loaned to us for our use. They do not need to reject non-Christian contributions to human life and culture in favor of embracing specifically "Christian" forms, since that would involve a rejection of God's earthly gifts and blessings. Instead, they are free to use their imagination or draw on the insights of a wide array of fields to build the human community, whether in business, church, the home, or society. Christians affirm the abilities of human reason the Creator has bestowed as they produce, for example, literature, science, social sciences, music, and art, among others.

29. Small Catechism, Ten Commandments, 22, *Book of Concord*, 354; *BSLK*, 510.
30. Thus, where Luther admits the impotency of reason in his explanation of the third article of the creed ("I cannot by my own reason or strength believe in Jesus Christ, my Lord, or come to him" apart from the call of the Holy Spirit), he readily acknowledges it as a good gift of God in the first article.
31. Rosin, "Christians and Culture," 58.

Faith Leavens Life within the Created World

At the same time that Christians embrace creation and the cultures that human beings have fashioned out of it, they may have to criticize a culture. In most of the Western world for the better part of the past thousand years, Christian churches have been dominant in the culture. As a result, Christians in North America have often been uncritical of societies' norms and structures, both in their callings and in the ways they accommodate the gospel to the culture. But that is changing. Increasingly, Christians will have to offer a cultural critique, but they must do so without losing their appreciation for God's gifts within their cultures, even in those cultures hostile to the Christian faith. Society will call on them to "exercise their critical skills to see problems and to work for corrections in those places where policies and practices are not serving God's creatures well."[32] The rapid shift to a land of many religions and cultures may be an occasion for thinking and speaking more critically about what Christian vocation might involve. Society is obviously different from the way we thought about it under the assumptions of culture in which Christianity exercised a dominant influence.

Luther believed that Christians should not try to bring about theocratic visions of society in order to manifest the hidden reign of Christ prior to the last day. Such visions have tempted the church periodically throughout Christian history to establish a distinctively Christian culture over against a world that it found to be in moral chaos. Even during the era of the Reformation, some theologians continued to propose a theocratic vision for a society shaped by Christian commitments, to take the place of a decaying medieval culture. Also in the American experience, "the Puritan vision transplanted to America proposed a theocratic vision (covenant) for a new culture that needed to overcome the chaos of the wilderness that surrounded their settlements."[33] In the wake of this heritage, some North American believers have promoted a Christian culture over against a world in moral chaos. The emergence of groups like the Moral Majority and the Christian Coalition reflects this Puritan tradition of establishing a "Christian culture."[34] These efforts often maintain that the best political values are those informed by faith in Christ, by faith in the gospel. And so they have treated the Bible as a book of regulations that gives directives on every aspect of life. Such theocratic visions often call for the transformation of society through

32. Kolden, "Earthly Vocation," 284.
33. Ellingsen, *Evangelical Movement*, 124.
34. Ibid., 124–25.

political action in the gospel rather than in creation and its orders, which are universally accessible to all. Luther and his colleagues believed that the gospel does not introduce new laws into the civil realm;[35] it sends Christ's people into the culture to recover the Creator's design and to recall the culture back to the Creator's intentions.

After the gospel freed Luther from the need to perform specifically designated religious works (carried out within the concomitant clerical careers) to acquire salvation, he was able to lift up the importance of every walk of life that had long been denigrated or regarded as inferior. Today, as they rediscover their vocations and embrace them as places of service to God, Christians can leaven them by modeling for the world how their vocations were intended to function when God established them.[36] As they do so, Christians may find it necessary to critique and warn the wider society of the dangers it brings on itself when movements and trends within the culture would undermine vocational structures. What are the long-term effects of divorce on couples and children? What kinds of habits and character are cultivated as "people are captured by the consumer ethos"?[37] As popular entertainment becomes the biggest business of the economy of North America, how does it shape culture and undermine traditional morality?[38] Similarly, the church needs to resist a culture that exalts a spirituality-centered and individualistic expression of the divine spark within each soul. It can begin to do so by cultivating Christian discipline through a Christian instruction that forms habits such as prayer for keeping the heart turned toward God.[39]

When the passive righteousness of faith allowed Luther and his colleagues to recover the law of creation (with its expression in the Decalogue), it also provided them with a basis for rejecting the medieval church's claim that the pope and bishops possessed the authority to establish laws binding on consciences. They affirmed an objective and universal moral order over against the subjective whims of the church's hierarchy. Thus, they argued that laws regarding celibacy and monasticism cannot and do not override God's created norms for life. Christian reception of natural law has prevented Christian ethics from absorbing itself totally within the realm of individual personal relationships or as

35. Apology of the Augsburg Confession XVI.3, *Book of Concord* 231; *BSLK*, 308.

36. See Alvin Schmidt's *Under the Influence: How Christianity Transformed Civilization* (Grand Rapids: Zondervan, 2001).

37. Robert Benne, "The Calling of the Church in Economic Life," in *The Two Cities of God: The Church's Responsibility for the Earthly City*, ed. Carl E. Braaten and Robert W. Jenson (Grand Rapids, Eerdmans, 1997), 98–99.

38. Ibid. See also Juliet B. Schor, *The Overspent American: Why We Want What We Don't Need* (New York: HarperPerennial, 1998).

39. Carl E. Braaten, *Mother Church: Ecclesiology and Ecumenism* (Minneapolis: Fortress, 1998), 145.

having no relevance for the world.[40] Christians again need to help society remember and discern natural moral orders in human affairs. They need to assist society in recovering natural law as an objective criterion for the validity of laws constructed by human beings in a society that has abandoned natural law out of the belief that the authority to construct laws is rooted in the individual, in a democratic majority, or in those who hold power.[41] When that happens, there can be no other "criterion of validity for the law than the will of those who had the monopoly of force."[42] In other words, "might makes right." In the twentieth century, this way of thinking has produced some of history's greatest legalized atrocities as societies and states have manipulated the law as a function of power.

So, as they return to creation, Christians may have to remind the world of the boundaries of human life and community given in natural law. The violation of these norms leads to the undoing of creation. The construction of positive laws within society sets boundaries so that the human community can be restrained from undermining human life and destroying itself. For this reason "a society must regulate sexuality by laws and customs, and whatever these laws are, the society cannot survive their widespread violation."[43] Robert Jenson argues that while we may hope that marriages in our world will reflect the biblical design for them, we cannot expect that. At most we can "tell a society like America, which is dismantling its laws of marriage and does not enforce those that remain, that it is undoing its own viability as a community."[44] Christians must contend for the value and nature of various social structures of life as of intrinsic value to the community, by which God sustains the community. In other instances, Christians will need to bring natural law into bold relief by stating the obvious. They may have to unmask the idolatries of culture and debunk the mythologies and ideologies of a society by stating what is morally obvious. "It is obvious that we cannot equate chosen or culturally accepted single parenthood with a family structure," Jenson concludes. Children generally do better in education and life when raised within a two-parent family. "It is obvious that homosexuals

40. Kolden, "Earthly Vocation," 287.
41. To recover natural law, Carl E. Braaten suggests the need for an ecumenical dialogue on the place of natural law in Christian ethics "as a kind of counterattack against the wholesale deconstruction of the classical moral and legal principles on which Western culture is founded" ("Natural Law in Theology and Ethics," in Braaten and Jenson, *Two Cities of God*, 49). On the individual level, he sees the recovery of classical virtues in virtue ethics as a step in the direction of recognizing that there is a design or purpose to created structures of life.
42. Braaten, "Natural Law," 47.
43. Robert Jenson, "The Church's Responsibility for the World," in Braaten and Jensen, *Two Cities of God*, 7.
44. Ibid.

cannot marry, so that homosexuality cannot be a social equivalent of heterosexuality."[45] Marriage is between a man and a woman. A society informed by the contributions of religion is better off than a society in which all discourse about God is ruled out of bounds.

Yet, as Christians carry out their work in this fallen world, they realize that all human activity has a penultimate value, and all human achievement has a provisional status. The righteousness of works does not serve creation for the purpose of establishing a utopian society on earth in the here and now. Rather, it serves creation in an interim fashion. We have to take into account the wild card of sin, which prevents and disrupts life from operating according to God's design. Thus, we will not attain perfect societies and laws this side of eternity. Christians have to tolerate some things in our horizontal relationships that cannot be allowed or permitted to encroach into the realm of spiritual righteousness. As Christians join hands with non-Christians in developing laws and customs for the sake of public morality within the world, we will at times have to make compromises because we are living in the overlap of two creations as the old is passing away and the new is coming. We have to make compromises as we deal with an imperfect world. In the Heidelberg Disputation, Luther argued that God often bears "lesser evil so that all is not destroyed by greater evil." It is like the wise magistrate who "winks at the bad and mischievous citizen for a while and allows him to enjoy citizenship for the good of the public peace."[46] For example, Christians must reject any and every ideology or theology that tries to find peace with God apart from Christ. But Christians may support the government's policy of religious freedom, which allows and encourages people to attend the church, synagogue, or mosque of their choice. Christians recognize that a society of religious people rather than religion-less people better serves public morality. Christians reject homosexuality as sin before God while supporting laws that provide civil rights and protect homosexuals from violence.

Faith Lets God Do the "God Stuff"

As Christians live in a fallen creation in which the moral order underlying society may be on the verge of collapse, faith frees them from the need to play God and thereby re-create the world or usher in a utopian society. Freed from the impossible burden of being God, faith lets God be the Creator and the human person be the creature. This is not an

45. Ibid.
46. Gerhard O. Forde, *On Being a Theologian of the Cross: Reflections on Luther's Heidelberg Disputation, 1518* (Grand Rapids: Eerdmans, 1997), thesis 14, 152.

easy task. Luther even contended that belief in the Creator and creation is the loftiest and most difficult article to believe:

> For without doubt the highest article of faith is that in which we say: I believe in God the Father, almighty creator of heaven and earth, and whoever rightly believes that is already helped and set right and brought back to that from which Adam fell. But those who came to the point of fully believing that he is the God who creates and makes all things are few, because such a person must be dead to all things, to good and evil, death and life, hell and heaven, and must confess from the heart that he can do nothing of his own strength.[47]

Why is it so hard to believe? Because it is the essence of our sinfulness that we want to be in control; we want to play god. Thus, in his Large Catechism Luther recognized that few believe that God is truly Creator and Lord. Most pass over that fact and give it no thought. "For if we believed it with our whole heart, we would also act accordingly, and not swagger about and boast and brag as if we had life, riches, power, honor, and such things of ourselves, as if we ourselves were to be feared and served."[48] Moreover, the devil would divert us from putting things into God's hands by inciting covetousness and lust and would resist our trust by throwing up obstacles in its way through trouble and adversity.

People continually make a grave error when they, as creatures who lack faith, seek to "usurp the power and authority of God the Creator" by shaping the future. Lacking faith, human beings want to plan and control events and things in order to obtain the results that they want. They want to define success and how to obtain it. They need to find meaning in the world and make sense out of life. In his preface to Ecclesiastes, Luther recognized that the human need to manage, to be in control of our plans and actions, is so deeply ingrained within every person that it will also at times characterize the Christian. Luther pointed out that things often turn out differently from the way we thought they would, which makes our planning and working seem futile and pointless. Retirement savings may be lost through corporate mismanagement (as in the Enron affair at the turn of the century) or diminished through economic recession and other factors, such as illness, accidents, storms, and war. According to Luther, Ecclesiastes teaches that "human calculations and plans dealing with creatures all fail and are worthless when one is not satisfied with what is presently at hand but instead wants to master and rule the future. So things always go backwards as a person has nothing more than lost effort and worry." When things do not turn

---

47. *WA* 24:18.26–33.
48. Large Catechism, Creed, 21, *Book of Concord*, 433; *BSLK*, 649.

out according to the best-laid plans of human creatures, they become impatient, disgusted, angry, disenchanted, and apathetic. Before long they want to give up and do nothing more, convinced that creation is meaningless when the fault lies with them and their scheming.[49]

As Christians carry out their responsibilities in the world, faith frees them from the bondage of caring for themselves and presiding over their own destinies. Christians no longer need to be masters of their fate. Their new relationship to God as the Creator and to the world as his creation no longer requires them to control everything that happens in their lives or in world history. It no longer requires them to predict the outcome of their planning and labors. Instead, faith lets God be God. It recognizes that he is the one who has a divine perspective and in his wisdom graciously guides creation according to his purposes. Faith then lets us be us, those who are fully human and accept our finitude and dependence on God. Luther comments on Ecclesiastes, "So [the Preacher] would teach us to let things be and to let God alone do all things over, against, and without our knowledge and advice."[50] Faith frees us from having to make sense of everything, for we know to whom we belong. Luther quoted Christ in Matthew 6:34, "Do not be anxious about tomorrow, for tomorrow will have its own trouble." "Worrying about us is God's business. Our worries fail anyhow and vainly produce wasted effort."[51] We do not need to understand everything or have the big picture in view in order to determine which actions will make sense or how they will turn out. Faith accepts our finitude even as it laments our transitory nature.

The human desire for control of the future also manifests itself in the human reaction to massive disasters and horrific evil within the world. In their desire to maintain a semblance of control, human beings have tried to make sense of things, to understand why things happen the way they do. Since long before the days of Job, human beings have complained against and railed against God. "Where is God when we need him most?" If God is present in everything we experience in this world, we want to know why he seems absent so often. "Where was God, and why didn't he do anything?" "Why do bad things happen to some and not to others?" People have always struggled with the seeming indifference of God. Especially since the time of the Enlightenment, however, people

49. Luther's Prefaces, ed. and trans. Robert L. Rosin, in Concordia Reference Bible: New International Version (St. Louis: Concordia, 1989), 785, 784; "Prefaces to the Old Testament," LW 35:264; WA DB 10.2:104, 106.

50. Concordia Reference Bible, 785; "Prefaces to the Old Testament," LW 35:264; WA DB 10.2:104, 106.

51. Concordia Reference Bible, 785; "Prefaces to the Old Testament," LW 35:264; WA DB 10.2:104, 106.

have tried to explain evil or explain God's indifference and his inactivity on our behalf. "If God does exist, how can we justify his treatment or neglect of us?"[52] About three hundred years ago the German philosopher Gottfried Wilhelm Leibniz coined the term "theodicy" to describe human attempts to justify God by explaining evil. Theodicies try to justify God and his way of doing things to human beings. The question "Why me?" can, among other things, imply that God is accountable to us. This immediately raises a question: Who is really God here? Who is accountable to whom? In the attempt to justify God's actions to us, theodicies often try to explain away God's involvement in tragedies, thereby letting God off the hook. If God is not responsible for tragedies in this world, the speculation suggests, it is safe to believe in him. Such theodicies appear to domesticate God by rendering him less frightening.

Luther refused to answer such questions even though he confessed that one time they had brought him to the brink of despair.[53] He stopped posing such questions and left God alone in the face of little tragedies and large ones, letting it up to God when he seems unfathomable, even frightening. For Luther knew that God never leaves his people, even when appearances are to the contrary; we know that he continues to love us. Luther knew that if God is in some way involved in the evil, then we have no hope. But if we do not affirm his power, then we also have no hope. As creatures who live from the passive righteousness of faith, we can only confess that, as sole Creator of all that exists, he is not the cause of sin or evil within the world, that he remains Lord of all even on the evil day, and that his way of doing things simply lies beyond our grasp.[54] We may not know why God allows things to happen, but we do not have to question how he regards us. Instead of relying on the explanations that humans may fashion for themselves, the Christian relies on the person of the rescuer, the restorer of human life. For God did not send Christ into the world to explain evil but to destroy evil in the cross. Meanwhile, "waiting on God in the midst of the shadows creates patience that endures and fosters hope when believers can listen to his voice through the darkness."[55] We live by faith, not by sight (2 Cor. 5:7).

What do these things mean for the ways Christians carry out their responsibilities within creation? Luther taught, "Whatever your hand finds to do, do it with [all] your might!" (Eccles. 9:10). He insisted that true service consists in taking up one's responsibilities in the world while at the same time realizing that human reason cannot orchestrate

---

52. Robert Kolb, "Luther on the Theology of the Cross," *Lutheran Quarterly* 16 (2002): 453.

53. "The Bondage of the Will, 1525," *LW* 33:190; *WA* 18:719.9–12.

54. "The Bondage of the Will, 1525," *LW* 33:289–92; *WA* 18:784.6–785.38.

55. Kolb, "Theology of the Cross," 457.

events. "Our inability to foresee, let alone to predetermine the results of our actions, should not prevent us from attending to the needs of our neighbor." Instead, Luther expressed it in even more shocking terms: Christians "should proceed as if there were no God and they had to rescue themselves and manage their own affairs; just as the head of a household is supposed to work as if he were trying to sustain himself by his own labors."[56] At the same time that Christians go about their work with all their might, they must be careful to watch their hearts so that they do not rely on their own works and become arrogant when things go well or worried that there is no help when things go wrong.[57]

Luther certainly did not mean to imply that faith is absent in the practice of our daily callings in life. On the contrary, in faith Christians with gratitude accept the responsibilities of our vocations and carry them out to the fullest of our abilities. "Those whom God justifies 'will always be content to do what lies at hand today.' They must not seek to 'master and control' what things and relations will be in the future."[58] They leave the rest in the hands of their Creator. As they strive to do their best in the various roles they find themselves, they let God crown their efforts with success when, where, and how he sees fit.

> For God rules us in such a way that he does not want us to be idle. He gives us food and clothing, but in such a way that we should plow, sow, reap, and cook. In addition, he gives offspring, which are born and grow because of the blessing of God and must nevertheless be cherished, cared for, brought up, and instructed by the parents. But when we have done what is in us, then we should entrust the rest to God and cast our care on the Lord; for He will take care of us.[59]

"So [we] Christians should regard ourselves and our activity as being the work of our Lord God under a mask, as it were, beneath which he himself alone effects and accomplishes what we desire."[60] Do what God wants and leave the rest to him. Thus, Luther advises, "Labor and let him give the fruits. Govern and let him give his blessing. Fight, and let him give the victory. Preach, and let him win hearts. Take a husband or a wife, and let him produce the children. Eat and drink, and let him nourish and strengthen."[61]

56. "Exposition of Psalm 127, 1524," *LW* 45:331; *WA* 15:372.22–373.17.
57. "Exposition of Psalm 127, 1524," *LW* 45:331; *WA* 15:373.5–9.
58. Bayer, *Living by Faith*, 38.
59. *LW* 8:94 (on Gen. 46:28); *WA* 44:648.21–24.
60. "Exposition of Psalm 127, 1524," *LW* 45:331; *WA* 15:373.5–9.
61. "Exposition of Psalm 147, 1531," *LW* 14:115; *WA* 31:436.27–30.

Luther's embrace of creation as a gift is evidenced in a well-known apocryphal story.[62] When asked about what he would do if knew that the world was going to end the next day, Luther replied that he would go out to his garden and plant a tree. The point of the story is that since the kingdom of God is coming, and there is nothing anyone can do about that, it is too late for prayers, piety, repentance, or acts of religious devotion. We are turned back into the Garden (Gen. 2:15) so that "when the good Lord shows up one might be found doing what God intended: taking care of creation."[63] Luther said the same thing about his marriage. He shocked the sensibilities of many when he got married during the German Peasants' Revolt in 1525, a time when the Reformation itself was hanging in the balance. Luther replied that he had done this because it would make the angels laugh and devils weep. But Luther insisted if the world were about to come to an end, the Christian would do the opposite of what one would expect. One would not forsake creation by going up on the rooftops to watch and await the Lord's return. Instead, the Christian turns back to creation all the more. So he said of his marriage that when the Lord comes, he was determined to be found doing what comes naturally, obeying the commission to be fruitful and multiply in spite of all the nonsense of popes, princes, and peasants.

Faith and Sanctification

So, does the living out of faith within the world have an impact on the Christian person in the sense of moral improvement or sanctification? Can and does Luther speak in terms of growth in sanctification? And if so, how? Good places to turn for a summary of his thinking are his catechisms. Luther organized his explanations to each of the articles of the Apostles' Creed around a single word that becomes the theme. In the first article he selected the word "Creator," and in the second he selected the word "Lord." The third article gave him the most difficulty since it dealt with what had been considered five disparate items in something of an appendix. He eventually settled on the word "holy," taken from the "Holy Spirit," but in such a way that the Holy Spirit (*Spiritus sanctus*) of the Apostles' Creed becomes the sanctifying Spirit (*Spiritus sanctificator*) in Luther's explanation. In other words, the Holy Spirit is the one who sanctifies us. Whereas in the first article God creates out of nothing, in

---

62. See Martin Schloemann, *Luthers Apfelbäumchen? Ein Kapitel deutscher Mentalitäts-geschichte seit dem Zweiten Weltkrieg* (Göttingen: Vandenhoeck & Ruprecht, 1994).

63. Forde, "Luther's Ethics," 149.

the third article he does something even more wonderful: "He makes saints out of sinners."[64]

In the opening passages of his explanation to the third article in his Large Catechism, Luther defines sanctification as a complete and already-given gift. "Therefore being made holy is nothing else than bringing us to the Lord Christ to receive this blessing [redemption], to which we could not have come by ourselves."[65] Yet a little later in that same discussion, Luther speaks of sanctification as a beginning that is not yet brought to completion. He observes, "Holiness has begun and is growing daily." The Spirit "creates and increases holiness, causing it daily to grow and become strong in faith and in its fruits."[66] A few sentences later, he adds that now we are only "halfway pure and holy."[67] And so we "await the time when our flesh will be put to death, will be buried with all its uncleanness, and [we] will come forth gloriously and arise to complete and perfect holiness in a new eternal life."[68] Luther frequently speaks of faith as the beginning of fulfilling the law.

These seemingly contradictory statements make sense when considered within the matrix of the two kinds of righteousness. The righteousness that we have been given by faith is a complete righteousness, and the righteousness we manifest in love is a partial righteousness. It is complete when viewed as God's approval of us and as our possession of the righteousness of Christ; Christ's righteousness is a totality, and the believer participates in it totally. It is partial when viewed from the standpoint of the world's approval of us and as a new beginning for human beings along with a new obedience. Another way to consider it is grammatically. God's acceptance of us must be described in the perfect tense: we have been made righteous in ourselves, and now we are righteous. The condition of being righteous in ourselves can be described in the present tense only as having begun; its completion lies in the future; we are only becoming righteous. In this sense, the Christian still waits for righteousness. It rests on hope. God accepts the person and the works of the believer. Just as God accepts the sinner for Christ's sake, so he also accepts this broken, halfway, and blemished obedience; he accepts it as total obedience.

We must not deem any talk of sanctification to mean a progressive emancipation from divine imputation.[69] In that case the passive righ-

---

64. Søren Kierkegaard, quoted in Martin E. Marty, *The Hidden Discipline* (St. Louis: Concordia, 1962), 58.
65. Large Catechism, Creed, 39, *Book of Concord*, 436; *BSLK*, 654.
66. Large Catechism, Creed, 53, *Book of Concord*, 438; *BSLK*, 657–58.
67. Large Catechism, Creed, 53, *Book of Concord*, 438; *BSLK*, 658.
68. Large Catechism, Creed, 57, *Book of Concord*, 438; *BSLK*, 659.
69. Gerhard O. Forde, "Forensic Justification and the Christian Life: Triumph or Tragedy?" in *A More Radical Gospel: Essays on Eschatology, Authority, Atonement, and*

teousness of faith would be merely the starting point and then gradually recede into the background. To speak of growth in the way of Aristotle (*ad modum Aristotelis*) calls passive righteousness into question and undermines its reality. We dare not consider sanctification one-dimensionally in terms of an ascent from unrighteousness to righteousness. Luther refuses to view the Christian life in terms of partialities, quantities, or percentages. In such a schema we can keep something of a balance sheet or ledger. Thus one can keep score by balancing the number of good works over against the number of sins committed. A person then thinks in terms of partialities, being partially sinful and partially sanctified. As I grow in works and decrease in sins, I can slowly stand on my own two feet, seemingly, with less need for forgiveness (I have fewer sins that need to be forgiven). For Luther, sanctification cannot be seen in the sense that our passive righteousness is "more and more replaced and limited by an active righteousness; the alien righteousness is not more and more replaced by man's own."[70] The Christian remains a sinner his whole life long and cannot possibly live and have worth before God except through this alien righteousness. And so the Christian does not need Aristotle's model of increasing holiness, the use of which implies that we need increasingly less of Christ's righteousness because we can stand more and more on our own two feet.

Luther speaks of sanctification in a different way. "Luther's approach to sanctification is unlike any other, *sui generis*." Rather, it must be viewed as a descent of the entire person into the world. "Furthermore: wherever that progress takes place—whether in the beginning or farther on—it always happens as a whole."[71] The Christian possesses the complete righteousness of Christ—possessing it as one's own—and reenters creation in order to serve. This view of growth affirms that we never leave behind the need for the total righteousness of Christ because the righteousness of Christ is the very power of sanctification. The gospel of Christ's righteousness strengthens faith and its fruit. The passive righteousness of faith is complete. Faith itself may be weak or strong, but in both cases faith makes the Christian completely righteous. Within the world, faith may grow and produce more and more fruit. But faith (like a cell with DNA) is whole and entire. Thus, if growth "takes place extensively only in little steps, or in isolated actions against particular sins, intensively the whole is always there, the total crisis, the entire transformation of the person, death and becoming new is wholly

Ecumenism, ed. Mark C. Mattes and Steven D. Paulson (Grand Rapids: Eerdmans, 2004), 126.

70. Paul Althaus, *Theology of Luther*, trans. Robert C. Schultz (Philadelphia: Fortress, 1966), 229.

71. Wilfried Joest, quoted in Forde, "Forensic Justification," 127.

present."[72] We can further consider two aspects of Luther's approach to sanctification.

First, the entire tree continues to grow. Using Luther's analogy of a tree, one could say that whether it is small or large, it is an entire tree. So also with faith. Whether it is weak or strong, faith possesses the complete righteousness of Christ and so the person is completely righteous in God's sight. As faith grows, one could say that the Christian grasps more firmly the righteousness of Christ. As faith grows, just like a tree, it does not become more righteous, but it does produce more fruit. And so in this sense justification becomes the power of sanctification. But in every case, it is a whole tree. Sin tries to restrict it and constrain it. But sanctification is not a process whereby we move from 57 percent holy to 58 percent holy. The Christian is 100 percent holy and now tries to manifest that righteousness, to make it known in daily life, in spite of the resistance of sin. Faith grows as it breaks free from its bonds of encumbering sin. For Luther, one can speak of more works or fruit, but this does not imply growth in sanctification. The growth is simply the new creature evermore breaking out of (or rising up from) the shackles of sin in this world. The new creature expresses itself in new and more works. But these works are not making the Christian into a new creature. The Christian is already a completely new creature in Christ. And yet, the Christian is hindered and resisted by the old Adam, which constricts works. As the Old Adam is drowned, the new creature comes forth. Forgiveness removes the sin. Daily forgiveness is a daily attacking and pounding away at the old Adam. "Forgiveness is constantly needed, for although God's grace has been acquired by Christ, and holiness has been wrought by the Holy Spirit through God's Word in the unity of the Christian church, yet we are never without sin because we carry our flesh around our neck [Rom. 7:24]."[73] We await "the time when our flesh will be put to death, will be buried with all its uncleanness, and will come forth gloriously and arise to a complete and perfect holiness in a new, eternal life."[74]

Second, as a tree grows, more fruit grows on it. Faith brings with it new desires: out of love and trust in God, one desires to do the will of God and conform to God's created intention for us. Faith produces new desires, attitudes, and dispositions to align one's life with God's design; new willingness to cooperate with God; recognition and gratitude for his many gifts, in both creation and redemption. Faith awakens character traits and may even free those character traits from their bondage to

72. Joest, quoted in Forde, "Forensic Justification," 127.
73. Large Catechism, Creed, 54, *Book of Concord*, 438; *BSLK*, 658.
74. Large Catechism, Creed, 56, *Book of Concord*, 438; *BSLK*, 658.

the flesh. In this way we can understand the "fruit of the Spirit." Faith does not suddenly make a person completely and perfectly patient. As one desires to become patient by overcoming impatience, one may use techniques such as counting to ten before speaking impulsively and saying something that one would rather not say. In other words, through faith the Spirit utilizes the personality, DNA, and character traits of the individual in helping the Christian become the person God wants one to be. We do not check our creaturely gifts and talents in at the door of the third article. Nor does the Spirit ignore or override our talents and abilities as he produces fruit within our lives. Instead, the Spirit uses them and develops them so that we each become conformed to Christ in distinctive ways.

This does not happen all at once or take place without resistance. These new spiritual impulses continually clash and collide with the old desires and addictions to sin. Christians begin to abandon and put to death the old ways of thinking and acting. Such abandonment of the old ways and walking in the Spirit do not grow steadily and unhindered in such a way that we need less and less forgiveness *coram Deo*. Nor does it occur without serious setbacks. In this life Christians remain addicted to sin no matter how long we are "on the bandwagon." Our carnal nature is addicted to lust and lasciviousness, evil and egoism, perversion and pathos of untold dimensions. As children of the new age who still live in the old age, the development of new attitudes, thoughts, and actions is not marked by consistent, steady, and unimpeded steps forward. Frequently, it will also be marked by significant steps backward. Even the best of persons, the "heroes" of the Bible—Abraham, David, Peter, and Paul—sinned spectacularly from time to time. However, as new creatures given birth by the Holy Spirit, we are prone also to love, goodness, sacrifice, virtue, and peacefulness.

This battle between the old creature of sin and the new creature of faith is related to the already and not-yet dimension of Christian existence. The battle between the old Adam and the new Adam resembles the Battle of the Bulge during World War II. Just as the Allies might push forward a few miles and hold their position for a time, the Germans would then push back and reclaim the ground plus gain a little bit. And so it went back and forth for six weeks. In an analogous way, so it is for the Christian. One may make progress in controlling one's temper, but then something happens and it gets away from the person. Immediately the Spirit rushes in, producing repentance so that one says, "I'm sorry, I didn't mean that," and resolves to work harder in controlling the temper. The Christian seeks absolution through the means of grace. As long as the struggle is evident, a person can take assurance that the Spirit is still present and active. The time to worry is when the struggle ceases, when a person no longer cares whether one is sinning or not. In the meantime, we "await the time when our flesh will be put to death, will be buried with all its uncleanness, and will come forth gloriously and arise to complete and perfect holiness in a new eternal life."[75] Then we will arise to a complete and perfect holiness in a new, eternal life, completely freed from sin, death, and all evil. Here and now we cannot see the righteousness with which the gospel has clothed us. We believe it on account of faith.

To use Luther's language, Christians live in two worlds, one heavenly and the other earthly. Into these we place the two kinds of righteousness, which are distinct and separate from each other. Both kinds of righteousness are God's will, and both kinds are necessary for us to live as fully human creatures restored in Christ. A whole, healthy human being must exist fully in both! And so Christians live deeply in both aeons. "Belonging wholly to Christ," the Christian "stands at the same time wholly in the world."[76] The earthly world is part of the old creation that extends until the last day. The heavenly is part of the new creation that has already begun with the resurrection of Christ and extends into eternity. For a Christian on earth, the active righteousness of works thus spans the whole field of reality from God's first creation to his new creation, from the first line of the Apostles' Creed to the last line of the creed.[77] The passive righteousness of faith brings about a new identity and a restored humanity that God will preserve beyond the resurrection of the body, through the last judgment, and into eternity.

---

75. Large Catechism, Creed, 57, *Book of Concord*, 438; *BSLK*, 659.
76. Bonhoeffer, *Ethics*, 198.
77. Braaten, "Natural Law," 56.

PART TWO

WHEN THE WORD IS SPOKEN, ALL THINGS ARE POSSIBLE

Luther and the Word of God

At the beginning of June 1535, Martin Luther launched a new course offering in Wittenberg that would take him ten years to complete, his lectures on the book of Genesis. This epitome of his theology began with, and revolved around, his concept of God's Word and how it works in God's world. "God speaks a mere word, and immediately the birds are brought forth from the water," he commented on Genesis 1:20. "If the Word is spoken, all things are possible." He called the creatures of God "nothing but nouns in the divine language," and he defined God's Word as the instrument of his power. That power expresses itself in promises to his people, the professor told his students: "We must take note of God's power that we may be completely without doubt about the things which God promises in his Word. Here full assurance is given concerning all his promises; nothing is either so difficult or so impossible that he could not bring it about by his Word."[1]

1. "Genesis Lectures, 1535–1545," *LW* 1:49; *WA* 42:37.5–24.

The people of the Wittenberg tradition have both expanded and shrunk Luther's insights in various ways over the past 475 years as they have tried to bring the Christian message to their own times and situations. In this essay (part 2), we present a summary and application of Luther's own insights, with help at points from other writers in the Lutheran tradition, for twenty-first-century readers. We all must appropriately translate these insights into our own contexts. When we do so, it is our conviction that we will be able to serve God faithfully in bringing his Word to our neighbors. This essay does not trace the development of Luther's view of God's Word in a strictly disciplined, historical fashion. In the context of our commentary, it lets Luther speak about his basic ideas as they apply to the world in which God has called his people to serve at the beginning of the twenty-first century.

Scholars have labeled and packaged Luther's theology under many topics, but the sinews that hold together the body of his gospel proclamation were fashioned from his perception of God as the Creator and Re-Creator, who acts by speaking. Luther's understanding of what the apostles and prophets meant when they spoke the Word of the Lord in various ways, and his understanding of what God meant when he spoke to us through his Son (Heb. 1:1–3)—all of this constitutes the nervous system that gives the impulse that makes his public teaching function in the lives of his hearers.

Luther's way of thinking is framed and permeated by his multifaceted understanding of the Word of God. God's first "spoken" Word was the creative "Let there be . . . ," the mysterious way in which God formed all that exists. From that point on, God talked his way through the entire Bible. His Word came to his chosen spokespersons as they delivered his message and effected his will among the Israelites (e.g., Jer. 1:4; Ezek. 1:3; Mic. 1:1). The Holy Spirit moved them, and therefore the interpretation of what they spoke and wrote is no human being's private domain (2 Pet. 1:20–21). The God who used the prophets as his mouthpieces breathed into them the words of Scripture as well (2 Tim. 3:16). The Word then became flesh and made his home among fallen human creatures as God himself, in his divine Second Person, assumed the human person, Jesus of Nazareth (John 1:1–18). The Word whose name is Jesus was God's medium for communicating his will and his essence, his very person, to sinners, and he was at the same time God's message of cruciform, self-sacrificial love for them. His dying and rising has atoned for the sins of humankind (Rom. 3:21–26) and reconciled sinners to God (5:9–11; 2 Cor. 5:17–21). Jesus Christ sends forth his Word through his Holy Spirit in oral, written, and sacramental forms.

6

THE FUNCTIONS
OF THE WORD

> God created all these things in order to prepare a house and an inn, as it
> were, for the future human creature, and he governs and preserves these
> creatures by the power of his Word, by which he also created them. . . .
> By speaking God created all things and worked through his Word. All his
> works are words of God, created by the uncreated Word.
>
> Luther, "Genesis Lectures, 1535–1545"

Each instance of the phrase "Word of God" formed an essential element in Luther's understanding of how God works in his world. He
developed his understanding of God's Word within the specific historical context of the late-medieval European academic world. His
conception of the person of God and his use of the terminology of the
Christian tradition had roots in his education, his engagement with the
biblical text, and his personal experience. All three contributed to his
understanding of how God's Word functions in all its forms, including
human language. Recognizing this setting in Luther's own time helps
twenty-first century readers comprehend what the reformer taught
regarding God's Word and how the church is to live under his Word
in this new millennium.

The Historical Background of Luther's Understanding of the Word of God

Luther was born into a world that had held on to some elements of ancient German religious practice. This world of medieval presuppositions retained aspects of traditional pagan religious belief that words can have magical powers. Many regarded certain words or phrases as magical formulas through which they could manipulate divine power. This point of view survived Christianization and embedded itself even within the practice of the church.[1] Many German peasants, probably Luther's kinfolk among them, regarded the words of the Mass, for instance, as working automatically, mechanically, or magically—*ex opere operato* is the theological term—to dispense God's favor or power on those who attended the most enchanted moment of the medieval week, the recital of the canon of the Mass. Luther rejected elements of medieval piety that employed certain phrases from the Bible or pious usage in such a magical way. He could not conform the magical use of language to his understanding of the person of the Creator, who wants to converse with his people in love and trust rather than place his power at their disposal in response to their external, ritual actions.

However, the reformer of Wittenberg refused to rush into a favorite option for some of his contemporaries. Among the biblical humanists there were those who appealed for the reform of education and life out of their conviction that true learning and piety should be grounded on knowledge of the biblical texts and other ancient works, both Christian and those of the Greek literary and philosophical authors. Some of them adopted the belief that human words are at best only symbolic shadows of some distant, heavenly, ultimate realities. They chose to retreat into a spiritualizing of God's Word that exiled its reality to heaven. They reacted sharply against medieval superstition by separating all things religious as far as possible from the material or created order.

Some of these theologians (including Ulrich Zwingli and Johannes Oecolampadius), devout and dedicated to biblical learning as they were, accepted much of the spiritualizing worldview of Plato and his disciples in the ancient world as it was being revived and revised in the contemporary milieu of Renaissance scholarship. At key points this profoundly shaped their reading of Scripture. For example, they could only conceive of the realm of the material as somewhat inferior to the realm of the invisible or spiritual. These thinkers believed that the nature of things,

---

1. On the implications of this and related late medieval religious phenomena for the Reformation, see Scott H. Hendrix, *Recultivating the Vineyard: The Reformation Agendas of Christianization* (Louisville: Westminster John Knox, 2004).

as Plato had understood it, drew a sharp line between the material or created order and heavenly reality. In his allegory of the cave, Plato had taught that reality rests in eternal ideas. He compared them to the real life that might be going on before the mouth of a cave. Prisoners chained in the cave see the shadows of reality taking place outside the cave as these are cast on the cave's walls visible to them. Because they do not realize that these shadows only reflect the true reality, these prisoners believe that the shadows themselves are real. So human beings on earth encounter here only shadows of the heavenly or eternal reality. With such a presupposition about reality, cast into a Christian mold, many of these humanists believed that the material order can at best only offer a glimpse, a shadow, of divine ideas. They thus held that the fundamental principles of the universe prevented God from actually delivering his forgiveness of sins and the life and salvation he gives, on the basis of Christ's death and resurrection, through human words and sacramental elements. These earthly, material things could only point to a heavenly reality or make a spiritual connection with divine intentions.

These biblical humanists shared Luther's view, to be sure, that the decisive line of demarcation runs between Creator and all creatures, but they still drew a hard boundary between material creation and the spiritual realm. They did not fully digest the fact that according to the biblical writers, God freely enters into his creation to do his will through material, created means, as well as through the purely spiritual. These learned, devout Christian theologians believed that human words and the objects of the material reality could only be shadows of heavenly reality. Their presuppositions deflected their vision from understanding how God had used material objects to convey his actual presence among his people in the Old Testament. They believed that the Word had become flesh as God assumed humanity in its fullest for his purpose of saving sinners, but they did not believe that the incarnation is a model for God's working with his world. They overlooked God's habit of selecting elements of his created order to accomplish or effect his saving will.

Luther used many of the tools the biblical humanists had prepared for the study of Scripture, for he shared their conviction that meaning and truth inhere in human language.[2] Most of his students can be classified as members of this movement, for they practiced its art of studying the ancient sources and its commitment to use them for learning

2. Lewis W. Spitz Jr., *The Religious Renaissance of the German Humanists* (Cambridge: Harvard University Press, 1963); Helmar Junghans, *Der junge Luther und die Humanisten* (Weimar: Böhlau, 1984); Leif Grane, *Martinus Noster: Luther in the German Reform Movement, 1518–1521* (Mainz: Philipp von Zabern, 1994).

of all kinds.[3] But Luther and his followers rejected the spiritualizing presuppositions of those who had absorbed ideas from Plato in a different manner than he had. His orientation for reading the Bible came from professors trained in the philosophical and theological system called Ockhamism and sometimes associated with the more general philosophical stream called nominalism.[4] (William of Ockham, a fourteenth-century theologian, had situated reality not in a supernatural pattern or form but rather in the created objects of the created order as God had made them.)

Luther's relationship with his Ockhamist instructors and their tradition is complicated. At the very heart of the Wittenberg professor's reform lay his sharp rejection of Ockhamistic views of salvation, which required human contribution and counted human merit as in some way necessary for establishing a relationship with God. However, his Ockhamist instructors had cultivated in their students a way of looking at God and his creation that shaped Luther's mature theology in positive ways. They convinced him that in his ultimate power, God had not been restricted by any laws of reason or nature. They also persuaded him that human creatures were totally dependent on the Creator's revelation of himself through the church for their understanding of things divine.

Luther's Ockhamist professors taught him that God in himself is unlimited and according to his absolute power could have constructed any sort of world he wanted. Yet this almighty God had bound himself to follow the rules he had set forth for his creation and for his human creatures. By binding himself with such a pledge or promise, God had established his "ordered" or "ordained" power, on which the daily functioning of the world is based. Therefore, people can be certain of what God shows them, through natural knowledge gained by simple observation of the natural world or through God's Word delivered by the church in regard to things above the mastery of human reason. The Ockhamists believed that God remains faithful to these rules and structures. They did not propose that he acts in arbitrary fashion toward his creation. These late-medieval intellectuals indulged in speculative debating to prove their logical prowess, but they did not presume to assert alternatives to the reality God had actually determined with their speculations over what God might have done or might be capable of doing according to his absolute power. They believed that human reason can never penetrate the mystery of God behind his revelation. That meant that human beings

3. Lewis W. Spitz Jr., "The Third Generation of German Renaissance Humanists," in *Aspects of the Renaissance: A Symposium*, ed Archibald R. Lewis (Austin: University of Texas Press, 1967), 105–21.

4. Oberman presents the teaching of Luther's intellectual grandfather, Gabriel Biel, who represented this way of thinking, in *The Harvest of Medieval Theology*.

must be satisfied with what God himself has revealed concerning himself even though they can exercise the gift of reason to explore the world he created and placed within their sphere of responsibility.

Luther left behind and/or rejected much of what he had learned from his Ockhamist teachers, but his thought consistently reflected the presupposition that he was completely dependent on God's revelation of himself for his knowledge of God and the divine plan for human living. The Wittenberg reformer was convinced that the Word made flesh, Jesus Christ, was the center and climax of God's disclosure of his person and the delivery of his love and new life to his people. He was also convinced that Scripture, given by God to the prophets and apostles, is the only reliable source for the continuing disclosure and delivery of God's mercy to human creatures. In it and the proclamation based on it, Luther experienced the power and presence of God.

Therefore, as the Wittenberg professor began to lecture on biblical texts, he had learned and presupposed that in the pages of Scripture the almighty Creator was telling him what he needed to know about God and about being human. Jesus Christ came to reveal both God's gracious disposition toward sinners and his expectations of performance from his human creatures. Luther presumed that in the biblical text, God would address him with the truth. He came to recognize that God's almighty power works in his world through his Word, and that God's word-actions not only describe but also determine the reality of his creation.

Luther's Understanding of How God's Word Functions

Luther thought that when God selects human words to serve as agents of his will and power, they accomplish what God wants them to achieve. When the Holy Spirit fashions the message of Christ in human language, these words are God's Word and an effective expression of his power. They do what he wants them to do. God acts through the words that he calls "gospel" to do more than inform human beings about his own disposition toward them. His Word is what modern linguists call "performative speech." Indeed, it is "creative speech." It accomplishes his will and actualizes his presence in human lives.

The Word Creates

The reformer's understanding of the Word as an instrument of God's power was grounded on the report of Genesis 1 on God's initial engagement with the world he created. There God spoke, and everything that exists began (1:3, 6, 9, 11, 14, 20, 24, 26). God's speaking is the foundation of all reality apart from his person. This fact reminds human beings of their creatureliness and their limits. For human existence is not infinite; we had a beginning (1:1). There are limits to the world and the creatures in it. We are products of God's creative action; human creatures, along with the world and all that is in it, exist because God spoke us into existence. The Word of the Lord is a mighty and lively power. In lecturing on Psalm 2 in 1532, Luther commented that the biblical definition of God's speaking posits that his words are "related to a real thing or action [*verbum reale*], not just a sound, as our words are." God's words make mountains tremble, scatter kingdoms, and move the whole earth. "That is a language different from ours. When the sun rises, when the sun sets, God is speaking. When fruit on the tree grows in size, when human beings are born, God is speaking. Accordingly, the words of God are not empty air but things very great and wonderful, which we see with our eyes and feel with our hands." When the Creator said, "Let there be . . . ," things happened. His Word accomplished its intention.[5]

For Luther, God is always acting, and his action is speaking. So it was as the worlds began. Luther was reflecting his Ockhamistic linguistic training as he framed his point of view. The exact nature of this creative Word, as the very essence of God's action, lies beyond human comprehension. It is clear that God's Word functions in a mightier way than words that have only a human person behind them. On the basis of his conviction that God's words exist as the realities of his creation, Luther concluded that God "does not speak grammatical words; he speaks true and existent realities. Accordingly, that which among us has the sound of a word is a reality with God."[6] Luther held that reality issues from God's speaking. He believed that the Old Testament witness to God's way of doing things established reality from the Word of God.

The Creator continues to act through the Word. His creative Word brought everything that exists into being, and he also sustains all created things and beings through his Word. That Word not only set reality in place; it also preserves that reality and continues to keep it going. The preserving and providing activity of God in his world takes place through his Word.[7] Luther presumed that all reality proceeded from and rested on the Word of the Lord. He believed that God's creative utterance had brought reality out of nothing, and he believed that the Word of the Lord gives form to the continuing reality of his creation.

5. "Lecture on Psalm 2, 1532," *LW* 12:32–33; *WA* 40.2:230.20–231.28.
6. "Genesis Lectures, 1535–1545," *LW* 1:21–22; *WA* 42:17.15–23.
7. "Genesis Lectures, 1535–1545," *LW* 1:24; *WA* 42:19.16–33.

The Word Re-creates

God's original creation of all reality also served Luther as the model for God's re-creating activity in bringing sinners back to himself. A new chaos and emptiness (Gen. 1:2) had invaded human existence in the form of death (2:17; 3:19). Sin induced death by trespassing the limits God placed on human behavior and by the human failure to fear, love, and trust God above all things (Eph. 2:1). After the human rejection of the Creator as Lord, a new act of creation was needed to rescue corrupted humanity. In his lectures on Genesis 1, Luther observed that God had fashioned heaven and earth out of nothing, "solely by the Word which he utters." Paul, Luther said, had referred to God's creative commands in 2 Corinthians 4:6, where the apostle was reflecting the biblical conviction that God is by nature a Creator, and that he creates through the Word when he converts the wicked—"something which is also brought about by the Word—as a new work of creation."[8]

This act of re-creation, like God's person and his power, is a mystery. Luther recognized that God conveys something about his power by labeling it a "word." This terminology reflects reality even if it is cloaked in the mystery, as it must be for creatures who cannot hope to comprehend God fully. It does reflect the nature of God as a Creator who wants and loves to be in communication with his creatures. The mystery of the incarnation, the mystery of the atonement, the mystery of the justification of the sinner—all have to do with the way God works through his Word. Those who are given what the crucifixion of the Word made flesh has accomplished become new creatures (Gal. 6:15 WA DB). Conversion from being dead in transgressions and sin bestows new life in Christ (Eph. 2:1–10).

The Word Establishes the Relationship of Conversation between God and His Human Creatures

Not all religious systems believe in a Creator and in the fundamental reality of that Creator's Word. Many peoples have invented a religion that disperses divine power into various material elements. Thus the stones and trees or the stars in which special spirits of power dwell do not claim that they have ordered their little parts of the world through a mighty word. They simply radiate their divine power and manipulate or are manipulated by human actions. Other people believe that one impersonal mighty Spirit exudes its power through all things and sweeps us along on the basis of feelings or the overcoming of emotions—without

8. "Genesis Lectures, 1535–1545," *LW* 1:16–17; *WA* 42:13.31–14.22.

words. In the last century, some people in the West have become so blinded to reality that they think individual or collective human powers determine right and reality, and they put their trust in human deeds, much less often in human words. Luther and his students encountered Christianized forms of spiritualism in the revival of ancient philosophies from the Greek world, and Christianized forms of spiritism in religious practices among the populace—forms that relied on remnants of pagan perceptions of reality. The Wittenberg reformers rejected these other ways of looking at the absolute and ultimate in human life and the wider reality beyond it.

Luther insisted that God is a person, a person who speaks and enjoys conversation with the human creatures he fashioned to listen to him and talk with him. God created his human creatures to be his conversation partners. God claims to be our Father, and through his Word he claims our trust and obedience as his children. His first conversation with his human creatures continued as long as Adam and Eve trusted God and delighted in chatting with him. In our fallen world he addresses his human creatures throughout Scripture, confronting them, condemning their unfaithfulness to him, comforting and consoling them with his word from Christ's cross, commissioning them to bring his love into the world, conveying his love and caring for his world through them.

Precisely how human beings relate to their Creator on the basis of such conversation also remains in part a mystery. The Maker of all retains responsibility for all things, which are completely in his own hands; biblical writers insist in acclaiming him as Lord of all. Yet he who holds all things in his own hands has placed responsibility for much of the working of his world into human hands, in human "dominion" or "management." How God's total lordship is congruent with the full responsibility of human beings is not clear to rational human analysis. But human beings experience both the limits of their own mastery of God's world and their own inner sense of accountability for it.

Human beings no longer experience the conversation with their Creator and Lord as he designed it naturally. In the unexplainable mystery of evil's existence, the conversation was broken. Its basis in human trust in God is gone. Luther recognized that this experience goes back to Adam and Eve. When they no longer trusted his Word, their doubt destroyed that relationship of trust, love, and dependence on their Creator. They fled from his presence and did not want to talk with him or listen to him (Gen. 3:8–19). God had to take the initiative if the conversation was to be restored.

The breaking off of this fellowship of conversation between God and human creatures is the essence of sin. For the Hebrews, "sin" meant missing the mark God had set for life; it meant straying over the boundary lines in which God wanted his people to live; it meant being something other than the conversation partner the Creator had created human beings to be. The question "Did God really say?" (Gen. 3:1 NIV) opened a breach. Sin resulted from Satan's luring human beings to question whether God meant what he had said. Satan was cunning enough to attack the greatest human strength, faith in the Word.

Luther defined "the root and source of sin" as "unbelief and turning away from God, just as, on the other hand, the source and root of righteousness is faith."[9] Denial of the reliability of God's Word meant the cessation of the conversation, the end of the relationship. That doubt exploded into a variety of defensive actions, which divided Adam and Eve from their God and avoided his claim that their lives be centered in him, conveyed in his Word. By undercutting their faith in the Word, Satan deprived them of the basis and heart of their relationship with God and thus destroyed their trust in him. "Unbelief is the source of all sins; when Satan brought about this unbelief by driving out or corrupting the Word, the rest was easy for him. . . . Therefore just as from the true Word of God salvation results, so also from the corrupt Word of God damnation results."[10] As Luther told his students, "The source of all sin truly is unbelief and doubt and abandonment of the Word. Because the world is full of these, it remains in idolatry, denies the truth of God, and invents a new god."[11] When doubt clouded and crippled the minds of Adam and Eve, the conversation between Creator and human creature broke down. Adam and Eve had stopped listening to God. They had broken their relationship with him by doubting what he had said. Their refusal to stay on target with their thoughts and their very disposition for life resulted in death. Ignoring the Author of life produced existence in mortality. Adam and Eve became sinners, doomed to death. Their missing of God's mark for their lives earned them sin's wage, and sin's paymaster, the law, always gives the slaves of sin what is owed them (Rom. 6:23a). Since the fall into sin, anger, resentment, manipulation, and outright avoidance plague every human attempt to communicate with the Ultimate and Absolute power beyond.

But God does not let sinners have the last word. God intervenes in the lives of his children and the history of the peoples through his Word. God's Word makes the critical difference in human experience. In commenting on Isaiah 55:11, "My Word shall accomplish that which I purpose and prosper in the thing for which I sent it," Luther asserted that God's Word indeed overcomes all that resists his will. God means to comfort

9. "Genesis Lectures, 1535–1545," *LW* 1:162; *WA* 42:122.10–13.
10. "Genesis Lectures, 1535–1545," *LW* 1:147; *WA* 42:110.38–111.17.
11. "Genesis Lectures, 1535–1545," *LW* 1:149; *WA* 42:112.20–22.

his people by telling sinners who resist him, "Although the Word will not do what you want, it will do what I want, even when you are hostile and resisting."[12]

Nonetheless, the Creator does not manipulate human creatures as he might push around mountains or rechannel seas. God created his human creatures as thinking and willing beings. Just as God shaped Adam and Eve to converse with him in the cool of Eden's evening, so he makes sinners into his children by a re-creative act of his Word, on the basis of his unconditioned choice of his people, made without any reference to anything they might do; but he re-creates them to be the kind of human creatures he fashioned in the first place. His reborn children trust in him, with hearts and heads, emotionally and rationally. Human life is founded on and centers on the person of our God, as we have come to know him in Jesus Christ. Like modern students of what it means to be human, such as the psychologist Erik Erikson,[13] Luther believed that trust or faith stands at the center of human living. Trust grasps and clings to God. It is the human side of the special relationship between Creator and the human creature. "Faith is nothing else than believing what God promises and reveals. . . . The Word and faith are both necessary, and without the Word there can be no faith."[14]

The Word Elicits Faith

All human attitudes and actions flow out of the central, core trust that determines who we think we are. "A 'god' is the term for that to which we are to look for all good and in which we are to find refuge in all need. Therefore, to have a god is nothing else than to trust and believe in that one with your whole heart. . . . It is the trust and faith of the heart alone that make both God and an idol." So Luther asserted in what seems like an extremely anthropocentric definition as he began to explain the first commandment in the Large Catechism. According to the reformer, only faith in the true God delivers and expresses true human life. "The intention of this commandment is to require true faith and confidence of the heart, which fly straight to the one true God and cling to him alone." Again in this peculiar anthropocentric way, Luther told his students that faith in Christ "consummates the Deity; . . . it is the creator of the Deity, not in the substance of God but in us. For without faith God loses his

---

12. "Lectures on Isaiah, 1527–1530," *LW* 17:258; *WA* 31.2:460.21–25.

13. Throughout his work Erik H. Erikson has treated trust as the fundamental and foundational element of human personality; see, e.g., his *Insight and Responsibility* (New York: Norton, 1964), esp. 81–107; *Identity, Youth, and Crisis* (New York: Norton, 1968), esp. 91–141; *Life, History, and the Historical Moment* (New York: Norton, 1975).

14. "Proceedings at Augsburg, 1518," *LW* 31:270–71; *WA* 2:13.18–22.

glory, wisdom, righteousness, truthfulness, mercy, etc. in us; in short, God has none of his majesty or divinity where faith is absent."

Luther personalized his definition of who God is by letting God speak: "See to it that you let me alone be your God, and never search for another. . . . Whatever good thing you lack, look to me for it and seek it from me, and whenever you suffer misfortune and distress, crawl to me and cling to me. . . . Only do not let your heart cling to or rest in anything else."[15] This is a trust created by the person of the Creator. Faith restores the human beings who have fallen into sinfulness by rendering to God what is due him, the acknowledgment of his being God, the reliance on him as Creator, the confidence that he alone can put human life in order again.[16] This faith becomes the display case for the very power of God. "Whoever believes and trusts in him is thereby delivered from all sins, from a guilty conscience, a sorrowing heart, error, lies, deception, darkness, and all the power of the devil, and is led to grace, righteousness, truth, understanding, consolation, and the true light. Thus, through faith, God is our power. We do not live in ourselves but in him, and he acts and speaks all things in us."[17]

The Creator generates such trust at the center of his human creatures by speaking to them, through his commitment and promise to them in the various forms of his Word. His own person, the Word made flesh, stands at the center of the communication of the divine love that elicits human trust. The promise of Christ delivers the power to become the children of God by pronouncing rescue and rebirth on those who have strayed from their heavenly Father. A divine promise is a word that does not subject itself to proof or testing. It is a word that elicits trust from its hearers and binds them on the one who promises.

The reformer was convinced that the Creator God speaks to sinners through a promise that reflects the nature of the relationship God has established with his human creatures. This relationship between a promising God and creatures who listen to and speak with their Creator provided Luther with his fundamental understanding of who God is and what it means to be human.[18] God is the Creator, who promises all good things to his human creatures. To be human means, first of all, to be in conversation with God, trusting him, obeying him, reveling in his gift of our being his human children. At the heart of being a "well-adjusted" child lies the total confidence and utter reliance with which

---

15. Large Catechism, Ten Commandments, 2–4, *Book of Concord*, 386–87; *BSLK*, 560.

16. "Lectures on Galatians, 1531–1535," *LW* 26:227; *WA* 40.1:360.24–361.18.

17. "The Beautiful Confitemini, 1530," *LW* 14:82; *WA* 31.1:43.22–39.

18. Oswald Bayer, *Promissio: Geschichte der reformatorischen Wende in Luthers Theologie* (Göttingen: Vandenhoeck & Ruprecht, 1971).

the child believes and trusts parents and selected other bigger people with abandon. Human beings learn to trust only through the relationship that is initiated by the object of their trust. Psychologically defined, faith comes by hearing God speak and by experiencing, in that speaking and listening, the One who loves without limit. Yet faith clings to the object of its trust in the face of negative experiences as well. Such is the faith that the Holy Spirit effects.

No one can believe apart from the Holy Spirit (1 Cor. 2:14; 12:3). From the standpoint of the human observer, that trust coming from the creature fashioned in God's image is a product of the functioning of mind and will, of thinking and feeling. While they are being brought to faith as adults, human creatures experience those functions as if they were happening simply by human power, through normal actions of the human mind and will. Yet in the mystery of God's dealing with us as the human creatures he created us to be, it is the Holy Spirit who moves mind and will in his re-creative act. Therefore, receiving God's gift of trust and the new life it brings entails human actions that can be described psychologically, human actions for which we feel responsible, but which really are the products of God's acting through his Word. Because of this analysis of human life, trust or faith, as Luther and Melanchthon conceived of it, involves psychologically explainable conveying and apprehension of God's Word. Simultaneous with these human activities, however, the Holy Spirit is using the believer's witness—our speaking words of gospel—as his instrument for his sovereign act of re-creating new human creatures out of the chaos and nothingness of sinful lives.

Faith "saves" because faith is the restoration, on the human side, of the trust that provides the fundamental orientation for all of life. Faith saves because it places human beings in their proper place, in God's embrace, in the hands of the Savior with holes through his palms, the One whom, believers know, will never let them go.

Therefore, out of the confidence and trust that depend totally on God flows a believer's sense of core identity. Out of the reliance on God's pronouncement of our rebirth as his children arises the very breath that animates Christian thinking about God and his entire creation. Out of the assurance that Christ has buried our sin and raised us up with him to renewed human living flows the entire activity and performance of God's children. Faith fixes its vision on Christ. Freed from the power of every threat, faith knows the freedom of practicing God's design for humanity. God's chosen people know who they are, and they act like it. Like a good tree that produces good fruit, so obedience to God's commands arises out of faith. Faith does not arise out of such obedience. Christians recognize that God has done all for them, and they seek to serve others. "From faith flow forth love and joy in the Lord, and from love [flows] a joyful, willing, and free mind that serves the neighbor willingly and takes no account of gratitude or ingratitude, of praise or blame, of gain or loss."[19]

Luther noted how Hebrews 11 teaches that "faith holds on and refuses to doubt simply because it cannot see." Such faith clings to God in spite of appearances and against experience. Such was David's faith, Luther goes on to say: believers learn to trust on the basis of the Word but also from the examples of others. "David speaks with certainty and power [in Ps. 110] about something that had not yet appeared or assumed reality." His trust in the coming Messiah, his Lord, "is his only comfort and highest joy. This faith sustained him amid all the perils of life, against violence and persecution from the outside as well as the grievous temptations of the conscience and the sorrow of sin and death. . . . By this faith he conquered all," for he could confess his absolute confidence in the God who had pledged to remain his God and defend him no matter what.[20] With his description of Abraham's faith as the basis of his righteousness in God's sight (Gal. 3:6), Paul had made faith in Abraham's God the supreme expression of worship, the supreme act of allegiance, the ultimate act of obedience, the most complete sacrifice of self. Such faith attributes glory to God: it recognizes God as God, with the corollary realization that human beings are the dependent creatures that we truly are.

Because human life in this world stumbles over temptation and tribulation of many kinds, faith also needs constant reinforcement through the Word of promise. In such times believers are called to flee to Christ's bridal chamber. There Christ alone reigns, and he "does not terrify sinners and afflict them but comforts them, forgives their sins, saves them. Therefore let the afflicted conscience think nothing, know nothing, and pit nothing against the wrath and judgment of God except the Word of Christ, which is a Word of grace, forgiveness of sins, salvation, and life everlasting." Such reliance on grace is hard for those caught in the struggle to repent, but it is faith's way under the power of the Word.[21] In comments on Isaiah 66:13, "As one whom his mother comforts, so I will comfort you" (RSV), Luther depicted the parental love of God for the broken and distressed by staging a conversation, a rhetorical device he frequently used. As a mother might say, "Darling baby, my dear little mouse," so God comes to us in our tears to reassure us, and in trust we react with joy. For living by faith means trusting what God has to say. "Faith judges according to the Word and by the Word and faith perceives a profoundly paternal love and thoroughly maternal caresses."[22]

19. "The Freedom of a Christian, 1520," *LW* 31:367; cf. 31:361–71; *WA* 7:66.2–10; cf. 7:60–69.
20. "Sermon on Psalm 110, 1535," *LW* 13:241–42; *WA* 41:86.18–98.11.
21. "Lectures on Galatians, 1531–1535," *LW* 26:120; *WA* 40.1:213.28–214.24.
22. "Lectures on Isaiah, 1527–1530," *LW* 17:410; *WA* 31.2:580.14–18.

The Word Simultaneously Reveals God and Hides God

The Word of God invades the world of sinners to reveal who God really is. But God does not tell all about himself. He could not, for creatures can never completely grasp their Creator. By definition the Creator must remain beyond the full and complete comprehension of those whom he has created. Through the sin that has broken conversation with God, sinners have further diminished their ability to comprehend who God is and what his disposition toward his human creatures is. God does reveal all that his human creatures need to know about him, even if that is not always all we want to know about him. He entered into conversation with his human creatures immediately after they had broken off their relationship with him (Gen. 3:9–19), and God has continued to make contact with fallen sinners in order to reveal himself to them as well.

The reformer recognized that there is a lot more to God than meets the human eye, and even the human ear. We can know him only in part (1 Cor. 13:12). He also knew that human beings can and want to construct their own pictures of what God ought to be like, even if these pictures tell us more about those who are imaginatively forging their own images of the Ultimate than about the true God. For these two reasons, he distinguished God as he remains hidden from us (Luther used the Latin term *Deus absconditus*) in his majesty and power, which are beyond our comprehension, from God as he reveals himself to us (*Deus revelatus*).

This terminology reflects a bit of the contrast Luther's instructors drew between the mysterious God—who could have done anything according to his absolute power, whose nature is inaccessible to human wisdom and human investigation—and the God who has given his promise to human beings in covenants that set nature and the moral order within fixed bounds. As late as 1538, Luther continued to use the Ockhamistic term "ordered power" for God's promise in his revealed Word. In that year he criticized books that distract from a focus on God's revealed Word: "You should direct your attention to the ordered power of God and the ministrations of God; for we do not want to deal with the uncovered God, whose ways are inscrutable and whose judgments are unsearchable (Rom. 11:33). We must reflect on God's ordered power, that is, on the incarnate Son, in whom are hidden all the treasures of the Godhead (Col. 2:3)."[23] However, Luther did not duplicate this Ockhamistic distinction of the two powers of God precisely with his distinction of the Hidden God from the Revealed God. He did not posit two different Gods but one God, who remains in part hidden from his creature's understanding, in all his majesty, but who reveals himself through his prophets and finally in

---

23. "Genesis Lectures, 1535–1545," *LW* 3:276; *WA* 43:72.37–73.4.

Jesus Christ (Heb. 1:1–3), giving his people all they need to know about him. In contrast to his instructors' teaching, Luther's point of view was not focused on God's power and potential but on God's revelation of what he has done for his people and what he intends to do with those whom he has chosen to be his own.

To try to venture beyond what God has told us of himself can only lead human beings into the maze and abyss of their own imaginations, Luther insisted. As a young monk, the reformer had tried that himself. He learned that, as creatures, human beings could never fully comprehend the nature of their Creator. Part of his lordship is expressed in the fact that he is simply greater than the human imagination. But sometimes human imaginations redesign this hidden God into some kind of substitute for the Creator. These "hidden gods" may seem to serve sinful purposes more or less well, but they deceive their deceived creators. As apprentices of the father of lies (John 8:44), sinners fashion their surrogate deities according to their own desires and designs. Luther wanted to turn his hearers from the folly of their own fantasies to the God who reveals himself in his Word. Commenting on Genesis 1, Luther stated that God reveals himself only partially as he lets human beings understand his disposition toward them in his action in history and above all in his Word. However, "whatever else belongs essentially to the Divinity cannot be grasped and understood."[24]

Nonetheless, God enters into the midst of our world to reveal himself and what we need to know about him. To do so he chooses selected elements of his created order as instruments of his revelation. The reformer did believe that God as he has revealed himself to us is not different from the Creator who by definition must remain beyond our grasp. He rejected any suggestion that there is an angry God and an indulgent God at odds with each other about what to do with human creatures. Therefore, whatever we have to say about God should presume that the Hidden God, mysterious and contradictory though his actions might sometimes seem, is indeed the same God who has revealed himself as loving and merciful in Jesus Christ and in the pages of Scripture.[25] Luther insisted that only and exclusively in the various forms of his Word could human beings encounter God:

> It is folly to argue much about God outside and before time because this is an effort to understand the Godhead without a covering, or the uncovered divine essence. Because this is impossible, God envelops himself in his works in certain forms, as today he wraps himself in baptism, in absolution, etc. If you should depart from these, you will get into an area where there

24. "Genesis Lectures, 1535–1545," *LW* 1:11; *WA* 42:9.32–34.
25. "Genesis Lectures, 1535–1545," *LW* 5:46; *WA* 43:460.23–35.

is no measure, no space, no time, and into the merest nothing, concerning which, according to the philosopher, there can be no knowledge.[26]

After Adam and Eve had tried to break off human communication with their Creator (Gen. 3), God kept coming to human beings to revive the conversation. His final approach came in the word of the cross, a word that appears to sinners to be foolish and impotent but that expresses the wisdom and power of God (1 Cor. 1:18). Just as God revealed himself by placing his Word into human flesh, so he acted on behalf of sinners by submitting that Word to the condemnation the law places on every sin (Gal. 4:4). The Word made flesh became the crucified and executed Word, so that the law's condemnation of sin might be accomplished. From the cross and out of his empty tomb proceeds a new creative Word of God. Certainly no one wants to center attention, to say nothing of life, on a cross, among the most horrendous instruments of death invented by human imagination. But God chose the foolish and impotent way of the cross as his means of communicating life.

God had often communicated with human beings in a still, small voice rather than through grand displays of power (1 Kings 19:11–13). But his apparently imprudent and irrational effort to rescue sinners by joining them in death makes no sense at all in fallen and corrupted conceptions of reality (1 Cor. 1:18–25). Given that plan for salvation, it is no wonder that God's saving and life-restoring Word causes those whose minds are trying to master life on their own terms to stumble. People are accustomed to controlling their lives and their environments by learning through signs and empirical testing or through logical and rational analysis. Such people are offended by having to learn about the most important aspects of life, God, and their relationship to him just by simply listening and receiving God's gifts. They think the cross of Christ reveals nothing but the end or absence of wisdom and power. They are wrong. Into sinful chaos and darkness, God's Word speaks the might and the prudence of his way of re-creating fallen, straying human creatures in order to restore light and life (1 Cor. 1:22–25).

From Paul's description of God's saving way and Word in 1 Corinthians 1 and 2, Luther developed his "theology of the cross," or more accurately from Paul's perspective a "theology of the word of the cross." It proposes that precisely through the contradiction of power-in-dying and wisdom-in-weakness, God is present to lead people out of imprisonment to their own power games and to substitutes for genuine understanding. The word God speaks from the cross leads them back to listening to him and taking him at his word. It permits them to acknowledge him

26. "Genesis Lectures, 1535–1545," *LW* 1:11; *WA* 42:9.34–10.1.

as Lord in the midst of death and despair. This word from the cross enables them to fill in the blanks in their lives. It clings to his promise when everything else contradicts the word of his love from the cross. It enables his people to confront and describe themselves and the world around them honestly and forthrightly. The theology of the cross liberates God's children from having to construct falsehoods in order for life to make sense. The truth of the cross sets them free to speak the truth, no matter how bad it is, so that God's truth in Jesus may restore the good. The word of the cross enables us to "call a thing what it is."[27] Such honesty cost Christ his life and costs sinners their addictions to their own control of life. It costs sinners their identity as sinners, for Christ's death and God's Word in baptismal form buries them (Rom. 6:3–4; Col. 2:11–12).

This Word from the cross also comes as close as possible to answering the unsolvable problem of the existence of sin and evil in the world fashioned and cared for by the good and almighty God. That problem intrudes into daily life in the form of the grand "Why?!" regarding the very existence of evil; in the question of why some are saved and not others; in the anguish of searching for a reason for some particular illness, accident, or misfortune; in the despair of wanting to know why God has not ended some particular sin in the believer's life with the coming of faith; in the frustrating search for common definitions of biblical truth and clear formulations of his Word among theologians quarreling and contending for their own versions of God's message in ecumenical exchange.

At the end of his great work on the bondage of the will, Luther confessed his own despair over the seeming injustice of God. He suggested that believers approach this dilemma under the shadow of three "lights." The light of nature finds the question "How can the good suffer while the evil prosper?" to be insoluble, but the light of grace presents God's love in its everlasting dimension. The light of grace, however, finds the question "How can God condemn those who have no power to turn themselves to him?" to be insoluble. Thus, the lights of both nature and grace find God unjust. The light of glory, however, affirms that God's incomprehensible righteousness will be revealed. "In the meantime we can only believe this."[28] For "if his righteousness were such that it could be judged to be righteous by human standards, it would clearly not be divine and would in no way differ from human righteousness. But since he is the one true God, and is wholly incomprehensible and inaccessible to human reason, it is proper and indeed necessary that his righteousness should

27. "Heidelberg Disputation, 1518," *LW* 31:53; *WA* 1:362.20–33.
28. "The Bondage of the Will, 1525," *LW* 33:292; *WA* 18:785.26–38.

be incomprehensible," as Paul says in Romans 11:33.[29] The theology of the cross blocks the human glance into the depths of the mysteries of God and draws our gaze to the person of Christ. He is God's definitive answer to these dilemmas and all others.

God's Word Kills and Makes Alive

God's Word reveals who he is. God's Word establishes reality. God's Word institutes and constitutes the Lord's relationship with his human creatures. For Luther, God's conversational relationship with his people comes to its climax in his pronouncing sinners free from their sin and the death it brings. The work of the Word made flesh restores sinners to human life as God designed it to be. This restoration takes place on the foundation of the condemnation pronounced by God's plan for life, his law. God effects that restoration through the pronouncement of the forgiveness of sins that returns God's chosen people to communion and communication with him. This forgiveness reconciles as it removes the sinner's fear of God. Forgiveness of sins through Christ's death and resurrection is the heart of the gospel. Luther described the Word that brings death and resurrection to sinners as a pair of messages, delivered in what he designated as "law" and "gospel." Although he used each of these terms in the variety of ways in which the biblical writers do, when he used them together, they took on a specific, technical meaning and function.

With these two terms Luther both described and brought about two actions of God: his condemnation of sin and his restoration of human righteousness in his sight. The categories of "law" and "gospel" also function for Christians as a guide for their own witness as they deliver God's Word to others. With law and gospel as a guideline for applying God's active and effective language to people's lives, believers serve as God's agents to kill and make alive (1 Sam. 2:6; Rom. 6:3–4; Col. 2:11–15). Their words serve the Holy Spirit as means by which God's favor falls on sinners with the gift of death to their sinful identities and of new birth as children of God. The proper distinction of law and gospel helps us sort out what we say to others as believers, depending on what we want the Word of the Lord to accomplish in our hearers' lives. It also helps us sort out what other people indicate they have understood from us as we have been speaking of God's Word to them.

Usually Lutherans say that law precedes gospel, in accord with Luther's own observation that the diagnosis must provoke the desire for a cure.[30] To be sure, God's creative Word that gave human beings their

---

29. "The Bondage of the Will, 1525," *LW* 33:290; *WA* 18:784.9–20.
30. "Prayer Book, 1522," *LW* 43:13; *WA* 10.2:376.12–377.3.

existence came first. His gift of life sets our lives in motion. He identified us as his own people, fashioned for conversation and communion
with him. In Eden, God spoke and thereby bestowed existence, granted
life, gave the human being a special status as the dominion-exercising
creature among all his creatures. Human existence and human identity
are gifts from God. God's first word for humankind is a word of gift, a
word that bestows life, a word that grants us our fundamental or core
identity as creatures of God.

The Law Is God's Prescription for Human Life. For God did not simply
give us our core identity, he also shaped a good life for us. Like all parents, God has expectations for his children. He assigns us roles to play
as he provides for his creation and manages its resources. These roles
involve secondary identities within the warp and woof of societal life.
They come and go among the changes of life. Important as the roles are,
their departure results in only surface changes in our persons. Our core
identity as a child of God remains.

It is a sign of God's love for his human creatures that for them he
designed a life with a framework and boundaries. As Creator, God
had the burden of fashioning life; he gave to his human creatures the
"burden" of performing according to his definition of what it means to
be human. According to Scripture, what it means to be human is first
of all simply to be God's child. One can do nothing to be or become a
child. That fundamental identity, like our existence itself, is totally a
gift of the parent, of the Creator of life. The expectations that flow from
God's shaping of our human natures do require performance from us.
God made us to be his children and to act like members of his family. The gift of this identity leads to the expectations of performance.
Apart from sin this performance flows naturally from lives that cling
to God in trust.

Although we cannot create ourselves, we can corrupt ourselves. We
are not given an explanation for this fact in Scripture. The existence
of evil and the continuation of evil in the lives of the baptized remain
mysteries beyond our grasp, beyond the command of our reason. After
the countless examples of atrocities visited on one another by human
beings during the twentieth century, it is difficult to deny that potential
monstrous evils and also tawdry, cheap, banal wickedness reside deep
within every one of us, waiting to display their potential if not tamed.
Thus, although God's first word to human creatures was a word that
gave life, and this life-giving word will be for his chosen people his last
word, Lutherans have generally maintained that, in the context of our
fallenness, the demands of God's expectations, expressed in his law,
must precede the promise of salvation. This Word that restores life is,
in the strict sense of the term, gospel. Sinners must come to realize that

something is wrong in their lives before they can truly listen to God's Word of gospel that bestows life and salvation on those who had thrown it away in their doubt and defiance (Matt. 9:12–13).

The law, as a description of God's expectations for human action, can never—was never designed to—give life. It can coerce an obedience that preserves the external aspects of human order. Bestowing life is the business of the Creator alone. The law only describes human actions. It tells us what God's will for the good human life is. It evaluates our performance against the standard of God's plan for human living. The heart of the law is the first commandment, that we fear, love, and trust in God above all things. Thus, disobedience to other commands from God only betrays what is wrong at the heart of our lives' conduct: false belief, a false definition of life and of God. This means that the law operates according to a pass-fail system. Perfect obedience proceeding from trusting the Creator is a fundamental characteristic of life. Anything apart from such trust and obedience produces a mark of failure. The law's evaluation assesses our lives, either saying "Nice" or saying "Die!" It has not said "Nice" for a long time.

In addition to evaluating and judging, the law's description of God's plan for human living functions in various ways in sinners' lives, as well as believers' lives. Christians have often spoken of the "uses" of the law. Employing the term "use" this way goes back into the Middle Ages. Lutheran theologians have proposed a number of schemes for listing and analyzing the uses of the law. In the Formula of Concord (art. VI) a more or less standard set of three uses of the law is presented. The "use of the law" describes the way Christians employ the law as they speak it or demonstrate it to themselves or other people. Christians distinguish the use that the speaker makes of the law from the function the law actually performs in hearers' hearts and minds. They should not be surprised when their attempts to bring order and discipline to people's lives give these people new insight and instruction regarding how human life works best. And Christians should be particularly sensitive to the fact that what they intend as instruction in good living or a simple call for order and discipline can easily turn into a crushing message, perhaps even an accusation, for a tender conscience.

God's Word comes to kill sinners and to make his chosen children alive through Jesus Christ. Relying on Paul's assurance that God's Word in baptism has ended the sinner's identity as a sinner and raised up those who have died with Christ in baptism to new life (Rom. 6:3–11; Col. 2:11–15), Luther used the motif of God's killing and making alive as found in a number of Old Testament passages (Deut. 32:39; 1 Sam. 2:6; 2 Kings 5:7; Hos. 6:1–2). These passages reveal how God restores rebellious people to his own rule and family. In early 1518, Luther commented that when God begins to make a person righteous, he first of all condemns that person; those whom he wishes to raise up, he destroys; those whom he wishes to heal, he smites; and those whom he wishes to give life, he kills.[31] A few months later he explained 1 Samuel 2:6: "The Lord humbles and frightens us by means of the law and the sight of our sins so that we seem in human eyes, as in our own, as nothing, foolish, and wicked, for we are in truth that." But God uses the "unattractive actions" that humble his people to bring them to new life.[32] "Him whom I am to help, I destroy. Him whom I want to quicken, save, enrich, and make pious, I mortify, reject, impoverish, and reduce to nothing." Through the reformer's 1519 instruction for praying the Lord's Prayer, this is what God said to the faith-filled sinner struggling to return to conversation with God.[33]

The Smalcald Articles contain one of Luther's most succinct descriptions of the law.[34] There he stated that the law does several things. Luther posited a "political" or "external" use of the law that governs our actions in relationship to one another. He maintained that this use of the law has three functions or effects. It may indeed discipline public life, quite apart from the gospel. When it does, it serves a good purpose. It produces order in society, effects justice, and protects the weak and the vulnerable. Indeed, it may produce hypocritical good works, but even they help hold society together.

The law may, however, also provoke rebellious human creatures to disobedience, the spiritual equivalent of the "terrible twos." We like to assert our own control over life by defying the one who truly is the Lord of all life. Third, it is also possible that this use of the law to order human life will provoke people to take what is meant as a guide for our actions in relationship to one another, to other creatures of God, and make it into a motivation for trying to please God. They make the sad mistake of showing up on God's doorstep with a gift for God that is suitable for their human neighbors, but not for their Creator. Thus, the first use of the law produces not only obedience in the civil sphere, but also rebellion in some and in others a religion of works righteousness and idolatry of our own performance.

Luther's second use of the law is the so-called theological use. It accuses, to use Melanchthon's language,[35] or as Luther describes it in the Smalcald Articles:

31. "Resolutions on the Power of Indulgences, 1518," *LW* 31:99; *WA* 1:540.7–14.
32. "Heidelberg Disputation, 1518," *LW* 31:44; *WA* 1:356.33–357.17.
33. "Exposition of the Lord's Prayer for Simple Laity, 1519," *LW* 42:79; *WA* 2:128.29–31.
34. Smalcald Articles (1537) III.ii, *Book of Concord*, 311–12; *BSLK*, 435–36.
35. Apology of the Augsburg Confession IV.38, 167, *Book of Concord*, 126 (cf. 148, 166); *BSLK*, 167, 194.

The foremost office or power of the law is that it reveals inherited sin and its fruits. It shows human beings into what utter depths their nature has fallen and how completely corrupt it is. The law must say to them that they neither have nor respect any god or that they worship foreign gods. This is something that they would not have believed before, apart from the law. Thus, they become terrified, humbled, despondent, and despairing. They anxiously desire help, but do not know where to find it; they begin to become enemies of God, to murmur, etc.[36]

This use of the law prepares people for hearing the gospel by destroying their confidence in alternatives to God and revealing to them the inadequacy and falsity of the way of life they have chosen apart from God.

But this use of the law is not as simple as it seems. First, the revelation of inherited sin depends not only on the sinful nature's recognition that something is no longer quite right here. In the previous article, Luther had said, "This inherited sin has caused such a deep, evil corruption of nature that reason does not comprehend it; rather, it must be believed on the basis of revelation in the Scriptures."[37] If we do not know something of our Creator, we cannot know that what is wrong with life fundamentally is our rejection of the lordship of our Creator. And our knowledge of our Creator may well contain at least a touch of gospel, or of God's goodness as he exercises his lordship by sustaining and supporting us in daily life. Therefore, law and gospel may intersect in the completion of the theological, or second, use of the law.

The law always accuses, Melanchthon said. But people do not always hear its accusation. Another insight of Luther in the Smalcald Articles takes us to a deeper level of the law's theological use and at the same time helps us recognize a wider field for its application by our hearers, both those outside the faith and those in the daily struggle of the dying and rising of repentance. Luther noted that the law is like "the thunderbolt of God, by means of which he destroys both the open sinner and the false saint and allows no one to be right but drives the whole lot of them into terror and despair. This is the hammer of which Jeremiah speaks: 'My word is a hammer that breaks a rock in pieces.'"[38] More than just accusing, the law is always cracking our confidence and sometimes even crushes it. God's law is always tearing at our security with a variety of doubts, sometimes bringing terror to our hearts. Sometimes subtly, sometimes dramatically, it shakes the falsely laid foundations that sinners have constructed for their lives.

36. Smalcald Articles III.ii.4, *Book of Concord*, 312; *BSLK*, 436.
37. Smalcald Articles III.i.3, *Book of Concord*, 310–11; *BSLK*, 434.
38. Smalcald Articles III.iii.2, *Book of Concord*, 312; *BSLK*, 436–37.

If we take seriously Luther's definition of what is really wrong with human beings in sin as our failure to fear, love, and trust God above all things, as he says in the exposition of the Ten Commandments in the Small Catechism, then we see that beneath or behind our disobedience against each specific commandment from two through ten lies the fundamental rejection of God, the doubt that defies God, the failure to "fear, love, and trust in him above all things." Any action of the law that deprives us of the pretense that we or any other created object, human or animal, mineral or vegetable, can serve as our God, can control our lives—that action does the theological work of the law. It crushes our pretension; it crushes our defiance of God; it smashes to smithereens our idols of every kind.

Thus, by giving us an overview of God's plan and order for our lives, the Ten Commandments can show those that feel no guilt for their own actions that, through no fault of their own, they are victims of others' disruption of God's order for life. This can point them to their need for Christ's presence in their lives. Producing guilt or shame is not the goal of the proclamation of God's law. Guilt and shame are facts of fallen life, but the gospel has come to abolish them. The goal of pronouncing God's judgment is the death of idols, the death of false faiths, the death of sinners, so that life from Christ may triumph. Whether we encounter our own inability to function well as the source of our own identity, security, and meaning for life in our own disobedience or in someone else's—in our own defiance of God, or the neighbor's defiance that brings havoc and fear to our lives—we encounter the crushing power of the law. That crushing power brings with it fear: fear of our own inability to control the evil within us, and fear because of our inability to control the evil that threatens us from outside.

However we are crushed under the law's sentence, we finally realize that death is inevitable; it is necessary. Our false gods must die, and we must die as false believers and false practitioners of human life. There is no other way to receive life than through death. For sin pays but one wage: death (Rom. 6:23a). And sin is an honest employer. It never cheats its servants. It always gives just compensation to those in its employ. The law does not offer bargain rates on liberation and life. It cannot liberate us or give us life. It can only evaluate. It can only judge. Its sentencing procedure is not complicated. Its judgment is either guilty in even the tiniest degree or not guilty. Only to those who have died to sin does God give the gift of life (Rom. 6:23b).

The Gospel Is God's Gift of New Life in Christ. There is good news for sinners only in the One who has assumed our sinfulness, died our death, and reclaimed our life in his own resurrection. The gospel of Jesus Christ alone brings sinners back to life. According to Genesis 1, only the Word of God created what exists, and only his Word made flesh re-creates those dead in sin into those dead to sin. The law has several uses and functions. The gospel, in one sense, has only one use. It makes sinners who have been buried with Christ alive in him. The gospel is a single word: "Arise." This gospel takes away our sin. It removes our old life enslaved to idols. It does not bring the former sinner, re-created through the Word of the Lord (in the flesh, in the absolution), to some neutral ground between corrupted humanity and restored humanity. It takes us out of death and into life, out of idolatry and into trusting the Creator, who has come as Jesus of Nazareth and who breathes new life into us as God's Holy Spirit. Nonetheless, to bring us the comfort of God's love when doubts and troubles plague us, it is useful to distinguish what the gospel does in our relationship with God from what it does to empower love for the neighbor.

Medieval theologians used a variety of verbs as synonyms for "to save." Luther did, too, but he believed that God's saving action is best described or expressed by the words " to justify" or "to restore righteousness to" sinners. It is vital to recognize that God accomplishes his saving intention through an action, through the activity of his Word. "Justification" is not an abstract concept or a description of some heavenly reality from a distance. Justification is something God does to sinners, a lively event. The verb "to justify" had several meanings in the German of Luther's day, definitions parallel to those in ancient Greek. The word could mean "to make righteous," and that meaning carried with it connotations of righteousness on the basis of human performance in late medieval theological circles. "To justify" also meant "to pronounce righteous," a term from the lawcourts that designated a verdict of innocence from the judge. Finally the term also meant "to do justice to," as did δικαιόω in ancient Greek.[39]

Luther often used the verb in the second sense. Although one might misunderstand the concept of "pronouncing sinners righteous" as a divine shell game, Luther found the concept helpful in reassuring those who still found evidence of sinfulness in their hearts and minds, as well as in their actions. It assures them that God's love trumps their sinfulness. When hearers were concentrating on their sinfulness, Luther emphasized that God considered them righteous, or counted and reckoned them free from sin through his verdict of "Innocent!"—no matter how they felt about themselves. Regarding the mysterious continuing presence of

---

39. Werner Elert, "Deutschrechtliche Züge in Luthers Rechtfertigungslehre," in *Ein Lehrer der Kirche: Kirchlich-theologische Aufsätze und Vorträge von Werner Elert*, ed. Max Keller-Hüschemenger (Berlin: Lutherisches Verlagshaus, 1967), 23–31. Cf. H. G. Liddell and R. Scott, *A Greek-English Lexicon*, rev. H. S. Jones and R. McKenzie, 9th ed., 2 vols. (Oxford: Clarendon, 1958), 429.

sin in believers' lives, Luther argued that as we struggle with the sin still clinging to our flesh during this life and experience having the feeling that we are falling into sin because the Holy Spirit is no longer with us, "we always have recourse to this teaching, that our sins are covered and God does not want to hold us accountable for them." When God's children feel their sinfulness, they need to recognize that God no longer takes it into account. Christ the mediator blocks his view of our transgressions, and God regards us as his children because his Word has assigned or imputed to us his righteousness, with a Word that determines reality.[40]

This does not mean that Luther viewed justification by God's pronouncement as a contrary-to-fact statement. Those who see this form of forensic justification as merely a legal fiction do not share Luther's understanding of the power of the Word of God. The reformer knew that from the beginning of the world, God determined reality by speaking. Therefore, he was certain that God's word of forgiveness created a new reality in the life of the sinner. The reformer could not explain the mystery of evil and sin continuing in the lives of those God had claimed as his own in baptism. But he did not doubt that when God said, "Forgiven," the reality of human sinlessness in God's sight was genuine and unassailable. God's children must live with the mystery of the continuing sin and evil in their lives as they engage in the battle against their own sins. But they have no warrant to doubt that God has established the mightier reality of their innocence in his sight. And what he sees is real because he determines reality.

But Luther also recognized that God "does justice to sinners" in justification. Employing Paul's baptismal terminology in Romans 6:3–11, Luther taught that the Word of the Lord brings sinners into the death and burial that sin necessitates (Rom. 6:23a) and then raises them up through the Word of life that comes as a gift from the cross, in the sacrificed and risen Lord Jesus Christ (Rom. 6:23b).[41] In the twentieth century, scholars debated fiercely and at length whether Luther believed that justification was "merely" a matter of words from God, a purely "forensic" judgment, or whether it effected a "real" change in sinners and was constituted by this "effective" transformation. Gerhard Forde breaks through this long-standing debate: "The absolutely forensic character of justification renders it effective—justification actually kills and makes alive. It is, to be sure, 'not only' forensic but that is the case only because the more

---

40. "Lectures on Galatians, 1531–1535," *LW* 26:132–33; *WA* 40.1:233–35.

41. See Robert Kolb, "God Kills to Make Alive: Romans 6 and Luther's Understanding of Justification (1535)," *Lutheran Quarterly* 12 (1998): 33–56; Gerhard O. Forde, *Justification by Faith: A Matter of Death and Life* (Philadelphia: Fortress, 1982; repr., Mifflintown, PA: Sigler, 1991), 21–38; cf. Gerhard O. Forde, *Theology Is for Proclamation* (Minneapolis: Fortress, 1990), 72–85, 119–33.

forensic it is, the more effective it is!"[42] For "the death inflicted by the justifying word which reduces us to nothing is the *real* death, the true *spiritual* death, the death of sin, the death of all defiance against the God who 'will have mercy on whom he will have mercy' [Rom. 9:15]." God's Word "*is* the death knell of the old and the harbinger of the absolutely new. . . . The unconditional word, the promise, the declaration of justification is that which makes new, that which puts the old to rest and grants newness of life."[43] From God's execution of the sinner with Christ on the cross spring new creatures, faithful children of God, raised to new existence through their Lord's resurrection. Justification is not a fictive assertion, an "illusion of being 'as-if'" righteous. God's Word creates reality, and God's Word of forgiveness creates the identity of being God's child, an identity that brings with it expectations of performance of God's will.

God's Word of absolution, liberation, and re-creation does not function magically. Luther confesses God as the one who creates through communication and who has created the mystery of humanity in such a way that his human creatures are to be his conversation partners. The Word of forgiveness creates, awakens, and renews trust and the community of trust and love between God's reborn child and himself. The Word of forgiveness functions as a promise, a pledge from God that immediately changes the reality of existence, a guarantee of God's favor forever.[44] God's promise to re-create his children anew through his gospel means, as Luther concluded in comments on Galatians 4:7, "sheer liberty, adoption, and sonship." This comes about on the basis of God's fatherly promises. His status as Father invites and expects my response as his child.[45] This gospel is God's power and his way of ruling his kingdom. He exercises this rule or power by promising not only a pledge of future delivery of the Good, but above all an assurance that rests on the word of the King. This word from God has immediate effect and validity. That word of promise is a creative Word, which establishes the new reality that this child of God belongs to him and is no longer a sinner because God no longer regards him as a sinner. God's view of things, God's Word, determines reality. God stands by his Word, his Word of forgiveness. Through it he creates trust in the untrusting person.

---

42. Forde, *Justification by Faith*, 36; cf. Oswald Bayer, *Aus dem Glauben leben: Über Rechtfertigung und Heiligung* (Stuttgart: Calwer, 1984), 41–53; translated as *Living by Faith: Justification and Sanctification* (Grand Rapids: Eerdmans, 2003), 42–57.

43. Forde, *Justification by Faith*, 37–38.

44. Bayer, in *Promissio*, shows how Luther linked God's Word of gospel as promise with the faith that responds to and lives in the promise of God in Christ.

45. "Lectures on Galatians, 1531–1535" (on Gal. 4:7), *LW* 26:389–90; *WA* 40.1:593.20 –594.12.

His word, "Your sins are forgiven you," means "Stand up and walk" (Matt. 9:2, 5). The gift of new life means new living. Some distinguish the forgiving use of the gospel from the empowering use of the gospel. The gospel does indeed function both to comfort us with assurance of our new identity through Christ and to enable us to live as real human beings through our newborn ability to serve and please God. But essentially it is just one simple word from God: "You are my child!" He follows that up with a gentle parental "So act like it!" But the one word that bestows our new identity brings with it the expectation of our heavenly Father that we will live out our identity in the performance of his will.

There are a thousand ways to proclaim the gospel, but they all contain the name "Jesus Christ" (Acts 4:10, 12). God has good news for us in his creation, but for those who have fallen by trying to rise higher than they were created to be, Jesus Christ is the name of life and salvation. The forgiveness of our sins, which is the restoration of our humanity, constitutes the heart of the gospel he is and brings. Believers have recognized a variety of ways of expanding on "Your sins are forgiven" to proclaim the liberating power that Jesus's death and resurrection have fashioned.[46] The liberating power of forgiveness, or reconciliation, or adoption, or atonement, resting on what Christ has done for us, has brought us back to being real human beings. That is the identity he has given us, and from that identity flow the works that make his love and his will real in our world.

When we think about helping each other perform his will, we should recognize that this performance involves both motivation and instruction. Motivation of the Christian life stems from the gospel. We live as children of God because of the fact that we trust God's Word, which says that we are his children. That Word has established our identity anew as his children. But in the mystery of our continued struggle with sin, we can indeed hear that Word of forgiveness and life without automatically knowing how to please God, how to live like the authentic human being he has restored us to be.

Therefore, we need instruction. Because any description of the activities God wants us to do to fulfill our humanity speaks about the burdens that our humanity places on us, that instruction will necessarily be a form or expression of the expectations of God for his human creatures. We have called those expectations "law." Some Lutheran theologians react against the use of this word both for God's crushing demands for human obedience and for the instructions that God gives his chosen people. They believe that new obedience is necessary but that the

46. J. A. O. Preus, *Just Words: Understanding the Fullness of the Gospel* (St. Louis: Concordia, 2000).

instructions for it should be called "God's commands" or "the imperative of the gospel" to distinguish them from the killing function and power of the law. Others argue that God's plan is the law regardless of how it functions. So with Melanchthon they speak of a third use of the law, a term that Luther did not use even though he often preached the law of God to instruct his hearers in Wittenberg.

These terminological debates are significant discussions for pastoral care. They do not alter the fact that we must distinguish the instructions for our living as God's children from the motivation for our new obedience. That which moves us to do good works is rooted in the gospel of Jesus Christ. The gospel alone provides power for Christians to act out God's expectations for his creatures. Thus, the motivation arises out of God assuming the burden for us and liberating us from our idolatry and sinfulness. The expectations of God squarely place the burden on us and describe the actions he has designed to be the expression of our humanity. Motivation reflects and arises from faith in Christ and is a matter of attitude and orientation. Performance meets the needs of neighbors with deeds, perhaps identical to the deeds of those moved by something other than the gospel of Christ.

In the life of Christians, who are caught in the struggle between God's truth and Satan's lie, the rhythm of law and gospel sets the tone for their daily experience. For believers who wish to serve properly as servants of his Word, in a fallen world and speaking with sinners, it is necessary to distinguish two kinds of sinners. The first are those who are still secure, perhaps even arrogant, in relationship to God because they find that their false gods, their substitutes for their Creator, are functioning well enough in providing them a core sense of identity, security, and meaning to get along. The second kind of sinner consists of those whose false gods are obviously failing them, whose sense of identity, security, and meaning is beginning to crack or is in smithereens. That is why the answer to every religious question is, "Why do you want to know?" We have to know why people are asking, the question behind or beneath the voiced question, before we know which of God's topics, identity or expectations, is on the immediate agenda—which of God's words, law or gospel, needs to be spoken.

In the language of the last document the Lutherans took as a standard for public teaching, the Formula of Concord of 1577, God calls his newborn people to believe and then to teach and also to confess the gospel. Confessing the faith to fellow rebels and doubters means that we are called to be God's "hit men" and his "midwives," to help people see that they are dead in trespasses and sin, that their allegiance to false gods gives them no proper sense of identity, security, and meaning. God calls us to speak the Word of absolution, the Word that conveys the Word made flesh and his death and his resurrection, so that they may die to their sin and rise to live as children of God.

Therefore, we listen, and then we speak. We speak a word that seeks to bring the unbeliever into death to false gods or the rebellious believer to the mortification of the flesh. That word smothers the beasts within us that want to lead us out of our humanity and back into bondage to evil, the evil one, our own evil thoughts, the evil plans of the world around us. We speak that word if from our conversation partner we hear a sense of rebellion—arrogant and defiant, or modest and apathetic—though in different ways depending on the tone of what we hear. If instead we hear the bruised reed or the smoldering wick gasping for breath, flailing about and seeking something to hang on to, we bring the comfort of God's promise: a promise of death to old identities, to the denial of our identity as children of God. We deliver the Word that breathes life once again into souls as dead and dried up as dust, as ghastly as the grime. We console the disconsolate, and we shine the light of the new creative power of the risen Lord into their lives. We do so through our use of God's Word in the various forms of what Luther labeled the means of grace, the means or instruments by which God delivers his favor and his re-creating power to those who have turned their backs on him.

7

THE ENFLESHED AND WRITTEN FORMS OF GOD'S WORD

Messiah is God's only eternal Son, whom he sent into the world to take our sins upon himself, to die for us, and to vanquish death for us. . . . Therefore, we exult and rejoice that God's Son, the one true God together with the Father and the Holy Spirit, became a man, a servant, a sinner, a worm for us; that God died and bore our sins on the cross in his own body; that God redeemed us through his own blood. For God and Man are one Person. Whatever the Man does, suffers, and speaks, that God does, suffers, and speaks; and conversely, what God does and speaks, that the Man does and speaks. . . . To him Scripture must bear witness, for it is given solely for his sake.

Luther, "The Last Words of David, 1543"

From Genesis 1 to Revelation 22, biblical writers employed the term "Word of God" to express several concepts. The Word of God that created the worlds, the Word in a mysterious and uncreated form, is some sort of speaking but is also the Second Person of the Holy Trinity, according to John 1:1–4. The Word as a means of communicating with human beings takes concrete form in a number of manners and modes. God's

Word is the origin, not the object, of our thinking and our being, so we can only listen to what God tells us about himself and his Word through his Word. From all these usages of the term, what is clear is that God is a God who communicates and who thereby creates communion and community.

Luther believed that God's coming to us in external means, commandeering selected elements of the created order as the instruments and vehicles of his saving action, revealed his special love for the human creatures he had made from the dust of the earth and the breath of his mouth.

The Enfleshed Word: Jesus Christ

In 1517 Luther lectured on the Epistle to the Hebrews. His comments on 1:2, "In these last days God has spoken to us by his Son," emphasized that God's communication with fallen human beings climaxed when God the Son became human. Through him the worlds were created, the writer to the Hebrews reported, and through him is everything upheld. He is the reflection of divine glory and the image of God's essence, who humbled himself to become recognizable among his lost creatures and to purify them from their sins (Heb. 1:3–4).[1] This passage summarizes God's revelation of himself in the human being Jesus of Nazareth and in his acting through Jesus's death and resurrection to restore his relationship with his lost human creatures.

Twenty years later the reformer preached on the first chapter of John's Gospel and expanded his exposition of what it means that God's Word "became flesh" (John 1:1–4, 14). The Word that became flesh as Jesus of Nazareth is the Second Person of the Trinity, Luther proclaimed to the Wittenberg congregation. Conceding that the analogy between God's eternal, uncreated Word and human words was faint, inadequate, and vague, he explained that John was echoing Genesis 1 when he chose this way of describing God's coming as a human being to save his rebellious and doubting creatures. A word "is not merely the utterance of the mouth; rather it is [also] the thought of the heart." "Thus, God, too, from all eternity has a Word, a speech, a thought, or a conversation with himself in his divine heart, unknown to angels and human beings. This is called his Word. From eternity this Word was within God's paternal heart, and through him God resolved to create heaven and earth."[2]

1. "Hebrews Lectures, 1518," *LW* 29:110–13; *WA* 58:98–103.
2. "Sermons on John 1 and 2, 1537–1538," *LW* 22:9; *WA* 46:544.3–7.

By confessing that Jesus is the Word of God, through whom all things were created, John attested to his being true God, for "this word was in the Father's heart from all eternity."[3] God became one of his own human creatures in the mystery of the incarnation in order that he might rescue his people from their captivity in sin. God alone has the might to "save us from the power of this world's god and prince, the devil, that is, from sin and death." He must also be our brother, who is of our flesh and blood, who "became like us in all respects but sin" (though the preacher did not elaborate on the logic behind this assertion of the necessity of the incarnation). This Word of God sustains the universe he created, and in human form and flesh he gives life and light (John 1:3–5). He creates anew and reveals what it means to be God's creature as well as who God is and how God is disposed toward his human creatures.[4]

Luther shed light on the biblical concept of "flesh" to make clear why John described God's becoming human with that term. Biblical writers used the term to denote the whole human being. Therefore John 1:14 means the Second Person of the Trinity became a human being, "with flesh and blood like that of any other human," and he did so to restore us to the presence and family of God, with the result that "our flesh and blood, skin and hair, hands and feet, stomach and back might reside in heaven as God does." Christ's incarnation enables his people to defy Satan and all evils because Christ has suffered God's judgment on human sin in our place.[5]

Luther's convictions regarding this unity of God and human creature in the person of Jesus Christ turned the reformer's thinking to the ancient church fathers for help in describing the mystery of the incarnation. The creeds of the church taught that God and human creature were united in one indivisible person without any merging or fusion, blending or mixture of the two natures, as the ancient church had formulated its definition of the person of Christ. His divine nature remains divine, and his human nature remains human, but the two natures share characteristics with each other.[6] Relying on the Council of Chalcedon (451), Luther confessed that the personal union of the two natures was so complete and intimate that their sharing of their characteristics—*communicatio idiomatum* in Latin, the "communication of attributes"—means that "from the moment when deity and humanity were united in one person, the Man, Mary's Son, is and is called almighty, eternal God, who has eternal dominion, who has created all things and preserves them

---

3. "Sermons on John 1 and 2, 1537–1538," *LW* 22:13; *WA* 46:547.36–37.
4. "Sermons on John 1 and 2, 1537–1538," *LW* 22:36–37; *WA* 46:567.15–568.25.
5. "Sermons on John 1 and 2, 1537–1538," *LW* 22:110–11; *WA* 46:631.27–632.26.
6. "Confession Concerning Christ's Supper, 1528," *LW* 37:210–32; *WA* 26:320–43.

'through the communication of attributes' because he is one person with the Godhead and is also very God."[7]

Because his instruction in the Ockhamistic way of thinking had eliminated all "impossibles" when it came to God and his working in his world, Luther believed that nothing prevented the Creator from becoming the incarnate Word and joining his Second Person with this human being named Jesus. In that union as one person, both the human nature and the divine could not become the other, nor could either one lose its own identity. Nonetheless, this mysterious miracle of the incarnate God could function with the two natures sharing their characteristics. The two natures had become one person, and in that one person the human being and the Second Person of the Holy Trinity, though completely distinct, were inseparable. One person acted when Christ was doing something. One person, and therefore both natures, had the characteristics or attributes of both natures. Luther's students made certain to stipulate that this must be understood of the concrete natures that meet in the person of Christ, not of divinity and humanity in the abstract. Apart from this kind of personal unity, Luther was convinced, believers could not fully grasp the wonder and magnificence of God's plan for salvation in the incarnation of the Word, Jesus of Nazareth, the eternal Son of God and Son of Man.

God became incarnate to bring his human children to everlasting life and to give them the ability to cast aside Satan and all else that distracts them from being God's faithful people. He became an offering for sin (Isa. 53:10) and a curse (Gal. 3:13) for the creatures who had rejected his lordship. Not clinging to his status as God, he came to be Mary's child, so that he could become the servant who would "save his people from their sins" (Phil. 2:4–11; Matt. 1:21).[8] John concluded his introduction to his Gospel, Luther told the Wittenberg congregation, by affirming that "no one has ever seen God; the only Son, who sits in the bosom of the Father, has made him known" (cf. 1:18; 13:23 WA DB). He did this "to assure our hearts that the Word revealed by the Son must be absolutely trustworthy since the Son rests in the bosom and in the arms of the Father, so intimately close to the Father that he is reliably informed about the decisions of the Father's heart."[9] Through Jesus, believers "look directly into God's face." Only through Christ can sinners find rescue and release from their sins, for "God has placed his grace solely in the only Son. . . . All will be futile without the grace and truth of Christ. Life resides exclusively in the grace and truth of the dear Son of God, our Lord Jesus Christ."[10] Because

7. "The Last Words of David, 1543," *LW* 15:293; *WA* 54:49.37–50.3.
8. "Sermons on John 1 and 2, 1537–1538," *LW* 22:111–12; *WA* 46:632.33–633.35.
9. "Sermons on John 1 and 2, 1537–1538," *LW* 22:149; *WA* 46:666.5–10.
10. "Sermons on John 1 and 2, 1537–1538," *LW* 22:158; *WA* 46:673.19–30.

the two natures share their characteristics, believers can be confident of their own salvation, Luther believed. "We Christians must ascribe all the characteristics of the two natures of Christ to him. Consequently Christ is God and human being in one person because whatever is said of him as human must also be said of him as God, namely, Christ has died, and Christ is God; therefore God died, not the separated God, but God united with humanity."[11] For the sake of rebellious sinners and for their salvation, Luther believed, God had become one of them in this mysterious revelation of the Word made flesh.

Some twentieth-century theologians tried to describe the history of preaching on the atonement that Christ effected in his incarnation and life, in his death and resurrection. The Swedish theologian Gustaf Aulén argued that Luther returned to the teaching of the ancient church and taught that Christ won salvation through his victory over the enemies of the believer, namely, Satan, sin, death, the wrath of God, and the accusation of his law.[12] More accurate is Ian Siggins' observation that Luther had no atonement "theory," no presumption that he could explain how and why God accomplished the salvation of his chosen people through Christ's death and resurrection.[13] "Begin where Christ began—in the Virgin's womb, in the manger, and at his mother's breasts. For this purpose he came down, was born, lived among human beings, suffered, was crucified, and died, so that in every possible way he might present himself to our sight. He wanted us to fix the gaze of our hearts on himself and thus to prevent us from clambering into heaven and speculating about the Divine majesty."[14] Believers are dependent on God's revelation of himself and on his telling of what he has done for them.

Luther used the richness of the biblical proclamation of Christ's saving work, and he fashioned his own metaphors and descriptions from his own world to bring the forgiveness of sins to his people. Two of these descriptions illustrate how the Wittenberg reformer delivered the gospel of the Word made flesh to his hearers and readers. Christ has entered into a "joyous exchange" with sinners, the reformer taught. He became "a sinner, who has and bears the sin of Paul, the former blasphemer, persecutor, and assaulter; of Peter, who denied Christ; of David, who was an adulterer and a murderer, and who caused the Gentiles to blaspheme the name of the Lord [cf. Rom. 2:21–24; 2 Cor. 5:21]. In short, he has and bears all the sins of all people in his body—not in the sense that he has

11. "On the Councils and the Church, 1539," LW 41:103; WA 50:589.21–590.4.

12. Gustaf Aulén, *Christus Victor: An Historical Study of the Three Main Types of the Idea of the Atonement*, trans. A. G. Hebert (1931; repr., New York: Macmillan, 1961).

13. Ian A. K. Siggins, *Martin Luther's Doctrine of Christ* (New Haven: Yale University Press, 1970), 108–13.

14. "Lectures on Galatians, 1531–1535," LW 26:29; WA 40.1:77.28–78.13.

committed them but in the sense that he took these sins, committed by us, upon his own body, in order to make satisfaction for them with his own blood."[15] The law demanded the death of the sinner. Christ became sin for us (2 Cor. 5:21), and as the sacrificial offering for the sin of all humankind, he met the law's demand for the death of sinners in order that they might become the innocent and upright children of God.

A second picture provided Luther's students with another way of thinking about Christ's work. He came to combat sin in a duel. On his cross sin and righteousness collided with each other. "Sin is a very powerful and cruel tyrant, dominating and ruling over the whole world, capturing and enslaving all people. Sin is a great and powerful god who devours the whole human race." On Calvary, sin "attacks Christ and wants to devour him as he has devoured all the rest. But he does not see that his opponent is a person of invincible and eternal righteousness. In this duel, therefore, it was inevitable for sin to be conquered and killed, for righteousness to prevail and live. Thus, in Christ all sin is conquered, killed, and buried, and righteousness remains the victor and the ruler eternally."[16] With the images of "the joyous exchange" and the "magnificent duel," as they are often labeled, and with a host of other portrayals, Luther brought words of comfort and God's gift of new life to his people.

All other words from and about God are set in place by God's revelation and action in Jesus Christ. This Word from God, who is the Second Person of the Holy Trinity, restored the relationship broken by human rebellion and rejection of the Creator's lordship. For Christ reveals God's gracious disposition toward his people. More than that, Christ submitted himself to the law's condemnation of sinners and overcame it and every other enemy of his people through his justifying resurrection. God's Word in its oral, written, and sacramental forms delivers the benefits of what Christ accomplished in dying and rising. Each articulation of the Word in these forms aims at revealing God and his gracious will for his human creatures. Every use of God's Word is part of his plan to accomplish the death of the sinful identity of the hearer and the resurrection of the new creature in Christ.

The Inspired Written Word, Source of All Other Forms of God's Communication in Human Language

Although Luther believed that God had first spoken with his people through the oral proclamation of the prophets (Luther's designation for

15. "Lectures on Galatians, 1531–1535," *LW* 26:277; *WA* 40.1:433.28–434.12.
16. "Lectures on Galatians, 1531–1535," *LW* 26:281; *WA* 40.1:438.28–440.35.

all who spoke God's Word in the Old Testament), he also believed that the authority of the written Word in the Scriptures was primary and fundamental to all uses of the Word in God's world in the New Testament era. Only in the Bible could God's voice be heard with the certainty that tests its validity. All other writings that convey God's love and mercy, as well as all sharing of the gospel of Christ in preaching or conversation and the sacramental forms of delivering God's forgiveness and salvation, had to be derived from and faithful to the utterly reliable Scripture. In 1537 he told the Wittenberg congregation that he believed in the Trinity even though he could not comprehend how God could be three persons in one God because "Holy Scripture, which is God's Word, says so; and I abide by what it states."[17]

Because all Christians of his time found God's authoritative revelation in Scripture, Luther had little occasion or need to argue for biblical authority. He took it for granted. Nonetheless, it is clear from the ways he preached and taught that the Bible was the only ultimate, foundational source of his knowledge of God and the final judge in all matters relating to God's revelation of himself. Casual references confirm this throughout his writings: "Such is the firm and dependable foundation of Scripture, if we are to believe the Word of God," he commented in the course of his definition of the public ministry.[18] More specific formal statements affirm this presupposition. To find the basis of their faith, believers should turn to Scripture and think of it "as the loftiest and noblest of holy things, as the richest of mines which can never be sufficiently explored, in order that you may find that divine wisdom which God here lays before you in such simple guise as to quench all pride."[19] It provides the foundation and therefore the touchstone and test for all theology. Wittenberg hearers were urged to examine any idea regarding God that came to them "to see whether it is founded on Holy Scripture, whether or not God has commanded and ordered it."[20]

Luther placed himself under God's Word in Scripture. Called to be a professor of Bible, he felt himself bound to proclaim and exposit the text of Scripture for the good of the church and not according to his own whims or fancies. After twenty years of lecturing on the Bible, he told the congregation in Wittenberg to lay aside reason as a judge of truth and to ignore those who argue that God's Spirit could speak from within them. They were

17. "Sermons on John 1 and 2, 1537," *LW* 22:6; *WA* 46:542.5–6.
18. "Concerning the Ministry, 1523," *LW* 40:36; *WA* 12:190.32–34.
19. "Preface to the Old Testament, 1545 (1523)," *LW* 35:236; *WA* DB 8:12.1–5.
20. "Sermons on John 6–8, 1530–1532," *LW* 23:174; *WA* 33:275.12–14.

to look solely to Scripture. For if you fail to cling to it, both the factious spirits and your reason will soon mislead you. I myself am also a doctor and have read Scripture, and yet I experience this daily. If I am not properly clad in my armor, such thoughts come to me, and I stand in danger of losing Christ and the Gospel. If I am to stand my ground, I must constantly adhere to Scripture. . . . These articles of faith which we preach are not based on human reason and understanding, but on Scripture; it follows that they must not be sought anywhere but in Scripture or explained otherwise than with Scripture.[21]

In 1539 he wrote, "Scripture, too, must remain master and judge, for when we follow the brooks [that flow out of the spring of Scripture, the origin of God's Word; these brooks are pious writings of other Christians, especially the church fathers] too far, they lead us too far away from the spring and lose both their taste and nourishment."[22] Luther joined Augustine of Hippo in ascribing to Scripture the authority of God himself, who does not lie and err.[23]

Relatively early in his career as a reformer, Luther wrote a short treatise urging readers to "avoid human teachings." In it he made clear his view of the origin of the Scriptures. "The words of the apostles were committed to them by God and confirmed and proved by great miracles." Since the words of the apostles are from God, the reformer condemned papal teachings, for they were "contrary to Scripture and the gospel. . . . The Scriptures, although they too are written by people, are neither of human origin nor from human beings but from God."[24] Because of this, Luther rejected a Jewish interpretation of Genesis 19:23–25 that altered a particle into a pronoun with indignation: "Who ordered them to have the audacity to do this in the case of God's Book? For if one were at liberty to trifle in this way with Holy Scripture, no article of faith would remain intact. . . . But let us be and remain his pupils, and let us not change the Word of God; we ourselves should be changed through the Word."[25]

The church receives both truth and life from the Scriptures that the Holy Spirit gave his people.[26] Scripture was never for Luther a simple repository of information for God's people, or an earthly description of a heavenly or spiritual reality. Scripture is the living Word of the Lord, Luther was confident, as he lifted its words from the page to deliver God's condemning and saving will and activity for his students and the

21. "Sermons on 1 Corinthians 15, 1532–1533," LW 28:79–80; WA 36:504.13–32.
22. "On the Councils and the Church, 1539," LW 41:20; WA 50:520.6–10.
23. "On the Councils and the Church, 1539," LW 41:25–27; WA 50:524.12–526.10.
24. "Avoiding the Doctrines of Men and a Reply to the Texts Cited in Defense of the Doctrines of Men, 1522," LW 35:152–53; WA 10.2:91.12–92.7.
25. "Genesis Lectures, 1535–1545," LW 3:297; WA 43:87.35–40.
26. "On the Councils and the Church, 1539," LW 41:51–52; WA 50:545.35–547.11.

people of Wittenberg. Also in its authoritative and written form, God's Word is mighty and accomplishes his will.

All Christians have recognized that sinful minds and emotions misinterpret the Word of the Lord and twist it to their own devices. So all Christians always have some summary of God's Word to help guide public teaching and the congregation's public confession of faith. Scripture is indeed a primary authority for most Christians, but all Christians have secondary authorities alongside or directly under it. Early in the church's history the practice of identifying the church through a statement of faith, a creed, flourished. There are, to be sure, fellowships within the larger body of Christ that claim to have no creed but the Bible. Yet such groups automatically reject certain interpretations of Scripture and guide their people without discussion or contemplation to a specific construal of individual biblical passages. Whether formally codified and recognized or only informally put to use (and thus often in more arbitrary fashion), these secondary authorities assist believers in formulating their understanding of the biblical message and provide a vehicle for public confession of the faith and regulation of the church's life and teaching.

Because many of Luther's own contemporaries experienced him as a person whom God chose as successor of Elijah and John the Baptist, giving him a critical place in God's history of saving his people, the earliest followers of Wittenberg theology regarded Luther's own opinions as a secondary authority in helping them understand Scripture and from it to formulate God's message for their time. Others continued to use the ancient fathers of the church, above all Augustine, as a basis for figuring out how to solve problems in biblical interpretation. Though they used their patristic readings with a critical eye,[27] they sometimes forced the fathers into the Wittenberg analogy of faith, presuming that the ancient words would mean in the sixteenth century what Luther and Melanchthon were teaching them. By the end of the sixteenth century, the majority of German Lutherans had settled on the *Book of Concord* as their standard for public confession, their "symbol," in the sense of the Greek word used by the ancient church for "creed." They called its documents "the Lutheran confessions" because Philip Melanchthon had named his Lutheran creed, prepared in Augsburg as an explanation of Lutheran reform and a statement of Lutheran adherence to the universal tradition of the church, a "confession."[28]

In the concluding "confession" in the *Book of Concord*, the Formula of Concord of 1577, the Lutheran churches of Germany confessed that

---

27. Scott Hendrix, "Deparentifying the Fathers: The Reformers and Patristic Authority," in *Auctoritas Patrum: Zur Rezeption der Kirchenväter im 15. und 16. Jahrhundert*, ed. Leif Grane, Alfred Schindler, and Markus Wriedt (Mainz: Philipp von Zabern, 1993), 55–68.

28. The texts are found in *The Book of Concord* and the *BSLK*.

"the prophetic and apostolic writings of the Old and New Testaments" are "the pure, clear fountain of Israel, which alone is the one true guiding principle, according to which all teachers and teaching are to be judged and evaluated." The Bible is the only source and rule of the teaching that effects God's will and reveals his person to fallen humankind. Under the Scriptures the Concordists of this document placed the ancient creeds of the church as a correct summary "on the basis of God's Word in short articles or chief parts [topics] against the adulterations of the heretics." Alongside the ancient creeds as secondary authorities they set the Augsburg Confession. "In these last times our merciful God, by his special grace, has through the faithful ministry of that most outstanding man of God, Dr. Luther, once again brought to light out of the horrible darkness of the papacy the truth of his Word. This teaching, drawn from and in accord with the Word of God, is summarized in the articles and chief parts of the Augsburg Confession in opposition to the adulterations of the papacy and other sects."[29]

As interpretations of the "genuine and true meaning of the Augsburg Confession," the Formula of Concord adds its own text to the secondary authorities of its churches: the Apology of the Augsburg Confession, Luther's catechisms and his Smalcald Articles, and thus, by implication, Melanchthon's Treatise on the Power and Primacy of the Pope. These documents function as guides and referees for Lutherans as they seek to proclaim God's Word, as given authoritatively in Scripture, and teach it faithfully for the conversion of those outside the faith and for the strengthening and edification of those who already believe in Christ.

Doubts about biblical authority have always plagued the church. They may spring from the fallen human desire to avoid God's authority, or they may spring from the failure of Scripture to meet certain humanly devised standards for consistency or performance. It may simply seem foolish that God's message for humankind comes in a little book of some thousand to fifteen hundred pages, depending on the size of type and dimensions of the page. It may seem quite ineffective that God works through literary productions so easily challenged by human investigation based on standards of judgment from other ages and cultures. But by its nature, Scripture is God's testimony, and its power is derived from God's claim and promise, his command and threat. From a God whose modus operandi placed crucifixion in the center of his rescue of his people, one cannot expect more than this sort of book.

As the Word of God, the biblical text will not submit to human domination. God speaks his final word for human creatures from the cross and empty tomb and through the word he gave the prophets and the

29. Preface, *Book of Concord*, 5; *BSLK*, 3.

apostles. The words of Scripture cannot help but appear, like the God-man Jesus, to be weak and foolish to those who stand apart from the cross (1 Cor. 1–2). Often Lutherans, like other Christians, have experienced frustration with scriptural authority because it does not seem to accomplish the purifying of the church and the correction of false teaching in the way we wish to construct a secure world for ourselves. Therefore, it sometimes seems best to flee to other means of asserting ultimate authority in the church.

Some people use some form of rationality and logic at hand in their culture as, or delude themselves into thinking that their presuppositions provide, a key to Scripture. Others combine their culturally conditioned rationality with a stance of independence: "I can teach what seems best to me," say some. Others flee to "the long tradition" of the church through history and hope in some indefinite and indefinable core of fundamental teaching throughout the ages, to find security and intellectual assurance as well as good order for God's church. They appeal to the ancient "rule" or "analogy of faith." But historical blindness is required to propose that anything close to all Christians in all places at all times have agreed on any set or series of doctrines. To make such a claim demands beginning with one's own definition of the qualifications for being Christian and setting aside anyone who falls outside those parameters. Thus, the problem remains that in "the long tradition" or any given formulation of the "rule of faith," we find all sorts and manners of biblical interpretation, and we usually choose to cling to those citations that match our own predispositions. Looking to "the long tradition" is in the end not much different from declaring, "I can teach what seems best to me," because the tradition as a whole gives the individual countless options from which to choose what he or she prefers. The Wittenberg theologians seem to have been aware of this and therefore insisted that the practice of theology be disciplined by a spirit of repentance that repeatedly returns to the biblical text to test all formulations of its message.

The same can be said about resolutions of church bodies adopted or promulgated by ecclesiastical assemblies or ecclesiastical officials, and about bishops and all other human authorities, whatever lineage they may claim. They respond with what "we" think best, and indeed all believers are called to their best thinking at all times. But to assign our own proclamation and promulgation secondary authority in the church is a dangerous thing. The Holy Spirit creates "confessions of faith" (Acts 15:28). Individual believers and even entire churches are called simply to perform the act of confessing the faith, to continue to test their own confessions and their own secondary authorities, and to leave it to the Holy Spirit to make such confessions into useful subsidiary authorities for his church. Students of God's Word live a life of "repentance" that brings them to continual review of what they have been teaching and how they have formulated and delivered the content of Scripture to their hearers. For even when they know that their reproduction of its content is not false, they often recognize that the changing situation of the hearer compels a reformulation of the message of the biblical text, though always under the discipline of the text.

Lutherans have never officially determined a canon of Scripture because they have recognized the Holy Spirit at work in the biblical text apart from any decision of the church. The people of God have lived under biblical authority whether they had a formal doctrinal expression of that authority or not. The church proclaimed the Word of God orally before the canon of the New Testament was finalized, but never apart from the writings of ancient prophets and recent apostles and evangelists. The New Testament writers cited Old Testament passages authoritatively apart from explaining why those texts were authoritative (in the 433 verses of Romans are fifty direct citations of the Old Testament and many other allusions). The earliest practice of Christian worship followed synagogue practice by placing Scripture reading at the center of the believers' gatherings. Apostolic witness flowed from oral reporting to the use of the written testimony of those who had heard and seen the Lord. Today the written testimony serves as the authoritative basis and foundation for conveying God's Word of life in Christ in writing and by mouth, in print, in electronic form, in personal, face-to-face engagement with those who need to hear what God has to say to them so that they may receive life from him.

The proper confession of the faith is vital for the life of the church and the liveliness of each believer. Individual confessions in daily Christian witness or weekly preaching and teaching in the congregation usually emerge from the use of Scripture as primary authority. Each believer must face honestly the temptations to succumb to false voices from the culture. This makes it necessary to teach within the discipline of intellectual repentance. It often seems that the Holy Spirit has failed the church because of its struggle with its own errors. This is another sign of the apparent weakness and foolishness of the proclamation of the cross in the real life of the church. Our secondary authorities (such as the Lutheran confessions for Lutherans), individual rumination based on reading, prayer, and the wider experience of what is happening among God's people in our vicinity—these all combine with Scripture to guide our witness. In this rumination we also make use of what might be called "tertiary authorities," fellow Christians who have commanded our respect and elicited our confidence because of the wisdom we have found in their oral or written counsel. Luther and his colleagues often functioned as a team in just this way. The ideas of such tertiary authorities must always be submitted to the critical judgment of Scripture itself, even as they are aiding us in our understanding of the biblical text. Because God's Word is lodged in the biblical text, and because human minds will never truly master what God is saying to humankind, there will always be a circular movement in our communication of the biblical message. Our words spring from his Word, and we can check our words only against the Word we are trying to interpret and pass on to others. Such an operation goes on only under the guidance of the Holy Spirit within a community of Christ's people, and in a spirit of repentance that makes us ever ready to have the Spirit change our minds. Believers want to convey God's Word faithfully out of the Scriptures into their world since it is God's power to bring sinners to new life in Christ.

For Luther, Scripture and Christ could not be separated. Christ served as God's ultimate communication of his will for humankind and his ultimate power in transforming sinners into his own children. Christ, the enfleshed Word, acted to restore humankind through his life, death, and resurrection. Scripture, the voice of God through prophets and apostles, conveyed the saving message and its power to those who continued to deliver this saving Word through their proclamation. Not only God's action and power but also his authority rested in Christ and intervened in every subsequent age of human history through Scripture. Scripture provided the only authoritative source for the use of God's Word that, on the basis of Christ's death and resurrection, delivers life and salvation to sinners in ensuing ages, in Luther's time—and ours.

8

THE "MEANS OF GRACE" AS FORMS OF GOD'S WORD

One must learn that God is not uncertain, ambiguous, equivocal, and slippery like a wavering reed, but that he is unambiguous and certain. He says, "I baptize you in the name of the Father and of the Son and of the Holy Spirit; I absolve you of your sins, etc." Here the Father, Son, and Holy Spirit make no mistake; they are not tossed about by the wind but are rocks and Selah, as God is often named in the Psalms because he is absolutely firm. You may rely solidly on him and say, "I am holy and saved. I am God's child and heir because I have been baptized."

Luther, "Genesis Lectures, 1535–1545"

God acts by speaking. Luther recognized that Scripture presumed that reality from Genesis 1 through the end of the book of Revelation. But Luther also believed that oral speech comes more naturally to people than do reading and writing. He was convinced that the power of God to save rests in the proclaimed word of the gospel of Christ (Rom. 1:16) and that God has joined this Word of power and life to sacramental elements to accomplish his saving will. Luther's heirs believe that God, the Creator of all things, is at home in and with his creation. They believe that no eternal principle prescribes that God as a spiritual being cannot work in and through elements of his creation that he selects to

175

accomplish his purposes. They further believe that the human creature, fashioned as a material being, can be approached through components of the created order such as human words and what God has made to be sacramental elements. Lutherans exult in the fact that from several directions God comes near as our conversation partner. One of Luther's most significant contributions to biblical interpretation lies in his insight that God uses these selected components of his created world to effect his saving will.

God Uses His Created Order to Accomplish His Will

Luther was convinced that the Creator was quite comfortable operating within his material creation and that he used selected elements of it to effect his saving will and convey his saving power. God has always used such elements in one way or another, in the Old Testament primarily as indications of his presence or signs revealing his will. Apart from circumcision, which incorporated a child into God's people and gave him an identity as God's child, this use of created elements did not actually effect his saving will. But he revealed his will to Gideon through a fleece (Judg. 6:37). He confirmed kings in office by anointing them with oil and thereby giving them the Spirit of the Lord (1 Sam. 16:1–13). David recognized God's guidance in the rustling of the breeze under the balsam tree (2 Sam. 5:24). "Christ gave all such signs not only for the sake of love but also to confirm people in the faith," that they might believe in him and through him in God and thus have life (John 20:30–31). Luther maintained that the whole of salvation history unfolds through external signs: Mary's virginity, Pilate's administration, the church, the Word,[1] especially as delivered by the prophets.

What Luther and his followers called "the means of grace" in the New Testament have the power to save (Rom. 1:16) as God fills the various forms of his Word with power and meaning. In the completion of his design for human salvation, God placed his power within specific created agencies, the instruments or means by which his grace acts to restore human beings to himself. These all reflect his nature as a God of conversation, who creates through his Word. Luther insisted on this in order to offer troubled consciences confirmation and assurance from outside the control of their own emotions or reason. Hope and peace rest on the objective promise of God external to our own manipulation. This assurance comes in his promise because he is a God who delights in conversation and who determines reality by his

1. "Sermon on Luke 18, 1528," *WA* 27:57.6–29.

speaking. "You cannot give me a single example of a person who was made a Christian or received the Holy Spirit apart from something external. Where did these Christians get the information that Christ is their savior? Was it not from reading or from hearing? It did not drop down from heaven. It came from Scripture and the Word. . . . [God] always grasps something physical as a means by which he deals with you, something that is beneficial."[2]

The Wittenberg reformers found great comfort in the fact that their assurance of God's love did not rest on something inside themselves, something subject to their own emotional analysis, their own intellectual apprehension and evaluation. Luther commented on Exodus 15:17:

> In every age God has given a physical sign on this earth, a person, place, or location where he wanted to be found with certainty. For where we are not bound and [our attention] caught through a physical, outward sign, every person will seek God where it pleases him. Therefore the holy prophets wrote a great deal about the tabernacle, the dwelling and house, where he intended to be present. God acted in this way again and again, and in the same way he has also built for us Christians a temple, where he intends to dwell, namely the oral Word, baptism, and the Lord's Supper, which are physical things. But our false prophets, the sectarian spirits and ravers, have contempt for this Word and discard it as if it had no power, and they say, "Yes, I want to sit and wait until a flying spirit and a revelation from heaven come to me."
>
> Preserve us from that! We know well that water, bread, and wine do not save us, but how does it please you that in the Lord's Supper it is not simple bread and wine, or in baptism it is not merely just water? Instead, God says that he intends to be in baptism. It is designed to cleanse and wash us from sin. And in the Lord's Supper, under the bread and wine, the body and blood of the Lord Christ are given. Do you want to have contempt for God and his sign and concentrate on the water in baptism and regard it as the same thing as the water that flows in the Elbe or the water with which you cook? Or do you want to regard the Word of the gospel as the same as words or speech that a peasant would utter in a pub or tavern? For God has said, "When the Word of Christ is preached, I am in your mouth, and I go with the Word through your ears into your heart."
>
> Therefore, we have a sure sign and sure knowledge that when the gospel is proclaimed, God is present there. He intends to be found there. There I have a physical sign, by which I can recognize and find God. He is also in the same way in baptism and the Lord's Supper, for he has bound himself to be there. If I run to Saint James [that is, his shrine in Compostella in Spain] or to Grimmental [a Saxon pilgrimage locale], if I go into a monastery, or seek God somewhere else, I will not find him. When the sectarian spirits

2. "Sermon on Luke 18, 1528," WA 27:60.20–23.

preach that just as monastic life, invocation of the saints, the mass, and pilgrimages are nothing, and likewise baptism and the Lord's Supper are nothing, they miss the mark by far. For there is a big difference between that which God has ordained and established and that which human beings have set up. Indeed, you are to believe God's ordinances and what he has set up, revere them and hold them in great honor, as he said to Moses, too [in this text, Exod. 15:17].[3]

In the Smalcald Articles Luther wrote, "God gives no one his Spirit or grace apart from the external Word, which precedes" faith and any human action of turning toward God. Luther intended this statement as a rejection of those whom he called "Schwärmer," "enthusiasts" or "ravers," "the 'spirits,' who boast that they have the Spirit apart from and before contact with the Word." "On this basis they judge, interpret, and twist the Scripture or oral Word according to their pleasure. . . . This is all the old devil and old snake, who also turned Adam and Eve into enthusiasts, and led them from the external Word of God to 'spirituality' and their own presumption—although he even accomplished this by means of other, external words. . . . Cornelius had long since heard from the Jews about a future Messiah . . . [Acts 10:1–11:18]. Without such a preceding Word or hearing he could neither believe nor be righteous."[4] Luther believed that God does not abandon his people to the fickle flow of their own inner thoughts and feelings. Instead, he nailed down his promise in the body of Christ on the cross and in the Word that comes from the cross in oral, written, and sacramental form.

Luther exulted in God's grace, as he shows by addressing the five senses of the human creature. Through the hand and tongue of the minister of the gospel, God is at work.[5] "In baptism there is an oral word and a pourer, in the sacrament an oral word and a feeder, in preaching an oral word and a speaker, as is also the case in absolution." If God had sent our justification through an angel instead of through those who pour, feed, and speak, he would not have done it any other way. The angel, too, would have had to pour, feed, and speak. For God himself is pouring, feeding, and absolving. The angel would have been no more than his instrument.[6] God has so structured his world that the reality of salvation his Word effects is delivered and brought into being through selected elements of the created order. The Wittenberg reformer believed that God has placed his re-creating Word in various forms, which we can classify as oral, written, and sacramental.

3. "Sermon on Exodus 15, March 26, 1525," WA 15:209.21–210.31.
4. Smalcald Articles (1537) III.viii, Book of Concord, 322; BSLK, 453–55.
5. "Sermons on Baptism, 1538," WA 46:148.16–21.
6. "Sermons on Baptism, 1538," WA 46:149.23–150.30.

In preparing a text designed to aid believers in confessing their sins to their pastors and receiving absolution, written in 1529, Luther had the pastor ask the parishioner why he wanted to receive the sacrament on top of the absolution that he had just received. The parishioner is to answer that he desires the grace and strength that God's Word would give through the external element. The pastor is to reply by asking whether absolution has not already bestowed forgiveness. The parishioner retorts, "So what! I want to add the sign of God to his Word. To receive God's Word in many ways is so much better."[7] Hence, Luther could assure the people of Wittenberg, "You now have the Word of God in church, in books, in your home, and this is God's Word as surely as if God himself were speaking to you."[8]

In his Smalcald Articles, Luther composed a list of vital topics for discussion at the papally called council that eventually met in Trent. After his discussion of "the first and chief article" of the faith, regarding the "office and work of Jesus Christ and our redemption," he addressed the subjects of sin, the law, and then repentance, or the way in which law and gospel do their work in believers' lives. Following repentance came the topic of "the gospel." Luther's treatment of "the gospel" did not detail its content, which he had already addressed. It instead concerned how the extravagances of God's grace are conveyed to believers as "guidance and help" against sin. Luther listed five means by which that help comes: in the preaching of the forgiveness of sins, baptism, the Lord's Supper, absolution or the power of the keys, which takes form not only in formal absolution from the pastor but also in a fifth form, "the mutual conversation and consolation of Christians with each other."[9] Monks employed this latter term for the encouragement they gave each other through the gospel. The reformer and his disciples understood all these forms of the Word to be instruments through which God actually effects his saving will in the continuing struggle against evil that believers experience. "All these instruments ought to be placed before our eyes, and we are to grasp only the Word, which God gives through his means. It is God himself who is speaking when it is God's Word which someone uses to comfort you, and if it is God's Word, then God is acting here, so remember that God himself is doing it."[10] God blesses his people with the gift of restored life as children of God through his re-creative Word, as it comes in its several forms, oral, written, sacramental, in the means of grace.

7. "A Short Order of Confession, 1529," *LW* 53:118; *WA* 31.1:345.9–12.
8. "Sermons on John 4, 1537," *LW* 22:527; *WA* 47:228.22–24.
9. Smalcald Articles III.iv, *Book of Concord*, 310; *BSLK*, 438.
10. "Sermons on Baptism, 1538," *WA* 46:150.20–26, 150.33–38.

The Oral Word

Through these encounters with the Word, Luther believed that God delivers the blessing of new life. In commenting on Galatians 3:9, he therefore emphasized that the blessing of God came to Abraham through the promise, which created and sustained the patriarch's trust in the Lord. That trust, the human response to God's initiation of conversation between himself and his creatures, constitutes their relationship. In defining the church, Luther listed as its first "mark" or "sign" "the possession of the holy Word of God." Some Christians have it in purer measure than others, but in every case it is the foundation for the life of God's people. It sanctifies everything it touches and anoints people to life eternal.[11] God's people bring his blessings above all in teaching the gospel and confessing Christ in the various forms of the Word of God. There are no greater blessings than the forgiveness of sins and the assurance that we are God's children, liberated from sin, death, and evil for righteousness, and living under his rule.[12]

The Preaching of the Forgiveness of Sins Is the Oral Form of the Word That Addresses the Congregation of God's People. Luther presumed that God gathered his people into communities, into congregations gathered by and around his Word as it was proclaimed, read, and shared in sacramental form. God is a God of conversation and community. The reformer knew that the Holy Spirit had made him "a part and member, a participant and co-partner in all the blessings" of this community. "I was brought into it by the Holy Spirit and incorporated into it through the fact that I have heard and still hear God's Word, which is the beginning point for entering it. Before we had come into this community, we were entirely of the devil, knowing nothing of God and of Christ. The Holy Spirit will remain with the holy community or Christian people until the Last Day. Through it he gathers us, using it to teach and preach the Word. By it he creates and increases holiness, causing it daily to grow and become strong in the faith and in its fruits, which the Spirit produces."[13] The preaching of God's Word, as law and gospel, stands at the heart of the community into which God incorporates individual believers, and therefore this proclamation of his Word is constantly forming and strengthening the core of every believer's life. "The pupil must hear God's Word, and the teacher must proclaim it. Both must surrender to it; both are captive to it and bound to hear and to preach it. . . . For we

11. "On the Councils and the Church, 1539," *LW* 41:148–49; *WA* 50:628.29–629.13.
12. "Lectures on Galatians, 1531–1535" (on Gal. 3:9), *LW* 26:245–46; *WA* 40.1:387.21–30.
13. Large Catechism, Creed, 52–53, *Book of Concord*, 438; *BSLK*, 657–58.

are perfect in Christ and free from unrighteousness because we teach the Word of God in its purity, preach about his mercy, and accept the Word in faith. That does away with unrighteousness."[14]

Luther was soberly realistic about the fact that not all who preach God's Word are truly the agents of his re-creating activity. In commenting on John 3:34 (cf. *WA DB*), "Whoever God has sent utters the Word of God," Luther warned, "Although this text declares that he who is sent by God utters the Word of God, it often happens that many are preaching nothing but lies."[15] But when pastors faithfully proclaim what God has revealed in Christ and in Scripture, their words deliver the actual Word of God himself. "The oral Word [the sermon] and the ministry [of the Word, the position and activities of the pastor] [are] a treasure costlier and better than heaven and earth."[16] His test for true preaching was simple: "Scripture and the teaching of the gospel, however, instruct us that it is essential for us to be convinced first of all that God is our gracious Father. . . . Wherever there is the kind of preaching that assures hearts of how they stand with God, I can conclude that such a sermon is true and presents the pure Word of Christ."[17]

God has assigned the public proclamation to called ministers, who are the servants of God and of the congregation of his people. "There must be bishops, pastors, or preachers, who publicly and privately give, administer and use" the Word in sermon, sacrament, and absolution, the "holy possessions in behalf of and in the name of the church, or rather by reason of their institution by Christ. . . . Ephesians 4[:8, 11]. . . . The people as a whole cannot do these things, but must entrust or have them entrusted to one person."[18]

The reformer recognized that the pastoral office does confer special responsibilities (but certainly not magical powers or exalted status) on those who fill it. Pastors serve the congregation publicly with the Word. Indeed, Luther insisted, each baptized Christian is called by God to confess the faith and to forgive sins in Jesus's name. However, God structured human society in such a way that leaders bear responsibilities of serving in special ways, not lording it over others in the manner of the Gentiles (Mark 10:42–45), but as true servants, seeking and self-sacrificing that those entrusted to them may live forever as God's children. Luther called the pastors of Christ's church spiritual fathers, who are entitled to honor, but who also, like the physical parents of children, are not to exercise their God-given functions as "scoundrels or tyrants" might. Nor do they

14. "Sermons on John 6–8, 1530–1532," *LW* 23:234–35; *WA* 33:371.15–30.
15. "Sermons on John 3, 1537," *LW* 22:483; *WA* 47:192.16–18.
16. "Sermons on John 4, 1537," *LW* 22:526; *WA* 47:228.6–7.
17. "Sermons on John 15, 1537," *LW* 24:218; *WA* 45:660.4–12.
18. "On the Councils and the Church, 1539," *LW* 41:154; *WA* 50:632.35–633.11.

receive special homage because of their person or status. Instead, they carry out their office and functions as true servants or ministers.[19] In the twenty-first century these spiritual fathers know the difference between parenting infants and being the parent of a maturing or adult child, who helps with the task of the household in an appropriate manner.

Because God's power lies in his Word, not in the office or position to which God calls some of his people, whom he has chosen to provide service through leadership to the church, Lutherans have defined the ministry of the Word as one ministry, not as three (as is the case in some Christian churches, who have fashioned three distinct ministries, those of bishops, pastors, and deacons). The power that God gives to his people comes from the Holy Spirit and is exercised through the instrument of his Word in its various forms (Luke 4:14–15; 24:45–49; Acts 1:8; 1 Cor. 2:4–5; Eph. 3:7–9; 6:10–17), and that use of the Word is *the* prime ministry of his church. The fact that there is one ministry of the Word has never precluded Lutherans from appointing some pastors to supervisory offices, with titles ranging from the traditional "bishop" to its translation as "superintendent" or "president." It has also not prevented Lutheran churches from creating ministries that provide special services for the congregation or the wider church under the pastor's leadership. Such ministries can deliver a wide variety of spiritual and also physical help to the people of God and the communities in which they live. But the one ministry exists to proclaim the message of Christ because God ordained this ministry of the Word for the purpose of bringing the power of the saving message of Jesus Christ to those who had rejected their Creator's lordship. Whatever else is needed in specific cultural situations, whether "higher" leadership or practical servanthood, the church may well be categorized as a humanly devised institutional form. But God instituted the ministry of the Word for the purpose of returning life to sinners, and that stands at the heart of his enterprise. "For the proclamation of God's Word to function properly it must be distinguished as law and gospel. Therefore, the calling of the preacher includes carrying out the Holy Spirit's convicting the world of sin (John 16:9). God's kingdom, ruled by the Word and the ministry of the Word, must bring people to repentance so that they can understand why the gospel of forgiveness and new life is necessary for them."[20]

At the heart of the office of public proclamation and therefore at the center of caring for a congregation rests the gospel of Jesus Christ. It creates new life and salvation; it sustains that life in the faithful people of

19. Large Catechism, Ten Commandments, 158–66, *Book of Concord*, 408–9; *BSLK*, 601–3.

20. "Sermons on John 16, 1537," *LW* 24:336; *WA* 46:34.28–37.

God. Addressing the Wittenberg congregation, Luther explained Peter's admonition to declare the power and works of God (1 Pet. 2:9):

> I preach and you believe that you are redeemed by baptism, not from pestilence and leprosy but from death, sin, and the power of the devil, and that baptism works salvation and eternal life in me. It is a miracle that a person who is condemned and lost, who died and is stinking in his grave, should have this consolation: his sins are forgiven, grace and mercy will surround and shine on him, and he will be blessed eternally. This is the message which is to be preached. . . . Those are the marvelous deeds God effects through us by the ministry of oral preaching.[21]

The preacher does not make his hearers an offer, in reaction to which they can sovereignly make a decision to accept or reject. It is true that with the mysterious continuing sin in the lives of the baptized, Christ's people can ignore or reject what the preacher in God's stead gives them. But give them he must: "I dare not say, 'Do you want God's mercy, or do you not?' The preacher must say, 'Here you have the gospel, which gives you forgiveness of sin and does not judge your evil conscience, so that you need not fear sin and death.'" Those who refuse this gift stand condemned, but the preacher indeed passes on God's grace and goodness.[22] This Word that is preached indeed embodies God's power and Christ's presence, both as law and as gospel. "Christ himself is present when I preach. Not only am I aware that it is his Word that I proclaim, that this Word is true, and that you will be dashed to pieces; but I also know that he himself will enforce this Word. I know that the Word will be followed by the fist, that what I preach will happen, and that you will perish. For Christ is present and makes my words come true. Action follows upon the words."[23]

Luther believed that God's actions take place through his Word. Twenty-first-century speakers of that Word know that they are God's instruments for conveying his life-changing, re-creative message.[24] When God speaks through his people, sinners are changed into children of God. People around the world are thirsting for new information that can solve their problems. Much more, they are striving to find a place where they belong and can enjoy the support of a community. Even more, they long for assurance that they are acceptable to others, that their identity is secure, that they will not simply be swept away by events rushing beyond their control. Through the mouths of Christians, the Word of

21. "Sermons on John 3, 1537," *LW* 22:479–80; *WA* 47:189.31–41.
22. "Sermons on John 7, 1531," *LW* 23:341; *WA* 33:549.13–550.29.
23. "Sermons on John 8, 1531," *LW* 23:386–87; *WA* 33:629.4–16.
24. Forde, *Theology Is for Proclamation*, 57–146.

God brings to these people the very power of God to place them within God's family and to bestow on them the identity that God guarantees, their identity as his children.

Absolution Is the Oral Form of God's Word That Addresses Individual Believers. The mystery of continuing sin and evil in the lives of the baptized imposes on God's people a life of battle against temptation. The gospel of Christ combats the continuing re-emergence of sin in believers' lives, through each of its media. Critical for this battle in the opinion of the Wittenberg reformers are private confession and absolution. The power Christ had promised to his church (Matt. 16:19; 18:18–19; John 20:22–23), and the power to save that Paul had attributed to the gospel as it is spoken in Christ's community (Rom. 1:17)—all this power formed the basis of Luther's conviction that God acts through his absolving Word to abolish sin and bring life and salvation to light among his people.

What the medieval church had labeled the office of the keys, because of Christ's reference to the keys of heaven in Matthew 16:19, Luther celebrated as authority given to the church to bind and loose sins, to exercise law and gospel in believers' lives. Both because of "the wild young people" who needed to be confronted with their sinfulness and because of the weak consciences who need the reinforcement of absolution, he argued that private confession and absolution should be continued.[25] Amid the distractions and discouragement of daily life in a sinful world, believers ought not to abandon themselves to their own thoughts and feelings. It is the devil who turns people from the external Word of God to "spirituality" and their presumption that they can make contact with the Holy Spirit through such inner movements of the soul.

The external Word creates faith, Luther insisted in an addition to his treatment of confession and absolution in the Smalcald Articles.[26] Believers need the personal engagement with another believer in order to have the forgiveness of Christ prevail over their own doubts and uncertainty about whether God intends to give them, as individual sinners, his forgiveness and new life. Therefore, beyond the confession of sins in the heart that leads the faithful to cling to Christ's cross, and beyond confession to other people that leads to hearing God's word of forgiveness, Luther urged those who were using the Small Catechism to approach their confessor with the confession of their transgressions against the Ten Commandments. He advised them, in the presence of this confessor, to confront their abuses of the situations into which God had placed them in the family, in their occupations, in society, and in the church. Then they were to "receive the absolution, that is, forgiveness, from the confessor

25. Smalcald Articles (1537) III.viii.2, *Book of Concord*, 321; *BSLK*, 453.
26. Smalcald Articles III.viii.3–13, *Book of Concord*, 322–23; *BSLK*, 453–56.

as from God himself and by no means doubt but firmly believe that [their] sins are thereby forgiven before God in heaven."[27] The confessor should pronounce that absolution and then, with appropriate passages of Scripture, "comfort and encourage to faith those whose consciences are heavily burdened or who are distressed and under attack."[28]

God had commanded baptism; he had commanded prayer. Luther asserted, however, that command is not necessary in the case of absolution. All Christians recognize the reassertion of sinfulness in their lives. They do not like this sinfulness, or they recognize that they like it too much. In either case the believer realizes the need to combat the sin and to get rid of it. "Their own consciences would persuade Christians and make them so anxious that they would rejoice and act like poor, miserable beggars who hear that a rich gift of money or clothes is being given out at a certain place; they would hardly need a bailiff to drive and beat them but would run there as fast as they could so as not to miss the gift. . . . Thus we teach what a wonderful, precious, and comforting thing confession is, and we urge that such a precious blessing should not be despised." Luther concluded, "Those who really want to be upright Christians and free from their sins, and who want to have a joyful conscience, truly hunger and thirst already. They snatch at the bread just like a hunted deer, burning with heat and thirst, as Psalm 42[:1] says. . . . That is, as a deer trembles with eagerness for a fresh spring, so I yearn and tremble for God's Word or absolution and for the sacrament."[29]

The contemporary world's fixation on personal privacy locks many people in lonely cells, with only their own fear, guilt, or shame to keep them warm. The heat of self-recrimination and self-reproach can torment and finally smother those whose remorse and disgrace truly mortify them. God intervenes with his Word of life through Christ, with his promise of putting the sinner's identity as sinner into Christ's tomb. No imagination is required when a fellow believer expresses that promise in audible words. Only trust must be there, trust that the Holy Spirit creates and renews through the power of the Word.

The Mutual Conversation and Consolation of Believers Is the Oral Form of the Word That Takes Place in the Course of Daily Life. Luther believed that God had entrusted the Word to all believers for their use in their own lives and the lives of fellow Christians, starting with their family circle. For instruction in that circle he designed his Small Catechism, reminding readers at the beginning of each unit that he had written it "in a simple way in which the head of the household was to present them" to children

---

27. Small Catechism, Confession, 17–26, *Book of Concord*, 360–61; *BSLK*, 518–19.
28. Small Catechism, Confession, 29, *Book of Concord*, 362; *BSLK*, 519.
29. Large Catechism, Confession, 32–35, *Book of Concord*, 479–80; *BSLK*, 732–33.

and servants within that household.[30] Therefore, the reformer also strove to cultivate in his hearers in the Wittenberg congregation the practice of informally delivering the forgiveness of sins that he labeled the mutual conversation and consolation of believers with one another.

Luther explained that believers "have no other reason for living on earth than to be of help to others. . . . He permits us to live here in order that we may bring others to faith, just as he brought us."[31] He preached these words to his Wittenberg hearers some seven years before he composed his catechisms. As he continued his way through Peter's First Epistle, he came to 2:9. He equated Peter's words "You are a royal priesthood" with "You are Christians." He then explained to the people of Wittenberg what it meant that God had called and appointed priests to proclaim God's wonderful deeds that brought them out of darkness into the light and delivered them from all evils. "Thus you should also teach other people how they, too, come into such light. For you must bend every effort to realize what God has done for you. Then let it be your chief work to proclaim this publicly and to call everyone into the light into which you have been called."[32]

The Lord's commission of his people to speak his Word extended to all of them on the basis of their baptism, Luther was convinced. In his postil for the nineteenth Sunday after Trinity, he wrote that

> all who are Christians and have been baptized have this power [to forgive one another's sins]. For with this they praise Christ, and the word is put into their mouth, so that they may and are able to say, if they wish, and as often as it is necessary: "Look! God offers you his grace, forgives you all your sins. Be comforted; your sins are forgiven. Only believe, and you will surely have forgiveness." This word of consolation shall not cease among Christians until the last day: "Your sins are forgiven, be of good cheer." Such language a Christian always uses and openly declares the forgiveness of sins. For this reason and in this manner a Christian has power to forgive sins.[33]

The reformer elaborated on this "mutual conversation and consolation" of believers in his Large Catechism. When "some particular issue weighs on us or attacks us, eating away at us until we can have no peace," or when we "find ourselves insufficiently strong in faith," then

30. Small Catechism, *Book of Concord*, 351, 354, 356, 359, 362, 364; *BSLK*, 507, 510, 512, 515, 519, 521.

31. "Sermons on 1 Peter, 1522," *LW* 30:11; *WA* 12:267.3–7.

32. "Sermons on 1 Peter, 1522," *LW* 30:64–65; *WA* 12:318.26–319.6.

33. "Luther's Church Postil, Sermon on Matthew 9:1–8, 1526," in *Sermons of Martin Luther*, ed. John Nicholas Lenker (1905; repr., Grand Rapids: Baker Books, 1983), 209; *WA* 10.1:412–14.

Luther advised laying our troubles before another believer "at any time and as often as we wish." From fellow Christians, believers receive "advice, comfort, and strength." For "by divine ordinance Christ himself has placed absolution in the mouths of his Christian community and commanded us to absolve one another from sins. So if there is a heart that feels its sin and desires comfort, it has here a sure refuge where it finds and hears God's Word because through a human being God looses and absolves from sin."[34] Nearly a decade later, in preaching on John 14:13–14, Luther explained that Christians naturally want to help others receive deliverance and life in Christ as they themselves have. "A Christian cannot be still or idle but constantly strives and struggles mightily, as one who has no other object in life than to disseminate God's honor and glory among the people, that others may also receive such a spirit of grace."[35] While preaching to the Wittenberg congregation on Matthew 18:15–20 a few months later, the reformer provided concrete details about his vision of Christians sharing the gospel with each other individually or in small groups:

> Here Jesus is saying that he does not only want [the condemnation of sin and proclamation of the forgiveness of sins] to take place in the church, but he also gives this right and freedom where two or three are gathered together, so that among them the comfort and the forgiveness of sins may be proclaimed and pronounced. He pours out [his forgiveness] even more richly and places the forgiveness of sins for them in every corner, so that they not only find the forgiveness of sins in the congregation but also at home in their houses, in the fields and gardens, wherever one of them comes to another in search of comfort and deliverance. It shall be at my disposal when I am troubled and sorry, in tribulation and vulnerable, when I need something, at whatever hour and time it may be. There is not always a sermon being given publicly in the church, so when my brother or neighbor comes to me, I am to lay my troubles before my neighbor and ask for comfort. . . . Again I should comfort others, and say, "Dear friend, dear brother, why don't you lay aside your burdens. It is certainly not God's will that you experience this suffering. God had his Son die for you so that you do not sorrow but rejoice."[36]

Standing in the shadow of the cross, believers do not always have an explanation for the evil others encounter. They have something better. They bring the person of Christ and the restoration of life that flows from his empty tomb to those whose lives are ragged and torn. This model

---

34. Large Catechism, Confession, 13–14, *Book of Concord*, 477–78; *BSLK*, 728–29.

35. "Sermons on John 14, 1537," *LW* 24:87–88; *WA* 45:540.14–23. Cf. "The Sacrament of the Body and Blood of Christ—against the Fanatics, 1526," *LW* 36:359; *WA* 19:482–523.

36. "Sermons on Matthew 18–24, 1539–1540," *WA* 47:297.36–298.14.

of confessing the faith to others, which the princes and municipal representatives of Germany presented to the church in Augsburg in 1530, calls all of their followers to continue confessing the faith while conversing with fellow believers in their own congregations in edification, with those outside the faith in evangelization, and with the wider household of faith in ecumenical sharing of insights and concerns.[37]

God has woven his chosen children into a community of mutual love and support. In the torn and tattered societies of the early twenty-first century, this fact takes on new importance. Other natural and artificially constructed communities can do many things for people, but only within the church can people give each other the forgiveness and new life that Christ has won for them. At the very heart of such a community lies the power of God's Word to heal and reconcile, to regain the harmony among God's people through restoring the peace that God gives through Christ, to set loose God's power against the murderous lies of Satan. The Word goes forth among God's people in several ways, including their conversing with each other and consoling one another. The Word in the mouth of the called Servant of the Word, the pastor, is the same Word that the Holy Spirit places in the mouths of all believers. In their mouths it has the same power as it does in preaching and formal absolution. It forgives sins, defies evil, and bestows life and salvation.

The Written and Read Word

Luther paid much attention to proclaiming the gospel and instructing his contemporaries through oral forms of the Word, for the majority of Europeans in his day could not read, though a growing minority of them could. Luther was aware of that and did many things to cultivate the proper reading and use of Scripture as a "means of grace" (although he never called Scripture reading that), an instrument of salvation, as he trained his students, who left the University of Wittenberg to care for God's people in congregations. He also worked hard to bring the biblical message to those parishioners through writings especially designed for their use, devotional materials, hymns, his translation of the Bible, and his catechisms. Toward the end of his life the reformer also set forth advice for believers' daily engagement with the biblical text, facilitating conversation with God through study of the written Word because "you should know that the Holy Scriptures constitute a book which turns the wisdom of all other books into foolishness, because not one teaches about eternal life except this one alone."[38]

37. See above, Introduction, pp. 16–19.
38. "On the Councils and the Church, 1539," *LW* 34:285–87; *WA* 50:658.29–660.30.

The reformer suggested three elements necessary for fruitful listening to what God was saying in the pages penned under the Holy Spirit's guidance by the prophets and apostles. He summarized them in the Latin words *oratio* (prayer), *meditatio* (meditation), and *tentatio* (the struggles and temptations of daily life). This latter element in the reading of the Word of God replaced the reading of the text (*lectio*) in the medieval monk's program for approaching Scripture. Luther presumed that one would read the text before beginning to work on it. He knew that once the believer and God's Word engage each other, the struggles and temptations that the reader encounters in daily life form a significant part of that engagement.

Proper listening to God's Word begins with prayer. The processing of a reading from Scripture or other Christian literature derived from it is initiated when the reader follows Luther's suggestion: "Kneel down in your little room and pray to God with real humility and earnestness, that he through his dear Son may give you his Holy Spirit, who will enlighten you, lead you, and give you understanding. Thus, you see how David keeps praying in the above-mentioned Psalm, 'Teach me, LORD, instruct me, lead me, show me' [cf. Ps. 119:26–27, 33–35]." Believers pray for guidance in reading the text before they begin, for insight and inspiration while they are reading, and for proper use and application in their lives as they conclude their reading.

Second, Luther directed his students to concentrate on the text, for in it the living Word of the Lord comes to human creatures. Therefore, they should read and reread the biblical text aloud, as was still the custom in his time, giving the text careful attention and reflection, so that they might ascertain the Holy Spirit's message. God does not give his Holy Spirit apart from the external Word.

Luther presumed that this conversation with God that arises from reading the biblical text takes place amid a world in which evil is always at hand. Believers never come to the text outside of experiences that arise from their own sinfulness and their being plagued by the sinfulness of others. Therefore, Luther advised them that the reading of Scripture involved, third, *Anfechtung* (in German), the trials or temptations of daily life. "This is the touchstone which teaches you not only to know and understand, but also to experience how right, how true, how sweet, how lovely, how mighty, how comforting God's word is, wisdom beyond all wisdom."[39] The restored conversation with God takes place within the struggles and weakness of the human condition in a world beset by evil.

In the twenty-first century, believers can encounter God's Word not only by reading Scripture. The voice of God challenges and consoles

39. Preface to his German Writings, 1539, *LW* 34:286; *WA* 50:660.1–4.

them through texts that reproduce the biblical message for them, in hymns and catechisms, in poetry and novels or short stories. God comes to meet them in the graphic arts. They encounter his Word in electronic media of various forms. In each of these forms the message they hear or read can be falsely focused, as can their own reading of the Bible. Cultural misrepresentations of God's will and words slip into the minds of authors, artists, and those who view and listen to these presentations of his message for them. Because of this, believers who read or view alone want to take what they receive from private devotion into the larger circle of Christian friends. Sharing insights and questions in the congregation of God's people continues and completes personal meditation on the text.

Alone or in the congregation, believers listen to God's Word as it addresses them in its various forms. The God who initiates conversations with his children also wants to hear from them. Like a loving Father, Luther said, God wants to entice us so that, believing that he is our Father and we are truly his children, we may put the desires of our hearts before him boldly and with complete confidence.[40]

The Sacramental Word

Baptism is God's sacramental Word that initiates the relationship between the heavenly Father and his reborn child. As Luther asserted in his Small Catechism, children early in their lives should learn that baptism "brings about forgiveness of sins, redeems from death and the devil, and gives eternal salvation to all who believe it, as the words and promise of God declare."[41] In his liturgy for baptism, he added that in baptism God "showers upon us the vast and boundless riches of his grace. He himself calls it a 'new birth,' through which we, being freed from the devil's tyranny and loosed from sin, death, and hell, become children of life, heirs of all God's possessions, God's own children, and brothers and sisters of Christ."[42] In his Large Catechism he responded to those who doubted that God was at work, giving the gift of life in baptism. Some ask, he asserted, "How a handful of water could help the soul?" An indignant reply came from the reformer: "Who does not know that water is water, if it is considered separately? But how dare you tamper thus with God's ordinance and rip out his most precious jewel in which

40. Small Catechism, Introduction to the Lord's Prayer, *Book of Concord*, 356; *BSLK*, 512.
41. Small Catechism, Baptismal Booklet, *Book of Concord*, 359; *BSLK*, 515–16.
42. Small Catechism, Baptismal Booklet, *Book of Concord*, 373; *BSLK*, 535–41.

God has set and enclosed his ordinance and from which he does not wish it to be separated? For the real significance of the water lies in God's Word or commandment and God's name, and this treasure is greater and nobler than heaven and earth."[43] He elaborated:

> In Baptism, therefore, every Christian has enough to study and practice for an entire lifetime. Christians always have enough to do to believe firmly what Baptism promises and brings—victory over death and the devil, forgiveness of sin, God's grace, the entire Christ, and the Holy Spirit with his gifts. In short, the blessings of Baptism are so boundless that if our timid nature considers them, it may well doubt whether they could all be true. . . . Because of the throng of rich people crowding around, no one else would be able to get near. Now, here in Baptism there is brought, free of charge, to every person's door . . . a treasure and medicine that swallows up death and keeps all people alive. Thus, we must regard Baptism and put it to use in such a way that we may draw strength and comfort from it when our sins or conscience oppress us and say: "But I am baptized! And if I have been baptized, I have the promise that I shall be saved and have eternal life, both in soul and body."[44]

Baptism, like every other form of God's Word, is an act of God, according to Luther. He made that point in a sermon preached in 1528: "Baptism is not a human work, but it is God's work. . . . The divine majesty ordained it. It is his command, commandment, and word." That means that baptism will always remain an effective weapon in the battle against Satan.[45] Luther drew the specific parallel between God's creative action of the Lord's Supper, baptism, and absolution and his creation of heaven and earth and all creatures through his Word.[46] Because his thought was guided by an "ontology of the Word," he believed that God speaks, and the reality of salvation takes place in the life of God's chosen people. Baptism is a divine water because God has chosen to convey identity as his child under the blessing of his name. "God's name is nothing other than God's power. It is eternal salvation, life, purity. Does it not sanctify, vivify, and purify not only the body but also the soul? It does this not because it is water but because God's power is in it."[47] That power comes through the words of the sacrament. Luther explained this to his hearers in 1538 by affirming that "the priest who baptizes is an instrument which carries out the baptism. He lends God his hands and tongue, but the words are God's, not the person's. 'I baptize you' is not

---

43. Large Catechism, Baptism, 15–16, *Book of Concord*, 442; *BSLK*, 693–94.
44. Large Catechism, Baptism, 41–44, *Book of Concord*, 461–62; *BSLK*, 699–700.
45. "Sermons on Baptism, 1528," *WA* 27:33.3–14.
46. "Sermons on Baptism, 1534," *WA* 37:278.15–22.
47. "Sermons on Baptism, 1534," *WA* 37:264.34–265.5.

said by the one who is performing the baptism but by the Trinity. The Trinity is baptizing through this tool."[48]

Baptism is God's Word in the form of a promise. Luther usually shied away from using the term "covenant," perhaps because his instructors had used it to designate a deal between God and sinners that demanded some human contribution to their common cause of saving the sinner. But he did call baptism a covenant. In this instance he regarded the baptismal covenant as God's gift, totally dependent on his agreeing to restore sinners to life without any contribution from their side. Luther reaffirmed the objective nature of God's performative promise in baptism by labeling the baptismal Word a covenant. "No one can say [of baptism], 'I did this myself.' This covenant proceeds from God without our input."[49] Just as God had established his covenant with the Jews through circumcision, so his pact, treaty, covenant between himself and his people is a promise that he will be our God and that he takes the infant who was circumcised or who is being baptized into his people as his own child (Col. 2:11–13). This covenant regards the baptized as God's children and as innocent. Christ functions as chief priest of the new covenant just as Abraham did of the old. With the new covenant in baptism "God has established a covenant not just with one people but with the whole world."[50]

It is indeed a covenant that expects to produce results, namely, faith and the fruits that flow from faith in good works (Rom. 6:3–14). In the mystery of the continued power of sin in the lives of God's chosen children, believers are able to break the covenant and run away from home. Therefore, by God's law they must be called to turn back to God. Yet only the promise of life in Christ has the power to restore them to truly human living. Luther expressed this dialectic between law and gospel in the lives of the baptized in a sermon: "Baptism is an eternal covenant which does not lapse when we fall but raises us up again. If we fall out of the ship, God helps us on board once again. When Christians fall, they always remain under the promise God made to them in their baptisms. God binds himself to them so that he will help them when the baptized call upon him."[51] Luther commented further:

> You see! We make an eternal covenant with the Son in baptism, that he wants to be our God and Savior, whom God has given us as his only Son that we may dwell in his wonderful heaven. . . . He is eternal. Therefore, this

48. "Sermons on Baptism, 1538," *WA* 46:148.36–149.27. Luther repeated the point in 1539; *WA* 47:648.2–3, 648.23–25.
49. "Sermons on Baptism, 1528," *WA* 27:33.27–29.
50. "Sermons on Baptism, 1528," *WA* 27:50.16–52.25.
51. "Sermons on Baptism, 1538," *WA* 46:172.12–17, 29–35.

covenant is also eternal. Even though I fall away and break the covenant, he does not break it but accepts me again into his grace as soon as we come before his throne of grace. He will not be unfaithful even though we fall. Therefore, we should look to baptism and find comfort in it for our lives. Although we sin, we will always be accepted once again when we return. If we do not want to hold on to Christ and wander from this tabernacle, God's wrath is certainly upon us. But if we deviate from the covenant and fall outside his kingdom through our weakness, let us not remain outside it but come into it once again and ask Christ for forgiveness. He will not be able to deny it to us because he has made this covenant with us, and it lasts eternally and will not disappear. Do not accept the error that baptism only takes away original sin and that thereafter a person must make satisfaction. No! No! Baptism dare not be pressed into so narrow a spot! It is supposed to be our comfort our whole life long, that we may be restored and revived through it.[52]

God's baptismal word of promise, according to Scripture, kills and makes alive; it raises sinners from the dead, and it cleanses them of their sins (Rom. 6:3–11; Col. 2:11–15). There is no required act of satisfaction that merits baptism before or after the sacrament is administered. There is only the Lamb of God, sacrificed from the beginning of the world. He has the power to initiate life and to bring us into death. In his "Babylonian Captivity of the Church," Luther observed that while baptism is indeed an effective sign through which God washes away sins, its fundamental significance lies in the bestowal of Christ's death and resurrection on believers.[53] The description of God's saving baptismal action presented in Romans 6 and Colossians 2, along with the affirmation of its power to regenerate or give new life, based on Titus 3:3–8 and John 3:3–5, served as Luther's summary of what God does in the sacrament. Baptism is simply new birth, a bath of regeneration (Titus 3:5). Thus, Luther did not hesitate also to call it a washing in which God purifies his people (Eph. 5:26).[54] This flow of water is "the power and might which washes sins away and creates a new birth, draws us from the old [way of living] which we have from our parents and gives us a new birth into eternal life, adorning us with innocence and life."[55] It is a "bath which makes us young again, purges us from sin and transplants us into eternal life. Sin is washed away, as is God's wrath—these are the works of God."[56]

52. "Sermons on Baptism, 1538," WA 46:196.35–198.40; the concept of the baptismal covenant is treated throughout much of the sermon; 46:195–99.
53. "The Babylonian Captivity of the Church, 1520," LW 34:67–68; WA 6:534.3–20.
54. "Sermons on Baptism, 1538," WA 46:167.13–17, 167.29–31.
55. "Sermons on Baptism, 1538," WA 46:174.17–22.
56. "Sermons on Baptism, 1538," WA 46:175.1–2; Luther had already used the term "Ju[e]ngel Bad" in his preaching in 1534; WA 37:645.15.

Baptism brings these newborn believers "out of sin into righteousness, out of guilt and condemnation to innocence and grace, out of death into eternal life."[57]

In line with the passages from Romans 6 and Colossians 2, Luther bound both Christ's death and his resurrection to the Christian through baptism. God gives his children this bath of new life, in which we are washed with the blood of the innocent Lamb, who paid for sin and strangled death, who poured out his blood and conquered death. Baptism's power rests on God's arranging to convey Christ—with his death, passion, blood, and merits—to his people in this baptismal bath.[58]

> It is Christ himself, who has the power and will, which will not be obstructed, but provides salvation and generously gives the gift of eternal life. . . . Christ draws us out of unrighteousness, condemnation, wickedness, death. He draws us through baptism into righteousness, life, and goodness. Where does baptism get that kind of power? It has God as the one who is at work in it. Christ redeems us through his blood and death, and baptism makes us holy through his wounds.[59]

Luther could also say that Christ's blood functions as chrism: in baptism sinners are "anointed and seasoned with the blood of the innocent Christ." Luther reported that the ancient church fathers had said that all the sacraments—"baptism, chalice, absolution"—flow from Christ's blood, and that this bath was instituted for us as an ablution when we are born again and renewed (Titus 3:5) as "from another mother." For being washed in Christ's blood means "the presence of the mortification of sin and death as well as the gift of righteousness and life." All this is effected by the Trinity, as confirmed at Christ's own baptism.[60] "The Word of Christ brings the power of Christ's suffering into baptism. No other water designed to make atonement has the same power. For it effects the remission and washing away of sins, the drowning of death, and the putting on of the garment of eternal life because of the one who instituted baptism."[61]

This is possible because baptism is no merely human rite but a form of the Word of God. It is God who speaks the Word in baptism. God's Word remains valid for those who are sleeping; it aroused John the Baptizer in his mother's womb (Luke 1:44). It does its work also on infants

57. "Sermons on Baptism, 1534," *WA* 37:645.17–18. Cf. Jonathan D. Trigg, *Baptism in the Theology of Martin Luther* (Leiden: Brill, 1994), 92–97.
58. "Sermons on Baptism, 1538," *WA* 46:175.14–18.
59. "Sermons on Baptism, 1538," *WA* 46:175.31–37.
60. "Sermons on Baptism, 1538," *WA* 46:176.1–12.
61. "Sermons on Baptism, 1538," *WA* 46:195.4–7.

when God pledges his faithfulness to them in his baptismal Word.[62] Luther compared the state of the unbaptized, including children, and God's action toward them with the story of the Jewish people in the Old Testament. God had established his covenant with them through circumcision, and he delivers his covenant pledge to sinners in the New Testament through baptism (Col. 2:11–12). His pledge and promise that he will be God and Father to those whom he chooses is valid, whatever the recipient's ability to think. In the new covenant in baptism, "God has established a covenant not just with one people but with the whole world."[63] That covenant, to be sure, provides new birth but then expects maturing, in conscious faith in the promises of God as expressed in baptism, among other forms of the Word.

In 1539 Luther laid out the Anabaptist argument that children cannot believe because they do not exercise reason and therefore cannot say, "I believe." Luther replied, "Christ did not die for older people but for all of humankind. When a child is brought to baptism, the gospel says, 'Do not forbid this,'" "for of such is the kingdom of heaven" (Mark 10:14 KJV). Against the argument that the word "child" here refers to large children, Luther contended that their mothers had to carry them. More important was the theological understanding of what baptism, as a form of God's Word, is and does. "God is acting here, not the human creature. Father, Son, and Holy Spirit baptize. Baptism is true. If it is possible that children do not have faith—and that they cannot demonstrate [it]—nevertheless, we should piously believe that God himself baptizes children and gives them faith and the Holy Spirit. That follows from the text. Therefore, regard baptism as a divine word, for God himself does it." There would be no church at all on earth if God did not assemble it through baptism, Luther added.[64]

That baptism is God's action did not mean for Luther that the treasures of baptism remained at the disposal of those who had contempt for God's promise of life and salvation. Luther did not believe that God's Word works magically. It is his creative Word designed for conversation with his human creatures. Like Paul in Romans 6, the Wittenberg reformer believed that baptismal identity condemned "sinning the more that grace might abound." The reformer's entire understanding of the use of the means of grace was integrated into his proper distinction of law and gospel. According to Luther, God introduced the rhythm of dying under the accusation of the law and rising under the power of Christ's

---

62. "Sermons on Baptism, 1528," *WA* 27:49.12–50.3.
63. "Sermons on Baptism, 1528," *WA* 27:50.16–52.25.
64. "Sermons on Baptism, 1539," *WA* 47:655.1–657.3. Luther had made similar comments in 1528; *WA* 27:44.29–45.14, 50.4–52.25. Cf. Trigg's treatment of "baptism and ecclesiology" in *Baptism*, 174–203.

resurrection in baptism. That rhythm of life gives believers a new start each day, a start from the creative beginning that God gave life in the very beginning, with the creation of the universe, and in the beginning of our new life in Christ, whenever his Word in one form or another brought us into his family.

People at the beginning of the twenty-first century are hoping for new beginnings, for the ability to understand anew what life is all about in a world filled with failure and frustration. Our contemporaries are craving for cleansing from their shame, for a way of setting aside the wreckage of an old way of life, for a new approach to living that satisfies and fulfills the deep-seated longing for wholeness that God has planted in all people. Luther's reminder of God's great work through the baptismal form of the Word speaks to them.

The sacrament of the altar is God's sacramental Word that nourishes and sustains God's children during the course of life on earth. Because throughout the Middle Ages most people, including a majority of parish priests, could not read or write, and because the church had inadequately educated personnel to teach and preach God's Word effectively, the church of Luther's childhood made relatively little—and then often ineffective—use of the oral forms of communicating the gospel of Jesus Christ. In medieval Europe, as a result, celebrating the Lord's Supper in the liturgy of the Mass functioned as the chief presentation of God's Word in the typical week of the average church member. The Mass, however, was often interpreted and understood as a rite that dispensed God's presence and favor in a magical way, through the repetition of divinely instituted rubrics and actions. The summoning of divine presence and power into the village or town marked the center of the people's encounter with God. During the late Middle Ages, therefore, many small reform groups that arose out of the populace opposed any use of the sacraments at all or called for a simplified meal of fellowship in place of the widespread superstitious use of the Mass. These groups, for the most part ephemeral—sprouting and withering in less than a generation—were biblicists, who rejected the elaborate requirements of their priests and the superstitious legends of popular belief and practice, and in their place called for only a simple biblical faith. They were moralistic rather than ritualistic and awaited an imminent return of Christ, eager themselves to help him set up his kingdom on earth. They opposed the clergy and what they regarded as its tyranny, and therefore they rejected the sacraments, which they viewed as instruments of that oppression.

Luther's older colleague and doctoral adviser Andreas Bodenstein von Karlstadt, caught Luther's enthusiasm for reform but could not comprehend its dynamic, which was based on the power of God's Word in his conversation with believers. Karlstadt formulated his own theology according to this medieval model of protest, the only alternative paradigm for change in the church that he knew. Luther was drinking from the wells of the biblical text on which he was lecturing, with presuppositions framed from a different school than that which formed Karlstadt's way of thinking. He thus examined the medieval teaching on the Mass from another critical angle, his understanding of how God works through his Word. Luther called the church to use the Lord's Supper as a form of the Word of gospel that delivers forgiveness of sins, life, and salvation to God's people.

The Wittenberg reformer objected to three aspects of the medieval church's teaching on the Lord's Supper. He considered its attempt to explain how Christ's body and blood could be present in the sacrament through Aristotelian physics, the theory of transubstantiation,[65] to be false because it tried to place the mystery of God's sacramental action under the control of human rationalization. For the same reason he also rejected consubstantiation.[66] Aristotle's physics could not exercise mastery over God's modus operandi. Believers must receive his gracious favor in the Supper without mastering its mechanics.

In the later Middle Ages the laity was forbidden to receive the Lord's blood (the cup). This custom probably arose out of a concern for spillage of the sacred substance, but it had become a symbol of the priest's superiority over the laity, since the priest did receive Christ's blood in celebrating the Mass. This exercise of priestly tyranny in refusing to give the laity Christ's blood in the wine also offended Luther. Withholding the cup from God's people opposed God and suppressed his will because it nullified Christ's command that all Christians should drink of Christ's blood (Matt. 26:27). It subjected God's people to priestly tyranny and reinforced the claim of spiritual superiority for the one person in the parish who could receive the cup.

At an even more serious level of concern, Luther rejected the popular belief that the Mass automatically conveyed spiritual advantages apart from faith, and that through its reenactment of Christ's sacrifice it bestowed God's favor and benefits on all who attended the liturgy, whether they trusted in

65. According to Aristotle's theory of physics, all things consist of the substance, which determines their nature, and their accidents, their specific individual characteristics as individual representatives of their kind. The church's theological adaptation of this theory to explain how Christ's body and blood could be present under the bread and wine of the Lord's Supper taught that the substance of the bread was transformed into the substance of body of Christ, and the substance of the wine was transformed into the substance of the blood of Christ, while the accidents, or outward characteristics, of bread and wine remained.

66. Consubstantiation is an adaptation of the theory of transubstantiation by some late-medieval theologians, who taught that the substances of both bread and body and of both wine and blood were present in the sacrament.

their Savior or not. Against Luther and other reformers, Roman Catholic theologians protested that they did not teach an automatic, magical use of the sacrament.[67] They also argued that their concept of the sacrifice of the Mass did not distract from the work of Christ. Some of them taught that Christ's sacrifice on the cross sufficed for forgiving only original sin, while the Mass re-presented his sacrifice to take away the actual sins of daily life. Luther maintained that the vast majority of the populace had indeed turned the teaching of the church into a reliance on the sacrament as an automatic, mechanical power from God, which they could command by their own good work of attending Mass. Most, he argued, believed that their own coming to Mass earned them God's favor. Therefore, according to Luther's observation of parish life, such beliefs led laypeople away from relying only on Christ's mercy, to relying on their own ritualistic participation in the Mass and thus on their own activity for salvation.

According to Luther, God had made his re-creating Word available in the mystery of the Lord's Supper, the gift of Christ's body and blood, given and shed for his people, even as he worked in other forms of his Word. He explained in his Small Catechism:

> The words "given for you" and "shed for you for the forgiveness of sins" show us that forgiveness of sin, life, and salvation are given to us in the sacrament through these words, because where there is forgiveness of sin, there is also life and salvation. How can bodily eating and drinking do such a great thing? Eating and drinking certainly do not do it, but rather the words that are recorded: "given for you" and "shed for you for the forgiveness of sins." These words, when accompanied by the physical eating and drinking, are the essential thing in the sacrament, and whoever believes these very words has what they declare and state, namely, forgiveness of sins.[68]

In the Lord's Supper the Lord is setting the table. He is host. He gives himself in a mysterious way that conveys his forgiving and life-bestowing Word, through and with the gift of his body and blood in bread and wine, in the marvel and miracle of one more avenue for his gospel to enter into human lives.

Because reform brought revolt against many medieval conceptualizations of biblical revelation, some theologians in Luther's time rejected

67. This aspect of the dispute revolved around the understanding of the phrase ex opere operato, which literally means that something is "accomplished by the very fact of doing or performing an act." Originally intended to defend the biblical idea that the reality of the sacrament depends on God's Word rather than on the faith of the recipients or the moral character of the priests, by Luther's time it had come to mean in the popular mind that faith was not necessary for reception of the benefits of the sacrament.

68. Small Catechism, Sacrament of the Altar, *Book of Concord*, 362–63; *BSLK*, 520.

the scholastic explanation of Christ's presence in the Lord's Supper by taking an opposite tack. They moved in a spiritualizing direction. Luther combated this way of framing reality, particularly in the thought of two Swiss reformers, Ulrich Zwingli of Zurich and Johannes Oecolampadius of Basel, as well as his own colleague Andreas Karlstadt. Trained in the Ockhamistic way of conceiving of reality, Luther thought that God had had the power and right to create the world in any way he chose. At creation the Creator had not been bound by the rule that followers of the spiritualizing tendency of Zwingli and others later adapted: "The finite is not capable of bearing the infinite." Luther believed that the critical dividing line was not between spiritual and material, a line that made sense in the world of ancient philosophers, who had no strong concept of a Creator. For Luther, the critical dividing line came between Creator and creature, and the Creator was therefore able to place at his own disposal elements of his creation, both seen and unseen, for whatever purposes he chose. The Wittenberg reformer could not explain how it was possible that bread and wine could bear Christ's body and blood, nor did he devise a theory to explicate how Christ's body and blood could serve as vehicles for the Word that forgives sins and bestows life and salvation. But he was certain that with God even that is possible. He took Jesus at his word when he said, "This is my body, given for you," and "This is my blood, shed for you" (cf. Matt. 26:26–28).

Luther thought it sufficient that Christ had said it. He did not believe that God had never used simile, metaphor, analogy, or other figures of speech; he believed that God uses human language in much the same way that human beings do (yet without sinners' deceit). That meant that for the most part he interpreted biblical language literally, or more precisely, realistically (given the wealth of figurative speech that conveys reality with little difficulty in normal conversation).[69] God has his own grammar, however, as Luther had learned from years of intensive reading of the Bible. Human reason cannot always fathom and can never master God's syntax. Therefore, the Wittenberg reformer thought that there is no reason why the Second Person of the Trinity, who had assumed human flesh and blood, could not offer his body and blood for the forgiveness of sins, life, and salvation if he wanted to do so. The words of institution in Matthew 26, Mark 14, Luke 22, and 1 Corinthians 11 convinced him that was indeed God's will and way.

Zwingli objected that it was impossible for the human body and blood of Christ to be present on altars throughout Christendom since the spatially circumscribed and localized human nature of Christ had ascended into heaven to be at the right hand of God. This criticism of

69. "Disputation on the Divinity and Humanity of Christ, 1540," *WA* 39.2:92–121.

his own position forced Luther to defend his presuppositions regarding the possibility of Christ's body and blood being truly present in the Lord's Supper without somehow denying that Jesus Christ is both true God and truly human. When the Wittenberg reformer argued that in the personal union of the two natures the characteristics of each are shared with the other, Zwingli charged that Luther was reviving the view of the fifth-century heretic Eutychus, that Christ's human nature was swallowed up by his divine nature. Zwingli said that it was not possible to attribute to Christ's human nature the ability to be present in sacramental form all over the earth without threatening the integrity of his human nature. Luther insisted that the ancient teaching regarding the communication of attributes, particularly as taught by the Council of Chalcedon (451), affirmed precisely that. He summarized his presuppositions for affirming the true and authentic presence of Christ's body and blood in the Supper as follows:

> The first [basis for his teaching on the true presence of Christ's body and blood in the Lord's Supper] is this article of our faith, that Jesus Christ is essential, natural, true, complete God and man in one person, undivided and inseparable. The second, that the right hand of God is everywhere. The third, that the Word of God is not false or deceitful. The fourth, that God has and knows various ways to be present at a certain place, not only the single one of which the fanatics prattle, which the philosophers call "local."[70]

The third axiom posited that God had the power to deliver his favor and accomplish his plan of salvation in whatever manner he pleased; since Christ had said that in the Supper he delivers his body and blood for his people, that was proof enough. The second axiom dismissed Zwingli's objection by arguing that the biblical term "right hand of God" (cf. Ps. 110:1; Dan. 7:14; Mark 14:62; Acts 2:33–34) denotes God's power and glory, not a physical location "above the earth," as the reformer of Zurich had insisted. The first and fourth axioms affirm two aspects of his Christology. In the first Luther asserted, with the ancient conciliar tradition, that Jesus Christ is both truly God in his Second Person and truly human, the son of the Virgin Mary. The personal or hypostatic union of the two natures brings them together in such a way that they do not merge or mix but remain divine and human, ever distinct though inseparable. Because this union bonds them so completely, they share their characteristics even though the human nature never possesses divine characteristics as its very own, nor does the divine nature ever possess

70. "Confession Concerning Christ's Supper, 1528," *LW* 37:214; *WA* 26:326.29–327.20.

human characteristics as its very own. But inseparable, each nature can exhibit and exercise the characteristics of the other in the one concrete person of the incarnate Word of God. Therefore, the human nature can be present where God wills it to be present in the way in which God wants it to be present. It can be present as body and blood when the pastor repeats the Lord's words of institution so that the congregation may receive forgiveness of sins, life, and salvation through this sacramental form of God's re-creative Word.

Because God gives the Supper and because its reality rests on his Word, it is what God says it is, no matter what human beings think of it. Therefore, Luther was certain that Christ's words of institution bring his body and blood to the bread and wine even if its recipients refuse to receive its benefits through their lack of faith. "Even though a scoundrel receives or administers the sacrament, it is the true sacrament (that is, Christ's body and blood), just as truly as when one uses it most worthily. For it is not founded on human holiness but on the Word of God."[71]

The gospel is doing what the gospel does also in other forms when it is associated with the Lord's body and blood. In the Lord's Supper "we receive a great treasure, through and in which we obtain the forgiveness of sins. Why? Because the words are there, and they impart it to us! For this reason he bids me eat and drink, that it may be mine and do me good as a sure pledge and sign—indeed, as the very gift he has provided for me against my sins, death, and all evil. Therefore, it is appropriately called food of the soul, for it nourishes and strengthens the new creature."[72] Indeed, this sacramental form of the Word also re-creates; it restores and reinforces the baptismal identity as a child of God. Because it is God-given, this identity has staying power. Christ's body and blood transform believers who receive it into God's own people.[73]

This principle guided Luther's admonition in the Large Catechism regarding the Lord's Supper as well as other forms of the Word. On the "power and benefit" of the Word, he wrote:

> It is the one who believes what the words say and what they give [who receive that power and benefit], for these words are not spoken or preached to stone and wood but to those who hear them, those to whom Christ says, "Take and eat," etc. And because he offers and promises forgiveness of sins, it cannot be received except by faith. . . . The one who does not

71. Large Catechism, Sacrament of the Altar, 16, *Book of Concord*, 468; *BSLK*, 710.
72. Large Catechism, Sacrament of the Altar, 23, *Book of Concord*, 469; *BSLK*, 712.
73. "That These Words of Christ, 'This is My Body,' etc., Still Stand Firm against the Fanatics, 1527," *LW* 37:101; *WA* 23:205.20–25.

believe has nothing, for he lets this gracious blessing be offered to him in vain and refuses to enjoy it.[74]

Early in his career the Wittenberg reformer treated, in more detail than later, the communion that God created among the recipients of the Supper. The Lord's Supper creates communion or community between the recipient of Christ's body and blood and the Lord himself; it also creates community and communion among those who receive the sacrament. On the basis of 1 Corinthians 10:17, Luther compared the relationship among Christ and his saints to a city, the inhabitants of which are members of one another and of the municipality. He likened the sacrament to citizenship papers. Thus, believers are members of Christ and of the church, the city of God. The Lord's Supper was a reliable indication that its recipients had been brought into his fellowship, incorporated into the community of Christ and his saints.[75]

This community shares both the good and the bad. Christ shares his love and forgiveness with all the recipients, and they share that love and forgiveness with each other. But sins and sufferings are likewise shared as Christ takes sin on himself and calls his followers to suffer as they bring his love and forgiveness to the world.[76]

The Lord's Supper, as a dress rehearsal for the eschatological banquet (Matt. 26:29), conveys the promise of life everlasting. The Word of God that is accompanied by the Lord's body and blood provides comfort and hope for those who come to the Lord's feast because of its everlasting dimension. Believers at the beginning of the third Christian millennium gladly hear Luther's urging his contemporaries to take advantage of this offer of the Savior's mercy as well as all the others. "True Christians who cherish and honor the sacrament should of their own accord urge and constrain themselves" to receive it, both because of the Lord's promise and command and because of the believer's need for strength and life's renewal amid the struggles of everyday living.[77] The medieval church had cultivated concern over a person's worthiness to taste the Lord's body. The reformer told them, "This sacrament does not depend upon our worthiness. For we are not baptized because we are worthy and holy, nor do we come to confession as if we were pure and without sin;

74. Large Catechism, Sacrament of the Altar, 33–34, *Book of Concord*, 470; *BSLK*, 714.

75. "The Blessed Sacrament of the Holy and True Body of Christ, and the Brotherhoods, 1519," *LW* 35:51; *WA* 2:743.7–27.

76. "The Blessed Sacrament of the Holy and True Body of Christ, and the Brotherhoods, 1519," *LW* 35:51–52; *WA* 2:743–44.

77. Large Catechism, Sacrament of the Altar, 43–87, *Book of Concord*, 471–76; *BSLK*, 716–25.

on the contrary, we come as poor, miserable people, precisely because we are unworthy."[78] Here is a Supper Table at which members of the family always have a place, to which every prodigal may come in the new robe of repentance, with the ring of acceptance and the sandals of salvation (Luke 15:22). For those longing for community, new identity, acceptance, a new beginning—the Lord's Supper has something to give: the very body and blood of the Lord, as the means of God to forgive and restore, to make new what has been damaged or destroyed, and to bestow life within the family of God. It is a distinct form of God's Word, but it does what God's Word in all its forms does.

78. Large Catechism, Sacrament of the Altar, 61, *Book of Concord*, 473; *BSLK*, 720.

9

GOD'S WORD TAKES FORM AS HIS PEOPLE CONVEY IT TO ONE ANOTHER

Come, Holy Spirit, God and Lord,
Your grace and goodness on us pour.
In faithful senses, mind, and heart
Spark burning love and ne'er depart.
O Lord, the gleam of your bright light
Has gathered peoples out of night.
They come from ev'ry land and tongue.
This to your praise, O our God, be sung. Alleluia, Alleluia.

O holy light, our haven sure,
Your Word of life gives light so pure.
Teach us to know our God aright
And call him Father with delight.
O Lord, protect from teachings strange,
That we do not our masters change,
But with true faith and all our pow'r
Trust Jesus to our final hour. Alleluia, Alleluia.

O holy flame, sweet comfort, you
Must help us, joyfully and true,
To stay the course and serve you well.
Diverting sorrows in us quell.
Lord, by your power us prepare
Against the flesh's fear and care
Like fearless knights to nobly fight
And press through life and death to light. Alleluia, Alleluia.

Luther, "Come, Holy Spirit, Lord and God, 1524"

God gives his Word of Life to his people for their daily living. Their use of that Word brings about the death of their sinful identity, and it aims at the elimination of their sinful practices. It renews their identity as children of God, which God gave them in their first encounter with the Word. It renews the faith that seeks and strives to do God's will in thought, word, and deed. The use of God's Word in daily life involves the proper use of the Word in conveying its content to believers struggling between "the law of sin" and "the law of God" (Rom. 7:21–25). It involves responding in the faith that praises God and prays to him as well as serves the neighbors for their own sake. It involves the continuing battle against deceit and death, which are the coin of the realm of God's creature and opponent, Satan, and all his forces in our world and our own persons.

Pure Teaching

Because God's chief weapon against the devil and his chief instrument of new creation is his Word in its several forms, it is important that believers strive to convey this Word properly. Luther regarded the concept of "pure" teaching—proper, correct conveying of the content of Scripture—to be of vital importance. He believed that God's Word did not come via a magical formula or an approximate equivalence of some heavenly mystery in warm and uplifting feelings. God's Word is communication by conversation. People get to know the Creator by listening. His Word initiates conversation between us and him, a God who wants his people to get to know him by knowing what he has to say to them in the Word made flesh and in his expressions of mercy and love throughout Scripture. God's Word is not just a collection of symbols on a page but that active, two-edged sword (Heb. 4:12) that conveys a new reality. It delivers the reality of new life in Christ, even to those who have died to the possibility of conversation with God. Therefore, it was of vital (that is, life-giving) importance that the Word deliver God's intent. His intent is expressed in the content of our message. However, pure teaching is not only a matter of getting the content "correct." Our teaching also conveys his person and his intent to save. It is the method and means by which he creates conversation and through that conversation creates trust in himself. His people's communicating his Word is vital for the process.

Luther's scholastic training in the academic disputation sponsored by his teachers taught him the importance of precisely formulating the truth. His colleague Philip Melanchthon, as a leading biblical humanist, impressed on him the rhetorician's concern for accurate communication of ideas designed to move the human mind and heart. His conviction that God is a God of truth and that Christ's truth sets sinners free to live fully human lives once again required "purity" of teaching. It was a concept more important to him than that of pure foods and drugs in contemporary North American society. Luther wanted a "no contamination" label on the Word he heard. He sought to preach in a way that assured his hearers that his message was not new-life-threatening but new-life-giving. For false teaching "troubles the church and consciences,"[1] and the Wittenberg team was always most concerned about the tender conscience. Nothing, not even an angel or a holy office in the church, may override the pure presentation of the gospel of Christ.[2]

The purity of teaching that the Wittenberg reformer required meant communicating what Scripture said without domination by any other, extrabiblical, human presuppositions. Obviously, it is impossible to be completely free from humanly devised presuppositions. But these must be continually placed under the review and discipline of Scripture. Luther was aware that his own understanding of how God works through his Word fit neither into the Aristotelian logic he had learned at the university nor into the Platonic presuppositions regarding the separation of material and spiritual and the unsuitability of the material to serve as an instrument of God's gracious will. To be sure, God's Word is always conveyed in linguistic vessels and other forms of communicating that are fashioned by the culture in which God has placed his people. Believers are often drawn into subverting the message by tying it to cultural forms that belie or obscure what God wants to say to us. Believers must never stop searching the biblical text and striving to understand God's message in its original context. They must do so while always trying to discipline their own analysis and purge it of misconceptions bred by their own cultures. That is what Luther meant when he refused to be bound by human rules of reasoning.[3]

1. "Lectures on Galatians, 1531–1535," *LW* 26:52; *WA* 40.1:112.11–25.
2. "Lectures on Galatians, 1531–1535," *LW* 26:98; *WA* 40.1:179.12–19.
3. "Lectures on Galatians, 1531–1535," *LW* 26:227–28; *WA* 40.1:361.19–362.27.

Although human rationality, under the regulation of God's Word, is also a tool by which God permits his human creatures to understand what his spokesmen wrote in his behalf, Luther for his entire life remained convinced that sinful human reason will always regard it as a weak and foolish message (1 Cor. 1–2). Nevertheless, it is God's wisdom and power. Indeed, the human language of the gospel is God's power for the salvation of sinners precisely in these cultural vessels that take form in rational exchange. Thus, human reasoning is a necessary, though too-oft-untamed, implement for delivering God's forgiveness and salvation. The various forms of the Word in which this power is imparted convey meaning in propositions, composed of nouns and verbs, subjects and objects. The grammar and syntax of God's communication to his people are instruments through which the Holy Spirit creates a new relationship, a new conversation, between God and those who have been alienated from him, for those other people whom God has placed near to believers. Therefore, Luther strove to keep his teaching pure, that is, faithful to the intention of the biblical authors and the Holy Spirit, so that it might be effectively transmitted to his hearers and readers.

God's Word as the Body of His Teaching

The concept of the proper working of God's Word involves our understanding of how its whole relates to its various parts and how those individual "teachings" relate to his "teaching" or message as a whole. God teaches us: he teaches us who he is, and who we are, and what the shape of our human life is to be. God's teaching has sometimes been compared to a necklace stringing pearls, one topic after another, all of equal worth. This view defines doctrine as static, an object in my own power rather than a functioning tool under God's control. People who understand biblical teaching this way may wonder how many pearls— how many of the teachings of the Bible—they have to have on their necklace to be saved. Such a picture makes believing correct doctrine a work that human beings perform to earn God's favor. That is not what proper teaching is designed to do.

Luther and Melanchthon employed a different metaphor to describe biblical teaching: a body.[4] We could compare its head to our understanding of Christ and its heart to the teaching regarding the justification of the sinner before God. One arm might be the doctrine of baptism, the other the biblical teaching regarding the Lord's Supper; the circulatory

4. Irene Dingel, "Philip Melanchthon and the Establishment of Confessional Norms," *Lutheran Quarterly* 20 (2006): 146–69.

system represents the proper distinction of law and gospel, the nervous system the distinction of two kinds of human righteousness. With this metaphor we can answer two aspects of the question "How pure does our teaching have to be?" The metaphor helps us properly grasp the necessity of correctly understanding what the Bible teaches.

The first aspect of the question concerns matters of life and death. We can still be alive even though we are quite sick. People may misunderstand precisely how they are justified by God's grace through faith in Jesus Christ—they may have heart disease—and still be alive in the faith. But they are hindered in living the Christian life of peace and joy to the fullest. Their cultural presuppositions may obscure what the biblical doctrine of the person and work of Christ can fully mean for them—something like having a brain tumor—but they can still live and move as believers. No believer fully understands God's Word, and even some serious misunderstandings do not quench the faith that clings to Jesus the Savior.

But none of us is ever satisfied with being ill. None of us wants our friends to be ill. We worry that a friend's rejection of baptismal regeneration—comparable to the loss of a right arm—might mean hemorrhaging or even death, if the friend follows certain logical deductions from denying that God's Word in baptism saves and then altogether abandons faith in God. We want to avoid becoming lame by misunderstanding the doctrine of the church; we would rather walk boldly and surely among God's people on a sound right leg, a biblical understanding of the church. Our clearer concept of the church can enable us to stand steady and firm and thus be able to support others who are moving toward an ever fuller appreciation of God's Word. Therefore, we are concerned that we teach properly and that others do so as well. Genuine ecumenical conversation brings Christians together in the common search for the health of the body of biblical teaching.

Luther's and Melanchthon's concept of God's teaching as a body emphasizes the organic connection that links all its parts, its articles or members. If sin is not taken in all seriousness, it is difficult to develop a clear teaching on justification that frees from sin. If dramatic intervention from God is not needed for the salvation of the sinner, then the work of Christ will probably elicit only a shallow presentation. Cultural pressures to alter the understanding of sin would certainly alter the expression of how God saves his people. We cannot formulate the doctrine of salvation apart from the presuppositions laid down in Scripture about the nature of the fallen human creature, about the way God's Word functions, about the place of the church in human life.

Most of the vital elements in the biblical message are expressed in more than one way, and Christians in different cultures will emphasize one doctrinal synonym rather than another in order to bring the gospel clearly to their own contemporaries. For instance, the assurance of salvation to despairing sinners can be announced by reminding believers of God's unconditional choice of them in eternity (Eph. 1:3–14); yet it can also be delivered by focusing on God's will that all be saved through the death and resurrection of Christ (John 3:16) or by reiterating the promise of God that remains certain from its initial bestowal to the last moments of life on earth simply because God is faithful (2 Tim. 2:13).

In giving witness to the faith and in teaching the biblical message to others, believers think about the relationship among the various elements or topics of their teaching. They recognize that certain common beliefs in their culture may contradict certain parts of the body of biblical teaching even though they seem to be correct when viewed from another angle. Teachers of the faith are also aware that how we express one element of the body of teaching may alter the way in which hearers and readers understand other parts of teaching.

The cultural context of the hearers of God's Word is continually developing. That means that the task of proclaiming and explaining God's Word demands careful attention to new questions posed to the biblical text, by believers and unbelievers alike. It also requires continuing re-examination of traditional doctrinal language to make certain that it is conveying the message intended in the text. Because of this, we continually express the body of Christian teaching anew to serve the purposes of Christ's gospel in every place.

Conveying God's Word in Proclamation and Explanation

God's prophets in the Old Testament addressed his people directly with words of condemnation designed to call them to repentance, and with words of comfort and restoration designed to give them assurance that God is faithful and will not desert them. God cultivated the ongoing conversation with his people that had begun in Eden. For example, the prophet Hosea delivered the words of God in direct address: "Hear the word of the LORD, you Israelites, because the LORD has a charge to bring against you who live in the land. There is no faithfulness, no love, no acknowledgment of God in the land" (4:1 NIV). Hosea, however, also encouraged the candid and open exchange that results in forgiveness: "Return, O Israel, to the LORD your God. Your sins have been your downfall. Take words with you and return to the LORD. Say to him: Forgive all our sins and receive us graciously" (14:1–2 NIV). Through the words of Isaiah, the Israelites heard, "Your New Moon festivals and your appointed feasts my soul hates. They have become a burden to me. I am weary of bearing them" (1:14 NIV). And also, "Though your sins are like scarlet, they shall be as white as snow; though they are red as crimson, they shall be like wool" (1:18 NIV).

Gerhard Forde has pointed out that we can talk about the gospel of Christ from a more or less "objective" perspective, in what he labels "explanation," second-order discourse in the third person. In this voice believers may show one another and those outside the faith what God's actions on their behalf mean for their lives and what God wants them to be doing in their lives. But explanation is the form that believers and also those outside the faith may try to use in establishing their mastery over God's Word and applying their own rationalizing to its words in inappropriate ways, which misrepresent God's message.

Indeed, the most natural voice of the gospel is that embedded in direct address, when God's people deliver the message "straight" to the hearer.[5] In such direct delivery of the re-creative Word of the Lord, the Word performs its function of forgiving sin and bestowing life and salvation most clearly. One does bring comfort by standing alongside a distressed sinner, pointing to Calvary and to the empty tomb, and observing that Christ's death and resurrection bring new life to all who believe in him. To look that sinner squarely in the eye and declare, "The Lord says to you, 'Your sins are forgiven,'" has an even more powerful psychological effect, even though in both cases the effectiveness of the Lord's Word remains the same. In that psychological effect, faith, as the mysterious creation of God, grows stronger as it receives God's Word and knows that it is "for me."

Explanation serves a number of good purposes, including its service as a "grammatical" orientation for proclamation in the practice of learned theology. God's people often hear explanation as a word applying directly to them even if it comes in the "objective" tones of the third person. Explanation can become an exercise of shaping the biblical message into formulations dictated by our own cultural forms and our own personal imaginations. Placing what we have to say under the discipline of formulating God's personal conversation with others on his behalf has the healthy effect of forcing us to think through precisely what God wants specific hearers to receive from him at the moment.

Responses to God's Word

When God talks, his people listen—and respond. They respond by doing his will in this world, a topic that this volume has adequately

5. Gerhard O. Forde, *Theology Is for Proclamation* (Philadelphia: Fortress, 1990), esp. 87–190.

covered under the topic of active righteousness (in part 1). They also respond in direct prayer and praise to him.

Prayer

Luther did not list prayer among the "means of grace" since they serve as instruments for the Holy Spirit's delivery of God's life-giving Word of re-creation to his people. Prayer, in contrast, is the human reaction to God's coming near to his people in his Word. As mentioned above, Luther did not regard our act of praying as a "means of grace" because it is our act, whereas the means of grace are God's instruments administered through his people to bestow forgiveness on others. Prayer, Luther asserted, "is one of the precious holy possessions whereby everything is sanctified" (1 Tim. 4:5).[6] Because he believed that through prayer Christians place everything in God's hands, already early in his career he began to cultivate the public and private life of prayer among his followers.[7] Living in the image of God means, among many other things, reflecting God's voice back to him as his overflowing love is echoed in our praise and pleadings.

Luther prayed because God had commanded prayer, because God had promised to answer prayer, and because believers need to pray amid the temptations and terrors of earthly life—to be in conversation with their "loving Father" as "loving children" (in the words of the Small Catechism).[8] To pray in trust, to ask God or complain to him boldly and with complete confidence, as loving children ask their loving father, is an art that we must learn, the reformer believed. It grows out of confidence in him. Prayer turns to God constantly, with heartfelt longing,[9] relying "solely and confidently on the promise of grace, in the firm trust that God will hear us, as he has commanded us to pray and has promised to hear us."[10] Prayer rests on the foundation of Christ's name; God's expression of his love for his people through his Son assures them that he cannot give them anything but the very best.[11] From the cross comes God's pledge and promise that prayer will be heard. Certainly Luther addressed prayers often to the Father and sometimes to the Holy Spirit, but he believed that Christ had taken away the barriers that sinners erect as hindrances to their own approaching God. Therefore, Christians are to pray in Christ's

6. "On the Councils and the Church, 1539," *LW* 41:164; *WA* 50:641.25–26.
7. For example, in the "Personal Prayer Book, 1522," *LW* 43:11–45; *WA* 10.2:375–501.
8. Large Catechism, *Book of Concord*, 443–44; *BSLK*, 666–68; *Book of Concord*, 356; *BSLK*, 512.
9. "Personal Prayer Book, 1522," *LW* 43:12; *WA* 10.2:376.3–5.
10. "Sermon on John 14, 1537," *LW* 24:88; *WA* 45:541.7–9.
11. "Sermon on John 16, 1537," *LW* 24:392; *WA* 46:84.8–23.

name because they have confidence that they "are surely heard solely for the sake of Christ, our only Mediator and High Priest before God. Because of this our prayer must be centered in him alone."[12]

This trust in God's love permits the most extravagant prayers, for believers are confident that God will not submit to the dictation of their wishes. They can risk placing the wildest ideas before God because they know beyond the shadow of a doubt that he will not cave in to that which would harm them but will act faithfully in their behalf. "Since it is beyond and outside our knowledge when or how God should help us and grant our prayers, we should leave this to him and pray nevertheless. We should not stop for this reason or doubt that we are heard; for, after all, everything is done for our benefit. Even if God delays or does not give us exactly what we have mentioned to him, he is nonetheless well pleased with our prayer. Instead of what we have asked for, he wants to give us something that is far better than we can understand."[13]

Luther could regard prayer as "a sufficient exercise of faith,"[14] which seems something of an exaggeration since faith also exercises itself in deeds of love. But Luther could say that because, as the explanations for each of the petitions in his Small Catechism make clear, he believed that prayer will not be contained in the conversation with God but will spill over into the whole of life. The Holy Spirit brings the believer to pray without ceasing, not necessarily with prayers spoken aloud but also in the heart. The pulse of prayer is constantly repeating the plea that Christ put in his disciples' mouths for hallowing God's name, the coming of his kingdom, the performance of his will. Luther knew that amid spiritual struggles, prayer becomes more intense and frequent as believers place themselves firmly in God's hands.[15] So Luther could confess that the Lord's Prayer sustained him like mother's milk and nourished him in his old age.[16]

If Jesus's disciples had to ask for instruction in prayer, it is certain that many in twenty-first-century Christian congregations are also going to crave guidance for and practice at praying. For prayer is not a common occurrence in lives lived apart from Jesus Christ, at least prayer in a biblical sense. Even within Christendom there are some who practice mantralike praying in the hope, if not confidence, that they have figured out how to put a hammerlock on God with the right kind of prayer. Some like the public display of prayer as an exhibition of their own spiritual heroics, but the Lord recommended the closet for prayer (Matt. 6:7–8). Others are certain that prayer cannot change things but, with

---

12. "Sermon on John 16, 1537," *LW* 24:393; *WA* 46:85.17–22.
13. "Sermon on John 16, 1537," *LW* 24:392; *WA* 46:84.8–13.
14. "On Good Works," *LW* 44:61; *WA* 6:234.31–33.
15. "Sermon on John 14," *LW* 24:89; *WA* 45:541.37–47.
16. "A Simple Way to Pray, 1535," *LW* 43:200; *WA* 38:354.17–20.

a condescending attitude toward both God and his human creatures, recommend it anyway as a good psychological exercise for soothing or calming troubled nerves and revving up the emotional engines. All these interpretations of prayer miss the point. Prayer is the conversation of the dependent and trusting child, who is eager to voice both thanks and requests with the loving Father, who in turn is eager to hear from his children.

Talking about prayer is easier than praying. Sinners find it unnatural to talk to God, for such conversations recognize God's lordship in our lives and our dependence on God. Because prayer is a confession that we are children of the heavenly Father, it produces the pleasure of conversation between a doting Father and loving children. True prayer can be filled with the delight of a child (of any age) surprised by an unexpected gift from a parent or with the agony of the one praying in Gethsemane. Sometimes God's children overflow with praise and thanksgiving. Occasionally they may shy away from praying because they think their needs are unworthy of God's attention or that they are suspect in motivation or small in size. But no topic of conversation is off-limits in God's household. He likes to hear about all the problems that plague us; none is too large or too small (Matt. 10:29–31).

Sometimes God's children even pray in bitterness, complaint, and lament (Ps. 3; 10; 22; 69; 80). Even in those times God wants to be hearing from his children in spite of their pleading, protesting, and reproaching, for in prayer the conversation of the believer with God continues. Precisely when the believer's faith is weak and breaking, such faltering faith can overcome the anger, disappointment, or bitterness at God only by engaging and wrestling with the Father's love. Such praying can deepen trust. Christians of tender faith who quake at the thought of falling into such prayer can learn more clearly that boldness and confidence should mark the trust of sinners whom God loves. Bitter or angry prayers are not ideal or pious, but they nonetheless can be expressions of the fearlessness with which children cling to their Father even when feeling alienated from him. In the final analysis, this conversation with God expresses our longing to be cuddled on his lap and lose ourselves in his embrace. Even when initiated in resentment or fear, such conversation can lead to expressions of our gratitude, perhaps even of our delight, at his gift of fellowship with us.

The formation of a believer who prays can begin with the Lord's model, and the faithful can learn how to expand the simple words of the Lord's Prayer into an agenda for praying. Believers pray alone or with others; they pray free-form from the heart or with eyes on their prayer books. They turn to God with well-organized, somewhat sophisticated cadences of praise or request, but they also throw themselves into God's arms with the inarticulate groaning of a terrified or exhausted heart. Distracted, distraught, despairing, even driven to the verge of denying him, faith can be ignited by the Spirit's strength when human strength has ebbed. Believers pray from the heart because their hearts overflow with the pleasure of sharing with God the joys and the desires of the hour. Believers pray the printed or memorized prayers of others because they need all the help they can receive in formulating their thoughts and finding subjects for prayer. Our agenda for prayer is expanded when we use prayers prepared by fellow believers. As important as it is that Christians learn to pray from the heart, we also encourage them to make rich use of others' prayers in prayer books and devotional literature. My ability to express my own thoughts grows when I use the prayers of others. Particularly valuable are their prayers when my own spirit is so bedraggled and bedeviled that the words do not want to come. Praying with fellow believers who have previously written down their prayers strengthens the bonds that Christ uses to connect us with the faith of other times, places, and circumstances.

Prayer is never an escape; it engages life, and it engages God in our lives and the lives of others. We pray because we have confidence in God and because of the needs we and others have. We pray for them because we love them and because we know that God loves them. So we may even pray retroactively, such as when the horse is out of the barn and we want God to catch it and bring it back. For we know that he alone is the Lord even of history and can creatively counteract what has happened and seems beyond repair. We pray preemptively as well, using prayer as a weapon against evil and striking before the deed is done and disaster befalls. We pray proactively, engaging God in the strategic planning process of our lives. We may even join the psalmists in praying imprecatorily, putting the sins of others onto Jesus Christ, placing our hurts and envies and desires for revenge into Christ's wounds and his tomb as we pray for and against those who oppose us and frustrate us in the struggles of daily life. For we will be condemned if we permit others' failure to forgive us block us from forgiving them. We will be doomed to stew in the juices of defensiveness and desire to even the score until God frees us from that and calls on us to set aside these evils in prayer. We can do this by stealing our enemies' sins from them and commending them to Christ.

For God stands ready to listen to our needs and cries for help as well as our thanksgiving and delight in his blessings. He receives our complaints and our screams of pain and anger; he receives our gratitude and praise. That is part of the relationship that God created as he shaped the world and placed the human creature as its steward in the middle of it. God enjoys the conversation.

Liturgy

The conversation takes place not only between individual believers and their God. Christians, fashioned according to the Creator's plans for his human creatures, do not exist alone (1 Cor. 12:12–27; cf. Gen. 2:18). Life together in the congregation of God's people has many aspects, but it centers on God's delivery of Word and common response in liturgy. God gathers his church by preaching and bestowing forgiveness through the sacraments. God identifies himself as the one who forgives sins and bestows life and salvation. He identifies us as his children, who are filled with praise for him. Therefore, Luther included "prayer, public praise, and thanksgiving to God" among the fundamental characteristics of the church. "Where you see and hear the Lord's Prayer prayed and taught, or psalms or other spiritual songs sung, in accordance with the Word of God and the true faith, also the Creed, the Ten Commandments, and the catechism used in public, you may rest assured that a holy Christian people of God are present." He added, "We are speaking of prayers and songs which are intelligible and from which we can learn and by means of which we become better."[17]

Luther understood the liturgy of the congregation of God's children as a response to his action and his message, not as a work that human beings had to perform to win merit in his sight and command or manipulate his favor. Much of Luther's concern in reforming the church centered on worship practices, for he believed that medieval worship had silenced the Word of God, introduced "un-Christian fables and lies" in its place, and turned the divine service into "a work whereby God's grace and salvation might be won."[18] He strove to restore public worship to its central role in the conversation between God and his people.

Therefore, Luther regarded the preaching and teaching of God's Word as "the most important part of the divine service"[19] and the public absolution of the sins of the worshipers as "the true voice of the gospel announcing remission of sins."[20] Nonetheless, he also regarded the sacramental form of the Word in the Lord's Supper as an integral part of the central service of the congregation each week,[21] for it also formed a vital part of God's conversation with his people. In the medieval world, daily services had been available not only within the monastery but also at urban parish churches. Luther envisioned the continuation of

17. "On the Councils and the Church, 1539," *LW* 41:164; *WA* 50:641.20–34.
18. "Concerning the Order of Public Worship, 1523," *LW* 53:11; *WA* 12:35.15–16.
19. "The German Mass, 1526," *LW* 53:68; *WA* 19:78.26–27.
20. "An Order of Mass and Communion, 1523," *LW* 53:28; *WA* 12:213.9–11.
21. "An Order of Mass and Communion, 1523," *LW* 53:20–23; *WA* 12:206.15–209.10.

reading and prayer services on a daily basis "even though these daily services might not be attended by the whole congregation," but only by "priests and pupils."[22]

Luther's plan for reform envisioned a good deal of uniformity throughout Christendom and certainly within specific regions. At the same time he did not insist on complete uniformity in the liturgy. Such uniformity had not existed previously, he observed, and no reason made it necessary to impose that sort of uniformity in the future.[23] He even envisioned within one congregation worship in three different modes. Both the Latin service and the German service should follow the historical outline of the liturgy, he believed, but the German service should use hymns as alternatives to traditional chants. The third kind of service should take place as small groups of Christians meet in a house somewhere to pray, meditate, and plan the good works God is calling them to do.[24] Luther believed that the sermon should last about a half hour and that the entire service should "be completed in one hour or whatever time seems desirable, for one must not overload souls or weary them."[25] In this way the conversation between God and his people could continue in such a way that individuals received the support and encouragement of others in the formal exchange between God's Word in its several forms and the prayer and praise of the congregation.

The Word of God Struggles against the Lie

The conversation between God and his people is often interrupted, however, because God and his people have an enemy who wants to destroy the relationship between Creator and human creature. Luther did not believe that there is any biblical explanation for sin and evil mysteriously continuing in the lives of God's baptized children. He did recognize, however, the need to confront sin and evil and turn away from them. "The whole life of the Christian is a life of repentance," he stated in his Ninety-five Theses of 1517. Although his understanding of those words may have undergone change over the years, for his entire life he remained committed to enabling his hearers and readers to live that life of being turned from evil back to the Lord.[26] In setting forth the fundamental characteristics of the people of God, Luther noted that Christians always live under the cross, in the midst of struggle against

22. "Concerning the Order of Public Worship, 1523," *LW* 53:13; *WA* 12:36.27–31.
23. "The German Mass, 1526," *LW* 53:61–62; *WA* 19:72.3–23.
24. "The German Mass, 1526," *LW* 53:63–64; *WA* 19:75.3–30.
25. "Concerning the Order of Public Worship, 1523," *LW* 53:12; *WA* 12:36.13–17.
26. "The Ninety-five Theses on Indulgences, 1517," *LW* 31:25; *WA* 1:233.10–11.

the devil, the world, and human desires. Jesus had described the ongoing battle of the lying and murdering devil against the church (John 8:44). The early Christians had defined their enemies as the devil; the world about them, which the devil was able to marshal to deceive and kill them; and their own personal inclinations and desires, which had been perverted and contaminated by satanic lies (Eph. 6:11–12; 1 John 1:6; 2:16–17; 5:18–19).

Luther described the ongoing struggle of the daily life of believers as a continuation of God's baptismal action, in which he eliminated their sinful identity by laying it in Christ's tomb, out of his sight, and by raising them up to live a life of true human righteousness as his children, who walk in Christ's footsteps. Luther explained that this baptismal death and resurrection continues each day as "the old creature in us with all sins and evil desires is . . . drowned and dies through daily contrition and repentance, and on the other hand a new person . . . comes forth and rises up to live before God in righteousness and purity forever."[27] Repentance takes place as the Holy Spirit leads believers to say "no" to every lie from Satan and to take comfort in the gift of the new identity God gives them through Christ as his chosen child.

The struggle of the Christian's daily life involves receiving the forgiveness of sins, which banishes the thought that we might still be children of Satan and establishes firmly once again our trust in the Word of our heavenly Father, who claims us as his own children. It also restores our ability to serve him in praise of his name and in love for others without any thought of gain for ourselves from either kind of action. In our horizontal relationships, this renewal of his promise and our life dictates a battle against habits that do not serve him. The church has traditionally called this action "the mortification of the flesh." It demands the vision of faith to identify the things we are doing wrong and to find courage and strength to break with these habits of mind and action. At the same time believers are practicing a new lifestyle, which follows the shape of human life as God designed it. From faith in Christ and the perception of life he has provided proceeds the character of the new person who walks in his footsteps, practicing the fruit of the Spirit in the disposition of love, joy, peace, patience, kindness, goodness, faithfulness, gentleness, and self-control (Gal. 5:22–23; cf. Col. 3:12; the disposition of those who have died with Christ: Col. 2:12, 20; and have been raised with him in baptism: Col. 2:12; 3:1). Through the use of the Word in its various forms, the re-creative power of Christ is turned loose in both dimensions of human existence.[28]

---

27. Small Catechism, Baptismal Booklet, 12–14, *Book of Concord*, 360; *BSLK*, 516–17.
28. See the essay on two kinds of righteousness (part 1, above).

A special aspect of the struggle between God's truth and Satan's lies appears throughout the history of God's people in persecution. In the execution of his followers by Roman Catholic authorities and in the threats and slanders Luther endured, the Wittenberg reformer experienced the conflict of God and Satan, of truth and lie, in a quite personal way. Luther defined martyrdom as a gift from God, not a meritorious accomplishment of those who had cultivated a special strength through their own powers. His student Ludwig Rabus collected stories of Christian martyrs and witnesses to the faith; Rabus also described two ways in which the devil attacks God's church: through the violence of persecution and through the deception of false teaching.[29] Luther, too, presumed that believers "must endure every misfortune and persecution, all kinds of trials and evil from the devil, the world, and the flesh, . . . by inward sadness, timidity, fear, outward poverty, contempt, illness, and weakness, in order to become like their head, Christ. And the only reason they must suffer is that they steadfastly adhere to Christ and God's Word. . . . No people on earth have to endure such bitter hate."[30] At the beginning of the twenty-first century, Christians look back on one century of immense and intense suffering for the faith, in the Soviet Union, in National Socialist Germany, and in Muslim lands throughout Asia and Africa, among other places. Persecution continues and will not cease. Neither will the devil's deception in the realms of our teaching and our living. Believers must prepare each other for the day when the Holy Spirit may give them the gift of martyrdom.

Amid this struggle against Satan's tricks and traps, the only thing that can truly help the believer and defend the gospel is the gospel itself. With the victory of his resurrection, Christ has assured his people's victory in the combat against persecution and deception. His Holy Spirit gives them courage and insight as well as the ability to cling to God's Word and to wield it as a mighty weapon against all whom the devil enlists in his attempt to suppress and drown out God's saving truth.

The promise of the gospel is not only carried by human voices announcing it but is also embedded and embodied in the creaturely elements of water in baptism and bread and wine in the Lord's Supper. Therefore, as meeting places between God and human beings, the sacraments also provide a place to encounter God's saving words and actions in the daily struggle against evil in every form. They have already incorporated us into the eschatological judgment Christ endured and

---

29. Ludwig Rabus, *Historien der Heyligen ausserwöhlten Gottes Zeügen: Bekennern und Martyrern* (Strassburg: Samuel Emmel, 1554–1558), IV:ija-)(a; cf. similar comments in his second edition, *Historien der Martyrer . . .* (Strassburg: Josias Rihel, 1571–1572), II:A2a–A4b.

30. "On the Councils and the Church, 1539," *LW* 41:164–65; *WA* 50:641–42.

into his resurrection, which has made us righteous heirs in hope of eternal life. Remembrance of our new birth in the waters of baptism and receiving Christ's body and blood make it possible for the church and all its members to persevere through our disappointment over the parousia's delay. Therefore, conscious of our place in God's history and the history of his people, we experience, amid the conflicts of daily life, the presence of the end of all things, as they have been and will be consummated in God's word made flesh, Jesus Christ.

At the beginning of the third Christian millennium, Lutherans around the world are not surprised to discover that the Lord's task involves confessing him in confrontation with opponents and challengers of various kinds. It has always been that way for the people of God. God is calling us, as he calls all Christians, to continue to confess this faith in Jesus Christ, as delivered to us from the past, in fresh ways to our contemporaries. The sword of the Spirit, the Word of God, brings the power of God for salvation and thus delivers comfort and peace, assurance of God's love, and assurance of our identity as his children. Christ has promised to be with us as we live as the instruments of his Word's power, baptizing and teaching on the basis of his authority as the Author of life (Acts 3:15) and on the basis of the new life we live, received from his death and resurrection.

CONCLUSION

THINKING WITH LUTHER IN THE TWENTY-FIRST CENTURY

Conversation with people who have died always poses special challenges, quite apart from the fact that we can only listen while they talk. Although we all presume that others should, and generally do, think just as we do, we notice in conversing with living people that gaps between us and our conversation partners interrupt and distort understanding. That problem is compounded when we try to hear and understand individuals who have lived and thought within a historical context quite different from our own. Martin Luther was such a person.

For all the distance that the technological, social, economic, and political changes of the second half of the twentieth century have put between us and all whose ideas arose before 1945, great minds of the past still intrigue us and command our attention. Luther's ideas fascinate many in our time and captivate our imagination, sometimes because of the twists and turns of his career, sometimes because his way of thinking and expressing himself offers a new, even if half-a-millennium-old, perspective on the human condition. Perhaps more than those who claim the name "Lutheran," those outside the community of faith that bears his name find reading Luther beneficial for making some sense of what it means to be human. Though perhaps with different words, he posed and answered questions such as these: Who am I? What *is* my purpose on this planet? What could make my life worth living? How do I find the proper boundaries to define my life? How can I be truly free?

But like all readers, we tend to fit what we absorb from Luther's pen into our own structures of thinking. We presume that he meant what we mean with familiar biblical expressions and the common words that people in all cultures use to describe and express the human experience. But that is a dangerous presumption for two reasons. The two thought worlds in which Luther grew up and in which he was educated framed their respective descriptions of reality on the basis of presuppositions that we do not readily grasp. (Luther's village of Mansfeld, within the context of a Christianity still shaped in significant ways by pagan as well as churchly antecedents, differed markedly at points from the university culture in which he learned the worldview of Aristotle as processed by Christian thinkers.) In addition, Luther himself formulated a substantial shift in his own paradigm for viewing God and humanity as he struggled with the implications of what he had learned about himself and his Creator from his parents and from his professors. Our ways of viewing and assessing reality, too, are shaped by our presuppositions. Study of any historical figure, particularly one who left behind so much to read, allows us to step outside our own situation and look at how we are sizing up the world from another perspective. Engaging his way of thinking provides a measuring stick for our own way of thinking.

In this volume we have not tried to offer a historical or systematic overview of all of Luther's thought. Readers can explore his way of studying Scripture, digesting the Christian tradition, and assessing the needs of his people by reading his extensive oeuvre and, if they must, bits and pieces of the secondary literature about them. In this book we offer orientation for such reading on the basis of its exploration of two fundamental presuppositions that guided what Luther proclaimed and recorded from the late 1510s onward. The first of these presuppositions defines what it means to be human. Luther's distinction of two dimensions of humanity, in relationship to God and in relationship to God's creation, determined how he viewed both his Creator and himself, along with other human beings (part 1). The second of these presuppositions describes God as he relates to his human creature, namely, through his Word in all its forms and functions (part 2).

Luther's faith viewed reality in an intensely personal way. For him, God is a person who wants to be conversing with his human creatures, who live in communion or community with both God and other creatures, human and nonhuman. Luther also held to a radical distinction between the Creator and his creatures. This led him to presume, quite naturally, that God had designed him and all other human beings to be in a relationship of dependence and trust with the one who had crafted them. For Luther, however, the heavenly Father had fashioned human beings to live in conversation and community with one another, in a relationship of love and caring for each other. From that delineation of how to be human, Luther ventured into the lives of hearers and readers with consolation for the disconsolate, rebuke for the arrogant, and instruction for those who wanted to live as God's faithful children. Many people in contemporary cultures seek to avoid the kind of personal contact or confrontation that Luther found so comforting. Others in our world long for more than impersonal "religious experience" and would like to hear from a God who likes to converse and enjoy community with his people. Luther's way of thinking invites us to engage another being, our Creator himself, in a personal way. Though some crave isolation, Luther's approach to presenting the God revealed in Scripture—by means of human language, human voices, human community—is attractive to many at the beginning of the twenty-first century.

Luther also believed that God was at work in his world chiefly through his Word. The Creator defied definition at the creature's hand, Luther was certain; but the Creator also loved to engage his human creatures in the dialogue of forgiveness and faith, between his own boundless love and human trust in him. Luther had learned that God's Word has the power to accomplish that for which he speaks it. He believed that God's pronouncement of a new identity on rebellious creatures and lost strays from his Garden bestows new life on them, a new relationship with the Author of Life. He viewed the richness of God's love in the various forms of his Word, oral, written, and sacramental, as the source and sustenance of "salvation," that is, of the humanity that sinners throw away when they turn their backs on the one who breathed human life into existence in the first place. This Word of life creates the faith or trust that provides the proper orientation for all of human living.

On the basis of these two presuppositions, Luther framed his application of the biblical message to the people of his day. Those called by God's claim on them as his children to do the same task in the twenty-first century will profit from conversing with Luther through the pages of his works. It is our hope that this volume will make those pages more understandable and thus more usable for the life-giving dispensation of God's Word in the twenty-first century. Such understanding and use should enable us to faithfully employ the biblical message for our own speaking of God's Word of life and salvation.

BIBLIOGRAPHY

Primary Sources

Martin Luther's works became the first "collected works" of a living author ever published. This was in part due to the fact that he lived only a little more than half a century after Johannes Gutenberg, inventor of the printing press. It was also due to the impact Luther had through the printing press on the European mind of the early sixteenth century. The first of his "collected works" appeared early in his career, in 1521, and in 1539 the first of two "rival" editions of his writings began to appear.[1] Throughout subsequent centuries, other editions of his publications made his ideas available, and in the twentieth century, translations into several languages made his works widely available in many parts of the world.

The standard edition of his writings is now found in the so-called Weimar Ausgabe (edition):

D. *Martin Luthers Werke*. 127 vols. Weimar: Böhlau, 1883–1993.

An index to Luther's writings in a wide variety of editions is available:

Aland, Kurt, ed. *Hilfsbuch zum Lutherstudium*. 4th ed. Bielefeld: Luther-Verlag, 1996.

---

1. See Robert Kolb, *Martin Luther as Prophet, Teacher, and Hero: Images of the Reformer, 1520–1620* (Grand Rapids: Baker Academic, 1999), 149–50.

Major libraries have the standard translation of Luther's published works in English:

Luther's Works. St. Louis: Concordia; Philadelphia: Fortress, 1955–86.

Not included in this translation were his postils, the collected sermons he issued for the instruction of pastors in how to preach the Wittenberg message. They are available in two translations; the first of those present sermons composed for preachers to use:

The Complete Sermons of Martin Luther. Edited by John Nicholas Lenker. 1905–9. Reprinted Grand Rapids: Baker Books, 2000.

Also helpful are his sermons edited to be used by families during home devotions:

Sermons of Martin Luther: The House Postils. Edited by Eugene Klug. Grand Rapids: Baker Books, 1996.

Translations of Luther's writings that his students regarded as formal standards of public teaching, or "confessions," appear in the following:

The Book of Concord. Edited by Robert Kolb and Timothy J. Wengert. Minneapolis: Fortress, 2000.

Those who wish to begin reading Luther's writings by sampling his catechisms or his sermons can consult the last three items listed above. Other good places to begin reading Luther are connected particularly with the discussions in this volume:

Heidelberg Disputation. 1518. In *Luther's Works* 31:39–70.
Two Kinds of Righteousness. 1519. In *Luther's Works* 31:297–99.
The Freedom of a Christian. 1520. In *Luther's Works* 31:333–77.
The Babylonian Captivity of the Church. 1520. In *Luther's Works* 36:11–126.
On Good Works. 1520. In *Luther's Works* 44:21–114.
Sermon on Monastic Vows. 1521. In *Luther's Works* 44:251–400.
Temporal Authority: To What Extent It Should Be Obeyed. 1523. In *Luther's Works* 45:81–129.
How Christians Should Regard Moses. 1525. In *Luther's Works* 35:161–74.

For further reading we suggest:

Lectures on Galatians. 1531–1535 and 1519. In *Luther's Works*, vols. 26–27.
Theses concerning Faith and Law. 1535. In *Luther's Works* 34:109–32.
Disputation concerning Justification. 1536. In *Luther's Works* 34:151–96.
Genesis Lectures. 1535–1545. In *Luther's Works*, vols. 1–8.
Against the Heavenly Prophets. 1525. In *Luther's Works* 40:79–223.
Against Sabbatarians—Letter to a Good Friend. 1538. In *Luther's Works* 47:65–98.
Bondage of the Will. 1525. In *Luther's Works*, vol. 33.

The works of Philip Melanchthon may also be read with profit, such as the following:

The Loci Communes of Philip Melanchthon. 1521. Translated by Charles Leander Hill. Boston: Meador, 1944.
Loci Communes, 1543: Philip Melanchthon. Translated by J. A. O. Preus. St. Louis: Concordia, 1992.
Commentary on Romans [1540]: Philip Melanchthon. Translated by Fred Kramer. St. Louis: Concordia, 1992.

Secondary Sources

The bibliography of works on Martin Luther and Wittenberg thought is immense. As foundations for further study, we recommend the following titles to readers of this volume.

Biographical Studies

Bainton, Roland. *Here I Stand: A Life of Martin Luther*. New York: Pierce & Smith, 1950.
Brecht, Martin. *Martin Luther*. 3 vols. Translated by James L. Schaaf. Philadelphia: Fortress, 1985–93.
Hendrix, Scott. "Luther." In *The Cambridge Companion to Reformation Theology*, edited by David Bagchi and David C. Steinmetz, 39–56. Cambridge: Cambridge University Press, 2004.
Lohse, Bernhard. *Martin Luther: An Introduction to His Life and Work*. Translated by Robert C. Schultz. Philadelphia: Fortress, 1986.

Kittelson, James M. *Martin Luther: The Story of the Man and His Career.* Minneapolis: Fortress, 1986.

Kolb, Robert. "Martin Luther and the German Nation." In *A Companion to the Reformation World*, edited by R. Po-chia Hsia, 39–55. Oxford: Blackwell, 2004.

Oberman, Heiko Augustinus. *Luther: Man between God and the Devil.* Translated by Eileen Walliser-Schwarzbart. New Haven: Yale University Press, 1989.

Schwiebert, E. G. *Luther and His Times: The Reformation from a New Perspective.* St. Louis: Concordia, 1950.

Overviews of Luther's Thought

Althaus, Paul. *The Ethics of Martin Luther.* Translated by Robert C. Schultz. Philadelphia: Fortress, 1972.

———. *The Theology of Martin Luther.* Translated by Robert C. Schultz. Philadelphia: Fortress, 1966.

Ebeling, Gerhard. *Luther: An Introduction to His Thought.* Translated by R. A. Wilson. Philadelphia: Fortress, 1970.

Lohse, Bernard. *Martin Luther's Theology: Its Historical and Systematic Development.* Translated by Roy A. Harrisville. Minneapolis: Fortress, 1999.

Specialized Historical Studies

Arand, Charles P. *That I May Be His Own: An Overview of Luther's Catechisms.* St. Louis: Concordia, 2000.

Bayer, Oswald. *Promissio: Geschichte der reformatorischen Wende in Luthers Theologie.* Göttingen: Vandenhoeck & Ruprecht, 1971.

Cargill Thompson, W. D. J. *The Political Thought of Martin Luther.* Sussex: Harvester, 1984.

Dingel, Irene. "Philip Melanchthon and the Establishment of Confessional Norms." *Lutheran Quarterly* 20 (2006): 146–69.

Edwards, Mark U., Jr. *Luther and the False Brethren.* Stanford: Stanford University Press, 1975.

———. *Luther's Last Battles: Politics and Polemics, 1531–1546.* Ithaca, NY: Cornell University Press, 1983.

———. *Printing, Propaganda, and Martin Luther.* Berkeley: University of California Press, 1994.

Elert, Werner. "Deutschrechtliche Züge in Luthers Rechtfertigungslehre." In *Ein Lehrer der Kirche: Kirchlich-theologische Aufsätze und Vorträge von Werner Elert*. Edited by Max Keller-Hüschemenger, 23–31. Berlin: Lutherisches Verlagshaus, 1967.

Estes, James M. *Peace, Order, and the Glory of God: Secular Authority and the Church in the Thought of Luther and Melanchthon (1518–1559)*. Leiden: Brill, 2005.

Flogaus, Reinhard. *Theosis bei Palamas und Luther*. Göttingen: Vandenhoeck & Ruprecht, 1997.

Forde, Gerhard O. *On Being a Theologian of the Cross: Reflections on Luther's Heidelberg Disputation, 1518*. Grand Rapids: Eerdmans, 1997.

Forell, George W. *Faith Active in Love: An Investigation of the Principles Underlying Luther's Social Ethics*. Minneapolis: Augsburg, 1954.

Grane, Leif. *Martinus Noster: Luther in the German Reform Movement 1518–1521*. Mainz: Philipp von Zabern, 1994.

Hagen, Kenneth. *Luther's Approach to Scripture as Seen in His "Commentaries" on Galatians 1519–1538*. Tübingen: Mohr Siebeck, 1993.

———. *The Theology of Testament in the Young Luther: The Lectures on Hebrews*. Leiden: Brill, 1974.

Hendrix, Scott. "American Luther Research in the Twentieth Century." *Lutheran Quarterly* 15 (2001): 1–23.

———. "Deparentifying the Fathers: The Reformers and Patristic Authority." In *Auctoritas Patrum: Zum Rezeption der Kirchenväter im 15. und 16. Jahrhundert*, edited by Leif Grane, Alfred Schindler, and Markus Wriedt, 55–68. Mainz: Philipp von Zabern, 1993.

———. *Luther and the Papacy: Stages in a Reformation Conflict*. Philadelphia: Fortress, 1981.

———. "Luther's Impact on the Sixteenth Century." *Sixteenth Century Journal* 16 (1985): 3–14.

———. "Martin Luther und die Lutherischen Bekenntnisschriften in der englischsprachigen Forschung seit 1983." *Lutherjahrbuch* 68 (2001): 115–36.

———. *Recultivating the Vineyard: The Reformation Agendas of Christianization*. Louisville: Westminster John Knox, 2004.

Junghans, Helmar. *Der junge Luther und die Humanisten*. Weimar: Böhlau, 1984.

———, ed. *Leben und Werk Martin Luthers von 1526 bis 1546*. 2 vols. Göttingen: Vandenhoeck & Ruprecht, 1983.

Kittelson, James M. "Successes and Failures in the German Reformation: The Report from Strasbourg." *Archiv für Reformationsgeschichte* 73 (1982): 153–75.

Kolb, Robert. *Bound Choice, Election, and Wittenberg: Theological Method from Martin Luther to the Formula of Concord*. Grand Rapids: Eerdmans, 2005.

————. "God Kills to Make Alive: Romans 6 and Luther's Understanding of Justification (1535)." *Lutheran Quarterly* 12 (1998): 33–56.

————. "Luther on the Theology of the Cross." *Lutheran Quarterly* 16 (2002): 443–66.

————. "Luther on the Two Kinds of Righteousness: Reflections on His Two-Dimensional Definition of Humanity at the Heart of His Theology." *Lutheran Quarterly* 13 (1999): 449–66.

————. "'What Benefit Does the Soul Receive from a Handful of Water?' Luther's Preaching on Baptism, 1528–1539." *Concordia Journal* 25 (1999): 346–63.

Lehmann, Martin. *Luther and Prayer*. Milwaukee: Northwestern Publishing, 1985.

Loewenich, Walther von. *Luther's Theology of the Cross*. Translated by Herbert J. A. Bouman. Minneapolis: Augsburg, 1976.

Lohse, Bernhard, ed. *Der Durchbruch der reformatorischen Erkenntnis bei Luther*. Darmstadt: Wissenschaftliche Buchgesellschaft, 1968.

————, ed. *Der Durchbruch der reformatorischen Erkenntnis bei Luther: Neuere Untersuchungen*. Wiesbaden: Steiner, 1988.

Oberman, Heiko Augustinus. *The Harvest of Medieval Theology: Gabriel Biel and Late Medieval Nominalism*. Grand Rapids: Baker Academic, 2000.

Ozment, Steven. *The Age of Reform (1250–1550): An Intellectual and Religious History of Late Medieval and Reformation Europe*. New Haven: Yale University Press, 1980.

————. *Protestants: The Birth of a Revolution*. New York: Doubleday, 1992.

————. *When Fathers Ruled: Family Life in Reformation Europe*. Cambridge, MA: Harvard University Press, 1983.

Saarnivaara, Uuras. *Luther Discovers the Gospel: New Light upon Luther's Way from Medieval Catholicism to Evangelical Faith*. St. Louis: Concordia, 1951.

Sasse, Hermann. *This Is My Body: Luther's Contention for the Real Presence in the Sacrament of the Altar*. Minneapolis: Augsburg, 1959.

Siggins, Ian A. K. *Martin Luther's Doctrine of Christ*. New Haven: Yale University Press, 1970.

Spitz, Lewis W., Jr. *The Religious Renaissance of the German Humanists*. Cambridge, MA: Harvard University Press, 1963.

———. "The Third Generation of German Renaissance Humanists." In *Aspects of the Renaissance: A Symposium*, edited by Archibald R. Lewis, 105–21. Austin: University of Texas Press, 1967.

Trigg, Jonathan D. *Baptism in the Theology of Martin Luther*. Leiden: Brill, 1994.

Vajta, Vilmos. *Luther on Worship*. Philadelphia: Muhlenberg, 1958.

Wengert, Timothy J., ed. *Harvesting Martin Luther's Reflections on Theology, Ethics, and the Church*. Grand Rapids: Eerdmans, 2003.

———. *Human Freedom, Christian Righteousness: Philip Melanchthon's Exegetical Dispute with Erasmus of Rotterdam*. Oxford: Oxford University Press, 1998.

———. *Law and Gospel: Philip Melanchthon's Debate with John Agricola of Eisleben over Poenitentia*. Grand Rapids: Baker Academic, 1997.

Wingren, Gustaf. *Luther on Vocation*. Translated by Carl C. Rasmussen. Philadelphia: Muhlenberg, 1957.

Wisløff, Carl F. *The Gift of Communion: Luther's Controversy with Rome on Eucharistic Sacrifice*. Translated by Joseph M. Shaw. Minneapolis: Augsburg, 1964.

Applying Luther's Thinking Today

Arand, Charles P. "Two Kinds of Righteousness as a Framework for Law and Gospel in the Apology." *Lutheran Quarterly* 15 (2001): 417–39.

Bayer, Oswald. "'I Believe That God Has Created Me with All That Exists': An Example of Catechetical-Systematics." *Lutheran Quarterly* 8 (1994): 129–61.

———. "Justification: Basis and Boundary of Theology." In *By Faith Alone: Essays in Honor of Gerhard O. Forde*, edited by Joseph A. Burgess and Marc Kolden, 67–85. Grand Rapids: Eerdmans, 2004.

———. *Living by Faith: Justification and Sanctification* (Grand Rapids: Eerdmans, 2003).

Benne, Robert. *Ordinary Saints: An Introduction to the Christian Life*. Minneapolis: Fortress, 1988.

———. *Reasonable Ethics: A Christian Approach to Social, Economic, and Political Concerns*. St. Louis: Concordia, 2005.

Bonhoeffer, Dietrich. *The Cost of Discipleship*. Translated by R. H. Fuller and I. Booth. 6th ed. New York: SCM, 1959.

———. *Ethics*. Translated by N. H. Smith. New York: Macmillan, 1955.

Elert, Werner. *The Structure of Lutheranism*. Translated by Walter H. Hanson. St. Louis: Concordia, 1962.

Forde, Gerhard. *Justification by Faith: A Matter of Death and Life*. Philadelphia: Fortress, 1982. Reprint, Mifflintown, PA: Sigler, 1991.

———. *A More Radical Gospel: Essays on Eschatology, Authority, Atonement, and Ecumenism*. Edited by Mark C. Mattes and Stephen D. Paulson. Grand Rapids: Eerdmans, 2004.

———. *Theology Is for Proclamation*. Philadelphia: Fortress, 1990.

———. *Where God Meets Man: Luther's Down-to-Earth Approach to the Gospel*. Minneapolis: Augsburg, 1991.

Giertz, Bo. *The Hammer of God*. 2nd ed. Minneapolis: Fortress, 2005.

Haemig, Mary Jane. "The Confessional Basis of Lutheran Thinking on Church-State Issues." In *Church and State: Lutheran Perspectives*, edited by John R. Stumme and Robert W. Tuttle, 3–19. Philadelphia: Fortress, 2003.

Koeberle, Adolph. *Quest for Holiness: A Biblical, Historical, and Systematic Investigation*. New York: Harper, 1936.

Kolb, Robert. "Christian Civic Responsibility in an Age of Judgment." *Concordia Journal* 19 (1993): 10–34.

———. "God and His Human Creatures in Luther's Sermons on Genesis: The Reformer's Early Use of His Distinction of Two Kinds of Righteousness." *Concordia Journal* 33 (2007): 166–84.

———. "God Calling, 'Take Care of My People': Luther's Concept of Vocation in the Augsburg Confession and Its Apology." *Concordia Journal* 8 (1982): 4–11.

———. "Mensch-Sein in zwei Dimensionen: Die zweierlei Gerechtigkeit und Luthers *De votes monasticis Iudicium*" In *Luther und das monastische Erbe*, edited by Christoph Bultmann, Volker Leppin, and Andreas Lindner. Tübingen: Mohr Siebeck, 2007.

Kolden, Marc. "Earthly Vocation as a Corollary of Justification by Faith." In *By Faith Alone: Essays on Justification in Honor of Gerhard O. Forde*, edited by Joseph A. Burgess and Marc Kolden, 167–88. Grand Rapids: Eerdmans, 2004.

Lumpp, David A. "Luther's 'Two Kinds of Righteousness': A Brief Historical Introduction." *Concordia Journal* 23 (1993): 27–38.

Meilaender, Gilbert. *Faith and Faithfulness: Basic Themes in Christian Ethics*. Notre Dame: University of Notre Dame Press, 1991.

————. "The Venture of Marriage." In *The Two Cities of God: The Church's Responsibility for the Earthly City*, edited by Carl E. Braaten and Robert W. Jenson, 117–32. Grand Rapids: Eerdmans, 1997.

Rieth, Ricardo. *"Habsucht" bei Martin Luther: Ökonomisches und theologisches Denken*. Weimar: Böhlau, 1996.

Schumacher, William W. "Civic Participation by Churches and Pastors: An Essay in Two Kinds of Righteousness." *Concordia Journal* 30 (2004): 165–77.

Schwanke, Johannes. "Luther on Creation." In *Harvesting Martin Luther's Reflections on Theology, Ethics, and the Church*, edited by Timothy J. Wengert, 78–98. Grand Rapids: Eerdmans, 2003.

Schwarz, Reinhard. "Luthers Lehre von den drei Standen und die drei Dimensionen der Ethik." *Lutherjahrbuch* 45 (1978): 15–34.

Watson, Philip S. *Let God Be God! An Interpretation of the Theology of Martin Luther*. Philadelphia: Muhlenberg, 1947.

Wingren, Gustaf. *Creation and Law*. Translated by Ross Mackenzie. Edinburgh: Oliver & Boyd, 1961.

INDEX

Abraham, 45, 51, 127, 143, 180, 192
absolution, 44, 99, 179, 184–88
Adam and Eve, 37, 60, 62–63, 95, 104, 138, 178
ad modum Aristotelis (in the way of Aristotle), 125
Aesop, 70
Agricola, Johann, 102
Alexander the Great, 71
American Protestantism, 91–92
Anabaptists, 41, 61, 109, 195
Anfechtung, 50, 189
anointing, 176
anthropological presuppositions, 12, 22
antinomianism, 92, 101
apocalyptic anticipation, 34
apologia (defense), 16
Apology of the Augsburg Confession (Melanchthon), 19, 25, 102, 170
Apostles' Creed, 68, 123
  first article of (creation), 38, 57, 69, 96, 112, 114n30
  second article of (redemption), 57
  third article of (sanctification), 57, 114n30
Aristotelian physics, 197
Aristotelian systems, 65
Aristotle, 65n, 71, 72, 74–75, 80, 94, 125
Asendorf, Ulrich, 9
Atlas, 92
atonement, 40, 157, 165
Augsburg Confession of 1530, 15, 16, 17, 102, 170
Augustine of Hippos, 34, 59, 109, 168, 169
Augustinian Neoplatonism, 44, 109

Augustus, 71, 73
Aulén, Gustaf, 165
aussz freyem synn (common sense), 72
authorities, tertiary, 172

"Babylonian Captivity of the Church" (Luther), 193
baptism, 44, 98–100, 177, 185, 190–96
baptismal liturgy, 190
Bayer, Oswald, 27, 51
Becker, Ernest, 79–80, 82
Bible. *See* Scripture
biblical humanists, 132–34
Biel, Gabriel, 84
body
  metaphor of, 14, 208–10
  mortification of, 108, 218
Boff, Leonardo, 9
Bonhoeffer, Dietrich, 92
Book of Concord, 169
Brahamanism, 86
Brief Form of Confession, 100
Buddhists, 107–8

Calvin, John, 83
Carthusian monastics, 112
celibacy, 111
chastity, 108
cheap grace, 92
chrism, 194
Christ, 34, 36, 39, 40, 49
  benefits of, 41–45
  blood of, 194
  dual nature of, 163–66, 200–201

Christian Coalition, 115
Christian ethics, 116–17
Christian freedoms, 101, 114, 120
Christian life, 97, 103
Christians, 22, 75, 172
church, medieval, 29, 111–12, 184, 202
Cicero, 71
circumcision, 176, 192
citizens and volunteers, 58, 62
civil righteousness, 57, 76, 96
civitas/politia. See citizens and volunteers
Cochlaeus, Johann, 29
"Come, Holy Spirit, Lord and God, 1524"
    (Luther), 205–6
communicatio idomatum (communication of
    attributes), 163
community, 109, 188, 202
confession, 99–100, 172, 184, 185
confessions of faith, 171, 172
Confucian systems, 65
consilia evangelica, 84
Constantine, 70
consubstantiation, 197
coram Deo (living in God's presence), 27
coram mundo (living in community), 27
Cornelius, 178
Council of Chalcedon, 163, 200
Council of Trent, 179
courage, 75
covenants, 192
creatio continua (ongoing creation), 55
creation, 17
    dominion over, 55, 138
    law of, 64–71, 73, 116
    Luther's theology of, 55–57
creatureliness, 38
creeds, 169, 170
cross, theology of, 146–47
cultural context, 209–10, 222
cultural criticism, 115

Daniel, 18
David, 39–40, 71, 73, 127, 143, 165, 176
day of wrath, 35
death, 34, 153
Decalogue. *See* Ten Commandments
Demosthenes, 71
Deus absconditus (hidden God), 144
Deus revelatus (revealed God), 144
Deuteronomy, Book of, 67
devil. *See* Satan
dies irae (day of wrath), 35
"Disputation on Faith and Love (1531)"
    (Luther), 74

divorce, 117
domus (marriage and family life), 58
Druids, 87

Eastern Orthodox, 39n26, 49
Ebeling, Gerhard, 29
ecclesia. See religious life
Ecclesiastes, Book of, 70, 112, 119, 120
Eck, Johann, 29
economic life, 58, 60–61
Elert, Werner, 96
Elijah, 71, 169
Emperor Charles V, 16, 102
Enlightenment, 92
environmental concerns, 87
epieikeia (equity). *See* wisdom, human
equitas. See wisdom, human
equity, 35, 72
Erasmus, 94
essential righteousness, 43
euangelion (gospel), 41
Eutychus, 200
evil. *See* sin
exchange, joyous. *See* joyous exchange
ex opere operato, 132

fabrica idolorum (factory of idols), 83
faith, 38, 45–46, 50, 77–78, 101–2, 211
    and creation, 106–11
    and daily life, 111–14
    and God's role in creation, 118–23
    and life in created world, 115–18
    and new life, 104–6
    psychological definition of, 142
    and sanctification, 123–28
    and Word of God, 143
fall into sin, the, 27, 56, 78, 95
family. *See* marriage and family life
Fichte, Johann Gottlieb, 80
Fletcher, Joseph, 91
Flogause, Reinhard, 9
Forde, Gerhard, 43, 92, 94, 155, 210
forgiveness of sins, 143, 148, 157
Formula of Concord of 1577, 34, 150, 158,
    169, 170
Fortuna, 71
Freud, Sigmund, 79–80
fröhlicher Wechsel (joyous exchange), 46
fruits of the Spirit, 218

Gaia, 87
Galations Commentary (1535) (Luther), 25
genera vitae (spheres of life), 58

Genesis Lectures, 1535–1545 (Luther), 131, 175
Gentiles, 40
German Peasants' Revolt of 1525, 29, 102, 123
Germany, 219
Gideon, 176
Giertz, Bo, 97
Gleichmut. See wisdom, human
Gnosticism, 85–86, 108
God
  acts through words, 135–36
  apparent injustice of, 147–48
  gospel as gift of, 153–54
  grammar of, 42, 199, 208
  hidden and revealed nature of, 144–48
  justice of, 35
  and law, 206
  ontological association with believer, 47–48
  ordained power of, 37, 144
  promises of, 42, 176
  relational character of, 42, 138, 176
  righteousness of, 35
  right hand of, 200
god, definition of, 140
God's Word. *See* Word of God
golden mean, 75
gospel, 21, 44, 84, 148, 153–54, 157
governments, 58, 61–62
grace, 34, 84, 92, 95, 143, 175–76, 178
Graham, Billy, 113
Great Commission, 113
Great Confession of 1528, 36n9
Gregory of Palamas, 9–10
guilt, 92, 153

habitus of love, 34–35
Hannibal, 73
Hebrew Scriptures, 35, 70, 176
Heidelberg Disputation, 25, 52, 89, 118
heresy, 92
Hidden God, 144
Hochstraten, Jacob, 47–48
holy orders, 63
Holy Roman Empire, 16
Holy Spirit, 45, 96, 123, 218
Homer, 71
homosexuality, 117–18
Hosea, 47
human beings
  as coheirs with Christ, 42
  and community, 26, 54–55, 58
  in conversation with God, 141
  questions of definition, 22

and reason, 84, 95, 207–8
  rebirth of, 94–97, 116
  responsibilities of, 138
  two types of, 73–74
  vocation and, 56, 74
human identity, 77, 88, 104, 149
humanists, biblical, 132–34
human righteousness, 76
human will, 95–96

idolatry, 79, 83, 99
image of God, 39, 94
incarnation, 39, 163
in relatione, 27
Isaiah, 71

Jabez, prayer of, 87
Jenson, Robert, 117
Jesus of Nazareth, 154, 157, 162, 164
John of Damascus, 14
John of Saxony, Elector, 16
John the Baptizer, 108, 169
joyous exchange, 45–52, 165, 166
Judeo-Christian heritage, 88
judgment, 34, 92
justification, 22, 27, 48, 107, 154–56

Kant, Immanuel, 90–91
Karlstadt, Andreas Bodenstein von, 196–97, 199
Kolde, Dietrich, 35
krisis, 10

language, 132, 133
Large Catechism (Luther), 36, 58, 78, 97, 98, 102, 112, 119, 124, 190, 201
larvae Dei (masks of God), 55
law
  as evaluator of life, 89
  and gospel, 179
  natural. *See* creation, law of
  as pass-fail system, 150
  political or external use of, 151
  precedes gospel, 148–49
  as prescription, 149–50
  righteousness of, 21
  Roman, 70
  as servant of God, 65
  uses of, 150, 151–52, 157
  See also written law
lectio (reading of text), 189
"Lectures on Galatians, 1531–1535" (Luther), 21, 33, 53, 77, 101
Leibniz, Gottfried Wilhelm, 121

lex semper accusat (law accuses), 89, 103
lex sola accusat (law only accuses), 103
Lindberg, Carter, 107
linguists, 135
liturgy, 190, 216–17
Livy, 71
Lombard, Peter, 14
Lord's Prayer, the, 62, 151
Lord's Supper, 177, 216
love, 34–35, 72
luck, 80
Luther, Käthe, 15
Luther, Martin
  cultural presuppositions of, 222
  life of, 64, 123
  relationship to Roman Catholic church, 10
  theological perspective of, 12, 25
Lutheran Confessions, 28n12, 41, 169, 172
Lutheran Formula of Concord, 104

MacIntyre, Alasdair, 91
Mammonites, 87
marriage and family life, 58–60, 63, 72, 111, 112
martyrdom, 219
Mass, 132, 196, 197–98
materialism, 86–87
meditatio (meditation), 189
Melanchthon, Philip, 12, 14, 25, 65–66, 102, 106, 207
Middle Ages, 58–59, 60, 63, 84, 103, 110, 195
military affairs, 63
ministries, 182
ministry of the Word, 182
Mirror of a Christian Man (Kolde), 35
modernity, 24
monasticism, 59, 84, 107–8
moral ground, 65
moralities, traditional, 65
Moral Majority, 115
mortification of the flesh. See body, mortification of
Moses, 36, 67, 71
mother goddess, 87
Mother Nature, 65

Narcissus, 80
Native Americans, 87
natural law. See creation, law of
neo-Gnosticism, 85–87
neomaterialism, 86
neopaganism, 87
Neoplatonists, 108
New Age, 86

New Testament, 62, 176
Nichomachean Ethics (Aristotle), 74
Niebuhr, H. Richard, 91–92
Ninety-five Theses of 1517 (Luther), 98–99, 217
nominalism, 11
North America, 115

obedience, 108
Ockhamism, 11, 37, 134, 164, 199
Oecolampadius, Johannes, 132, 199
oeconomia (economic life), 58, 60–61
Old Testament. See Hebrew Scriptures
On Good Works (1520) (Luther), 105
"On Monastic Vows" (1522) (Luther), 25
On Secular Authority (Luther), 72
opino legis (opinion of law), 79
opus alienum (alien acts), 37
opus proprium (appropriate acts), 37
oratio (prayer), 189
ordained power, 37, 134, 144
original sin, doctrine of, 22, 198
Osiander, Andreas, 39n26, 49
overpopulation, 59
Ozment, Steven, 112–13

paganism, 87
patres et matres familias (heads of households, employers), 58
patres patriae (fathers of the nation), 58
Paul, 11, 12, 39, 127, 143, 146, 165
Pelagianism, 81
performative speech, 135, 192
Peter, 39–40, 127, 165, 186
Peters, Albrecht, 98
Philip of Macedonia, 71
piety, medieval, 34, 132
Plato, 133
Platonic systems, 65, 132
Plotinus, 86
political action, 116
Pontius Pilate, 68
postmodernity, 24, 85
potentia absoluta (absolute power), 37
potentia ordinata (ordained power), 37
poverty, 108
power, 37
power-in-dying, 146
praecepta, 84, 109
prayer, 185, 189, 212–15
preachers, 181–82
preaching, 180–88
prepositional phrases, Luther's use of, 97
presuppositions of Luther, 12

promise, concept of, 41
proprium (personal belongings), 46
propter Christum (righteous because of Christ), 41
Protestantism, 90, 91
Proverbs, Book of, 70
Psalms, Book of, 101, 70
punishment, 35, 36, 76
Puritans, 115

Rabus, Ludwig, 219
reason, 65, 72, 79, 84n25, 114n30, 135
rebirth of human creatures, 94–97
Reformation, 22, 29, 34, 38, 41, 72, 115
regnum gratiae (realm of grace), 110
regnum naturae (realm of nature), 110
relationships, mutual, 58
religious life, 59, 62–63
Renaissance scholarship, 132
repentance, 13, 94, 98–100, 172
Revealed God, 144
righteousness
    active, 21, 25, 29, 54, 76, 91
    "alien," 39
    ceremonial, 63
    civil, 57, 76, 96
    concept of, 26–29
    essential, 43
    forensic, 43
    human, 76
    of God. *See* God
    of the gospel, 118
    of the law. *See* law
    passive, 28–31, 50, 76, 91, 103–5, 125
    as right relationship, 28
    two kinds of, 22, 25, 51, 104, 124
        relationship between, 29–31, 104, 110
    types of, 53
    works, 102, 118
right relationship, 28
Roman Catholic theologians, 47
Roman Empire, 59
Roman law, 70
rule of faith, 171

Sabbath, 68–69
sacraments, 44, 190–204
Saint Anthony, 106
saints, cult of, 40
salvation, 34, 37, 86, 143, 191, 209
    by transformation, 49
salvation history, 176
sanctification, 124–25
Sao Bento du Sul, 9

sapentia (wisdom), 72
Sarah, 51
Satan, 99, 119, 139, 184, 218
Schwambach, Claus, 9
Schwärmer, 178
scientia (fixed body of theoretical knowledge), 72
Scripture, 167, 169, 170, 172, 188
Scriptures, Hebrew. *See* Hebrew Scriptures
self-destruction, 88–94
semi-Pelagian systems, 81
Sermon on the Mount, 109
service, 121–22
shame, 92, 153
Siggins, Ian, 165
signs, physical, 176–78
simul justus et peccator (similtaneously righteous and a sinner), 49
sin, 78, 94–96, 126–28, 138–39, 146–49, 209, 217–20
Sinai, 67
sinfulness, 66, 92, 185, 189
sinners, 36, 39, 90, 94, 145, 158, 214
situation ethics, 91
Smalcald Articles (1537) (Luther), 39, 151–52, 170, 178, 179, 184
Small Catechism (Luther), 13, 37, 63, 97, 113, 114, 153, 184, 186, 198, 213
solas (alone), 78
Solomon, 71
soul, exiled, 108
Spiritus sanctificator (sanctifying Spirit), 123
status perfectionis, 109
Stoicism, 65, 72, 108
synagogue practice, 172
synergism, 81

Tao, 65n45
teaching, purity of, 206–8
temperance, 75
Ten Commandments, 61n33, 66–69, 100, 102–3, 153
    first commandment, 78, 99
    fourth commandment, 62, 72
tentatio (temptations of daily life), 189
tertiary authorities, 172
The Cost of Discipleship (Bonhoeffer), 92
The Hammer of God (Giertz), 97
"The Last Words of David, 1543" (Luther), 161
"The Me Decade and the Third Great Awakening" (Wolfe), 90–91
theocracies, 115
theodicy, 121

Theological Topics (Loci communes theologici) (Melancthon), 14
theologians, systematic, 22
theologies of glory, 80–83, 85
theology
  medieval, 94, 154
  of creation, 55–57
  of the cross, 146–47
  of the Word, 41
"Three Kinds of Righteousness" (1518) (Luther), 25
Trajan, 71
transubstantiation, 197
"Treatise on the Power and Primacy of the Pope" (Melanchthon), 170
Trinity, the, 167, 194
"Two Kinds of Righteousness" (1519) (Luther), 25

University of Wittenburg, 10

Vedantism, 86
verbum reale (real thing or action), 136
Virgil, 71
Virgin Mary, 200
virtue ethics, 74n82, 117n41
virtues, 74, 75
vocation
  doctrine of, 107
  human, 56, 63, 92, 107, 113–14, 122
volunteers. *See* citizens and volunteers

Walther, C. F. W., 96
Wengert, Timothy, 19, 72

Wicca, 88
will, bondage of, 147–48
Wingren, Gustaf, 56
wisdom, human, 71, 72, 75
wisdom-in-weakness, 146
Wisdom literature, 70
Wittenburg Reformation, 15
Wittenburg theology, 19–20
Wolfe, Tom, 90–91
Word of God, 41, 97, 130, 131
  authority of Scripture, 167–68
  as body of God's teaching, 208–10
  functions of, 135–59
  historical background of, 132–35
  inspired written word, 166–73
  in liturgy, 216–17
  as means of grace, 17, 175
  prayer as response to, 212–15
  preaching, 180–88
  proclaimed orally, 172
  in proclamation and explanation, 210–11
  pure teaching of, 206–8
  re-creative functions of, 137, 211
  responses to, 211–12
  sacramental forms of, 44, 190–203
  as Second Person of Trinity, 161–66
  in struggle against sin, 217–20
  written and read forms of, 188–90
works, 77, 78, 84, 89, 92, 102, 104
worship, modes of, 217
wrath, day of, 35
written law, 66

Zwingli, Ulrich, 132, 199–200

Printed and bound by CPI Group (UK) Ltd, Croydon, CR0 4YY

13/04/2025

14656460-0001